Notorious Prisons of the World

Notorious Prisons of the World

Stephen Wade

Wharncliffe Books

First Published in Great Britain in 2013 by
Wharncliffe Books
an imprint of
Pen and Sword Books Limited,
47 Church Street, Barnsley,
South Yorkshire. S70 2AS

Copyright © Stephen Wade, 2013

ISBN: 978 184563 164 2 Hardback
ISBN: 978 178303 017 0 Paperback

The right of Stephen Wade to be identified as author
of this work has been asserted by him in accordance
with the Copyright, Designs and Patents Act, 1988.

A CIP catalogue record of this book is available from the
British Library.

Typeset in Palatino by
CHIC GRAPHICS

Printed and bound in England by
CPI Group (UK) Ltd, Croydon, CR0 4YY

Pen & Sword Books Ltd incorporates the imprints of
Pen & Sword Aviation, Pen & Sword Family History, Pen & Sword
Maritime, Pen & Sword Military, Pen & Sword Discovery, Wharncliffe
Local History, Wharncliffe True Crime, Wharncliffe Transport, Pen & Sword
Select, Pen & Sword Military Classics, Leo Cooper, Remember When,
The Praetorian Press, Seaforth Publishing and Frontline Publishing

For a complete list of Pen & Sword titles please contact:
PEN & SWORD BOOKS LIMITED
47 Church Street, Barnsley, South Yorkshire, S70 2AS, England.
E-mail: enquiries@pen-and-sword.co.uk
Website: www.pen-and-sword.co.uk

Contents

Introduction 6

Chapter 1   The First Dark Places 28

Chapter 2   Judgement and Debt 41

Chapter 3   Prison and Imperial Power 59

Chapter 4   Europe: From Dungeons to Houses of
             Correction 72

Chapter 5   Work and Pain: From Penal Colonies to Gulags 89

Chapter 6   Reform and the Penitentiary: The American
             Experience 109

Chapter 7   Punishment as Commodity and Masterplan 127

Chapter 8   Politicals, Enemies and Doing Time 143

Chapter 9   A Short History of Modern Failures 165

Chapter 10   History from Inside 178

Conclusions 192

Glossary 195

Bibliography 197

Index 205

Introduction

In the course of my six years of work as a writer in various prisons, I constantly discussed, or was asked, if prison worked. The question echoed a constant will to succeed, a drive to prove that criminals could be contained in a community in such a way that they might be returned to society as good citizens. There was a massive amount of paperwork and there were endless meetings, several training initiatives and endless theoretical gambits, aimed at improving success rates, to say nothing of the impressive variety of professionals working within the prison walls. With all that effort and investment, prison should have 'worked' – but for who and for what purposes? The brick wall of failure was always there in the form of 'career criminals' whether they were the ones who saw crime as a career or whether they were the ones choosing a prison cell for warmth in the winter months.

Prison 'worked' for too many vested interests, and in too many ways. As a historian, I can see that same pattern in the houses of correction of the Georgian years, just as much as in the massive penitentiaries created by the Victorians. The only real differences between prisons c.1850 and those of today in this respect is that now they have a 'duty of care' and the social scientists inside and behind them.

AN OVERVIEW

On the walls of the prison at York Castle, there is a square of stone with these words carved into the surface:

> 'This prison is a House of Care
> A grave for man alive.
> A Touch Stone to thee, friend,
> No place for man to thrive.'

The lines hint at the layers of paradox behind the conception of a prison. They also record a revolution in penal philosophy. In the first place, the words stress care rather than the original meaning of a prison, from the Latin *prensio-ionis* , meaning 'seizure'. On the other hand, the York gaol is also a kind of 'grave' and warning to those reading the inscription. A criminal act could take them and seize them, and they would be in a 'grave' and yet in 'care'. The words were put there in 1820, in that period after the first flush of the Enlightenment, a time when the notion of a prison was a focus of great philosophical and reflective interest to writers and thinkers across Europe.

This book will relate the history of prisons and their punishment, assessing how these places gradually became far more than the original dark holes of oblivion in early civilizations. Yet that is too simplistic and Euro-centred because the world's great empires created prisons with attitudes varying markedly from the so-called 'civilised' world of the West. The clash of the empires in global invasions and settlements brought with it a notable set of differences in notions of what prisons are for and whether or not they 'worked'. My principal aims are to give an account of the prison systems across the world and to explain the thinking behind them, as well as the regimes of suppression and control inside the walls.

Contrary to popular belief, a prison is not, and has never been, a rational creation. In fact, the challenge for states and regimes over the centuries since the first black dungeons of oblivion has to attempt rationality. This has been against the grain of human community, with necessary bonds of friendship or mutual protection, and the imposition of order and routine has always been made on the shifting sands of human frailty, error and muddle. Even today, with the full armoury of technology behind prison management, the establishment has to function on the assumption that any new day might bring a tumult of rage and disorder, and that could happen through one small act of neglect or one waiving of a rule.

Before there was any attempt at applying an organising principle of uniformity on the feckless and wayward criminal population held forcibly behind the high stone walls, there was no concession to any principle of caring. The first penal ideas were founded on the destruction of the individual - sheer retribution - and the ripping away of the mind and the body, sometimes by attrition and sometimes by immediate application of the Mosaic Law.

These general thoughts suggest built-in failure, but in fact there has always been an instinctive belief in prison government that collectives of prisoners can easily be ruled and suppressed by means of ritual and psychological application – even more than by fear. In a prison community, the domination of the few over the many is applied through the use of a powerful combination of ritual methods. Working in prisons, I have stood with one officer, watching a line of 40 men walk in single file from a prison block to an exercise yard, in perfect order and with restraint. The first time I saw this, I sensed that if that group of prisoners had a means of united action, the officer and myself would be at their mercy. Why and how is the power of the oppressors, those who maintain the withdrawal of freedom from the imprisoned, held and retained?

The answer is in the fear of consequences and the virtual impossibility of action outside the sanctioned actions. Regulation is the seat of power and enforced in every single act of the prisoner. When a man in the British prison system *does* attempt an escape, for instance, symbolism and taboo come into play. He is forced to wear a parti-coloured outfit of yellow and blue. His stigma as the man who attempted to break the steel rules of regulation is displayed for all; his colour in sharp contrast to the dull green or grey of the other inmates.

Those who have conceived and established prisons from the first hellish pits and cages where torture and deprivation crushed the prisoner, have understood that the prison has to work by extreme suppression or by the exercise of what we would now call the psychology of group dynamics, but what was formerly conceived as a hierarchy of power, cowing the de-humanised victim of the system.

At the heart of this thinking about what makes a working and successful prison is the erasure of identity. Even today, the new arrival at a prison enters 'reception' and that entails a relentless and minutely-planned depersonalization. A person walks into the reception gate wearing his normal clothes and with pockets and possessions. After what the American language refers to as 'being processed' he is a non-person, an entity with a number and a regulation set of clothing. His possessions have been placed in a labelled bag along with his civilian clothing, until he is released. The prisoner has stepped into an alternative world: a place in which time is ordered differently and in a sense, stops, loses real meaning, as the days coalesce into months and the months into years. When Oscar Wilde entered Pentonville Gaol in 1895 he was transmuted from the fashion-loving, stylish writer and wit into a piece of government property and wearing the suit of black arrows to signify that fact. Wilde wrote of that first impact of 'being inside':

'The first evening they made me undress before them and get into some filthy water they called a bath and dry myself with a damp brown rag... The cell was appalling; I could hardly breathe and the food turned my stomach ... I did not eat anything for days and days... as soon as I ate anything it produced violent diarrhoea and I was ill all day and night.'

The uniform of the officers who control and regulate has also been, in most cases, very much a powerful symbolic element of that control. In the first dungeons and gaols, these professions would have been military or related to the livery of a specific lord and master. As time went on, the dress was entirely militaristic. Today it is relentlessly back and white in Britain, with a universal attire of white shirt and epaulettes, black trousers and shoes, and a buttoned, police-style jacket – again in black. The officers are ranked as in a military structure with those of a lower status in the hierarchy known as 'OSGs' – Officer Support Grade.

The prison has always had an ambiguous status too. It was always conceived as a version of limbo because it was a community outside the 'normal' community of citizens. Inmates are deprived of citizenship in most places; they become non-persons. It is easy to see why so much prison literature has reached for metaphors of a spiritual nature. Dante's circles of *The Divine Comedy* have a purgatory in which spirits trapped in non-time express the pain of their static condition and exist in a shadow-land created by someone else.

The massive corpus of prison literature provides my narrative with reminders of the fundamental facts of what a prison essentially is, regardless of where or when it was established. This writing constantly expresses the see-saw interplay of punishment and redemption. Prison has always been a place and a concept of spiritual activity and thought with the very word 'cell' suggesting a monkish life of course, and prisons from the early modern period to the present day have had chapels and chaplains. Since the modern prisons in Europe around the late seventeenth century, and even in the first Bridewells of the Elizabethan years, there has been an acknowledgement that a criminal incarcerated is in need of a knowledge of potential redemption.

Philip Priestley, writing about Victorian prisons, explains one prisoner's thoughts on what the chaplain said to him:

> '"You must, he said, consider yourself a slave until your time is out." But he added, "Though your body is condemned to slavery, your thoughts, your mind and heart are free to commune with God, free to pray, free to praise and free to repent. You may in after-life reclaim yourself…"'[2]

The ongoing debates and issues concerned with prisons and their social function are in relation to the dichotomies of rehabilitation and reform, retribution and care, social values and criminal justice systems. As these matters fluctuate according to changing governments and policies, or with the ever-shifting meta-narrative of a state or culture, the history of prisons in the centre of these ideologies will involve explanations of what may be learned from the past - surely a major function of history in all its expressions.

The historiography of penal systems has often concentrated on the punishments, abuses and inhumanity of those in power. In popular history this has often dominated, and documentary sources from the press and from memoirs explain partly why this has been so. In 1914, for instance, a report in *The Daily Citizen* carried one of the most horrendous prison reports ever in print when a female explorer who had been to Mongolia gave this information to the Royal Asiatic Society:

> 'She witnessed a triple execution and was able to photograph the terrible "Living God" at Urga during a great religious orgy. But her most terrible experience was a visit to the prison at Urga. "Within a small compound," she said, "Fenced in by high spiked palisades are five or six dungeons. There are human beings there… quite a number of civilised Chinese, who are

shut up for the remainder of their lives in heavy, iron-bound wooden coffins, out of which they never, under any circumstances, move. They cannot sit upright. They cannot lie down flat. They see daylight only for a few minutes when food is thrown into the coffins…"[3]

As usual, such horrendous stories of cruelty in relation to a specific penal system are not necessarily limited to past time as recent (July 2010) reports on Iranian judicial execution methods have shown.

Any history of prisons must necessarily consider the abuse of power, and the nature of punishment, and these matters are important in our understanding of the theory behind the institution. Michel Foucault's influential work on prisons, *Discipline and Punish* (1975) begins with an extensive account of a savage and prolonged execution in eighteenth-century France.

A major factor in my history will be the uneasy tug of war in a prison population between the natural anthropology of human co-operation and the artificiality of the edifice itself: a prison accommodates loners and those who wish to cultivate the social nexus of peers. A few hours spent in any prison will make it clear to an observer that the population mix is of a culture and a counter-culture; within the walls, there are clannish groups, racial and local allegiances, and obdurate loners.

From the very beginning of the more enlightened prisons, a fundamental problem has been what the Georgians called 'contamination' and so there have been various types of separation and isolation. Every theme in the following pages has its dimension of separation and integration – the eternal issues of male and female, remanded and convicted, old and young, elites and scapegoats. The typical British local dispersal prison today has the fundamental split of sex offenders and 'straight' cons. The prison ethos constantly denigrates and abuses the 'nonces' – paedophiles and rapists- and applauds the criminals with a code of honour. That has been there from the beginning.

It has often been remarked that a civilisation may be judged by its treatment of, and attitude to, its prisoners. My history will include that proposition, and do so largely by looking at prisoners' lives. The literature of prison often springs from the kind of thinking Shakespeare puts into the mouth of Richard II: 'I have been studying how I may compare/the prison where I live unto the world.' Historical scrutiny of what has happened inside prison walls, and to what extent prisoners have been allowed to think, feel, write and express their thoughts, will be an integral part of the story.

The spine of the narrative is the development of the prison from a place totally without definition and identity (represented by the Black Hole of Calcutta perhaps) to the self-conscious establishment of the sixteenth century, a domain in which those fallen from the status of respectable citizen – offenders, paupers and vagrants – were given a means of survival through social identity. They were people who appeared as simulacra of the free citizens outside the walls. Like the shadows outside Plato's cave, they moved, worked and spoke but were not alive in the sense of being participants in the social world outside.

Huge differences are apparent in the penal creations in which utilitarianism has governed the regime and the small-scale prisons within a small state or kingdom; in the great empires, prison is part of a structured criminal justice hierarchy and so innovation may happen, through dialogue and a learning process on the part of the imperialist. More often, in more tightly circumscribed states, prison will be in some ways a visible and acknowledged institution. A classic example of the latter is the King's Bench prison in Georgian London where there was a curfew system so that prisoners could walk out and work or socialize in certain hours of the day. The prisoner was still a citizen, rather than an invisible, forgotten entity quietly tucked away in the darkness.

Finally, there is the approach to understanding the history of prisons in terms of the massively imaginative dimension: this is about the prison as an expression of the dark side of humanity. In this respect, prisons across the world have been largely formidable in their very position and material construction. Hence the almost folkloric and mythic status of the 'Rock' of Alcatraz, the dungeon of Chillon, the tortured oblivion of the Lubianka or the Tower of London, and of course, the masterpiece of imperial imagination, the penal colony.

Prisons have been purposely made on mountains, on isolated islands, in plague-infested swamps and across thousands of miles of permafrost. Geography has in a sense provided the most awesome punishment available to those who have the responsibility of punishment. From this has come one of the most fertile and astonishing branches of world literature with works such as *One Day in the Life of Ivan Denisovich, Notes from Underground, The Pilgrim's Progress* and *In The Penal Colony*. Film has also exploited the possibilities of prison as a terrifying topographical creation from *Papillon* and Devil's Island to the fortress of Colditz.

The history of prisons is essentially about the solutions to the problem of human transgression with counter-arguments of destroy or reform, forget or care for, regulate or neglect, inflict pain or simply deprive of freedom. Transgression is of course, whimsical and many-sided. At any given point in history, and in any specified culture, transgression will be uniquely conceived, sometimes influenced by religion and sometimes by sheer exigency. Penal solutions tend to be more often pragmatic and thoughtless than humane and restorative. After the Great War, ex-soldiers across Europe were frequently to be found in the death cells after using cut-throat razors on wives and partners. Prison and/or the scaffold provided the simplest solution. Psychotherapy was a distant possibility too complex to contemplate.

The global history of prisons, then, is a chronology of pain, torment and oblivion in the mainstream, but along the way towards various stages of enlightenment, it has a contrary story of humanity's persistent will to believe in redemption. The true complexity and the real understanding, as history has shown, comes from answering the question; redemption to *what*? Answering that question has forced societies to look at themselves rather more profoundly, hence the closeness of philosophy, spirituality and imprisonment. They are rooms in the same mansion. Redemption to *what*? Even today, millennia after the first basic dens of torture, that question is fundamental to our search for human communities that actually work and succeed. The germ of any really constructive thinking on questions of redemption has to come from the answer to a simple question: Is prison created *as* a punishment or *for* a punishment? In some societies through history, prison has been an end in itself - simply a place of oblivion and despair, a location of non-persons. For other societies it has been merely the beginning of punishment, the deprivation of liberty being the platform for further suffering.

THE LABYRINTH OF IDENTITY

In January 2011 Zofia Evershed died in the village of Scotton, Lincolnshire. She was 87 and described by her son as 'Tough'. He added: 'Trying to stop her would be like trying to stop a steam roller.' Zofia's father was murdered by Stalin's secret police at Katyn and she was taken to a gulag, to the labour camp at Aktyubinsk. Between 1940 and 1942, Zofia lived in the labour camps. She travelled there in a cattle truck and when settled in, she worked at brick-making and later in the maize fields. She escaped because her uncle somehow obtained call-up papers for her so she could serve in the Polish army.

Her story is one of thousands upon thousands through history, in that any prison biography generates multiple stories. For most prisoners, the time inside is merely a period of their lives, a phase and, of course, an ordeal. It is easy to name several notable people – all criminals in the sense of having somehow transgressed laws of their time - for whom prison was a significant experience: Casanova, Bunyan, Dostoievski, Mandela, Gramsci, Wilde, Genet, Malory and Henry Hunt. But there have been innumerable people who form the textless history of the human experience for whom prison has been a penalty for political views, for minor crime, for debt or for the satisfaction of some local despot.

The history of prisons creates an infinite number of permutations of biography - life stories of states as well as of individuals. Zofia's story was also the narrative of a generation. With this in mind, the historian has to find a way to work that will enlighten the complexities involved. As G. K. Chesterton said: 'But though we cannot reach the outside of history, we all start from the outside.' If we do approach the 'outside' in terms of a general account of the growth of penology for instance, we do describe something, but it tends to blur the human story. Working with the 'inside' there is the massive literature of the prison to help.

Prison experience has been integral to some major events in history and often these have been formative in terms of philosophical or ideological systems and lines of thought. For a typology of this, we have the experience of Socrates. In choosing to stay in the Athenian prison and not accept banishment as expected, he had the impact of all great men against the orthodoxy of their age. Prison was part of his total effect on ideas. As the great historian, J. B. Bury explained:

'There have been no better men than Socrates; and yet his accusers were perfectly right. It is not clear why their manifesto for orthodoxy was made at that particular time; but it is probable that twenty years later such an action would have been a failure. Perhaps the facts of the trial justify us in the rough conclusion that two out of every five Athenian citizens then were religiously indifferent. In any case the event had a wider significance. The execution of Socrates was the protest of the spirit of the old order against the growth of individualism...'

Socrates drank the hemlock in the prison because he was, as he said, 'Released from trouble.' He was incarcerated because he was a danger to democracy and a bad influence on the youth of the city. His story represents one of the most notably problematic elements of writing on prison history with the widest possible scope - the fact that criminality has had shifting definitions, changing with the tides of ideology and authority across the world.

It is when we see the attempts to impose some kind of order and pattern on prison history that the immensity of the task becomes clear. One pattern might be that there have been ages of retribution, penitentiary and correction, in that order. But that does not include the frequency of anomalies within each period, culture and *Zeitgeist*
.

PENAL DILEMMAS

One way to illustrate why theories of prison history are so difficult to propose with any degree of confidence is to look at some case studies. However, it can be said with confidence that prison is there to incapacitate, to reform or to punish. Here are three accounts of imprisonment from British history, each illustrating a specific use of imprisonment.

First, prison *as the only conclusion*. It reads like such a simple, uncomplicated statement of a killing: 'York Assizes: Abraham Bairstan, aged 60, was put to the bar, charged with the wilful murder of Sarah Bairstan his wife, in the parish of Bradford.' In the busy, overworked courts of the regency, dealing with new and often puzzling crimes form the labouring classes in the fast-growing towns, it was maybe just another 'domestic' that went too far. But this is far from the truth, and the Bairstan case gives us an insight into the plight of those unfortunate people at the time who were victims of ignorance as well as of illness. In this instance it was an awful, anguished mental illness that played a major part in this murder.

When the turnkey brought Bairstan into the court he commented that he had not heard the prisoner say a word since he was brought to York and locked up. This was nothing new to the man's family. Mr Baron Hullock, presiding, was shocked but also full of that natural curiosity of someone who just does not understand something. He pressed the gaoler to explain. He asked if the man in the dock understood the spoken word, and the answer was 'no'. He also ascertained that Bairstan appeared to have no response to any sound whatsoever, nor any movement.

It makes painful reading in the court report to note that the prisoner was a 'dull and heavy looking man who… cast a vacant glance around the court.' The reporter in 1824 noted that the man 'appeared totally insensible of the nature of the proceedings.' Poor Hullock had a real challenge to try to communicate with the man, doing his best to make the prisoner make any sound at all, asking several questions but receiving no answer. When he asked 'Do you hear what I say to you?' Bairstan simply stared at the officer next to him.

It was obviously going to be one of those trials at which many people were thinking that this silence was the best ruse if a man wanted to avoid the rope. The judge had to instruct the jury about potential fraud and the possibility that this was a tough and amoral killer with a canny wit and impressive acting skills. In legal jargon, the point was, was the man standing there fraudulently, wilfully and obstinately, or 'by the act and providence of God?' It was going to be a hard task, one might think, but not so. Enter his sons and a close friend. They told a very sad story, and an astounding one, given that Bairstan managed to marry and raise a family.

His friend stated that he had known the prisoner for over five years, and that he was sure that ten years had passed since Bairstan had fallen silent. He explained that his two sons had been looking after the old man in that time. His key statement was that 'while he was sane, his wife and he had lived together very comfortably.' The man, Jeremiah Hailey, added that his friend had been capable of merely saying 'yes' or 'no', and that the last time he had heard the man speak was when he had asked him if he knew his friend Jeremiah. 'He said aye, but I think he did not know me.'

Bairstan's two sons confirmed that their father had been silent in that 10-year period, with the exception of one or two words. Henry said that since being locked up, his father had been pressed to speak and had answered something sounding like. 'Be quiet… be quiet'. The other son, Joseph, confirmed that his father had been 'out of his mind' for 10 years'.

There had been enough in him to marry and earn a living, but we must see with hindsight and more relevant knowledge, that Abraham Bairstan had been struck by a paralysis, perhaps combined with a depressive mental illness. In 1824 the most meaningful explanation was to put it down to God's will, so the jury found that the prisoner stood mute 'by the visitation of God.'

Or, if one is pressed to say that it had all been a wonderfully impressive family performance, then would not this be the sure way to keep the old man from the noose? On the other hand, being criminally insane, he was destined to be shut away for ever in awful conditions. The truth will perhaps never now be known. Whatever the reason, the destination of the prison cell was simply the way of dealing with an individual who presented a problem to the criminal justice system of the day.

Second, *social security*. Prison officers have not written many books about their lives. Maybe very few in their ranks have any urge to write down experiences. After all, who would want to take that line of work home with them and make books out of their lives? One person who has, thankfully, done so, is Robert Douglas. Not only has he given readers one of the very rare examples of a man being detailed to work with a condemned man back in the days of capital punishment; he has also left a memory of being on the Durham E Wing when John Straffen was there. As he looked out into the exercise area, Douglas saw a man who was a very striking figure. He wrote: 'A tall, solitary prisoner is exercising… striding out. He wears a blue cotton jacket, buttoned up under his chin. His head is shaved. All he needs are a couple of bolts through his neck and he'd be a dead ringer for Frankenstein.'[5]

The man watched the wire and when two birds landed on it, he shook the wire to chase them away. He was amused by doing that, Douglas noticed, and adds: 'I look at him as he passes by. He exudes strangeness, menace.' He asked the other officers if the man was out for a punishment. And anyway who was he? When Douglas was told it was John Straffen his response was: 'Straffen! Bloody hell! This is a name from my childhood. I would've thought this reptile would have died years ago… As I grew up, began to try and read the papers and saw news reels, now and again there would be some big murder case…' Thousands of people would agree with that. The name Straffen had become a word that was known through the tabloids and the broadcasts; a name to cause a shiver of revulsion.

If writing is largely about trying to apply some empathy to the subject and to imagine what another life would be like, then to contemplate what Straffen's mind must have been in 55 years of incarceration is surely beyond any writer's ability. When he was found guilty of the murder of a girl, Linda Bowyer, in July 1952, he was initially sentenced to death but that was reduced to life inside. He had already killed two young girls for which he had been tried at Somerset assizes in 1951. Straffen had been declared a 'mental defective' in 1947 and had been sent to an asylum. After being found unfit to stand trial for the first killings he was sent to Broadmoor.

In this way the massive stretch of fifty-five years began. He managed to escape from Broadmoor and he went out to kill again. Today, Broadmoor's alarm system is sounded every Monday morning at ten in the morning as a practice run for a real escape alarm. But when Straffen escaped there were no sirens and he was free to stroll into the nearest village and take a life.

In 1952 Straffen was doing cleaning routines when he found a way out. He clambered onto the roof of a hut, climbed to freedom, and then walked to the nearest village at Arborfield where he met five-year-old Linda and strangled her. His murderous tendencies were something that just a little earlier in history would have labelled him 'criminally insane' and that term certainly held good for his nature when he struck again after his escape.

Straffen's first murder happened when he came across little Brenda Goddard at Rough Hill, in Bath, where Straffen was born. He was just twenty-one and was compelled to go to children, place his hands on their necks and strangle them to death, as he did with

Brenda. Only a few days after that he came across Cicely Batstone, who was a little older. They met at the cinema, he walked out with her and then strangled her in a field. Straffen was woken up by police and had no idea what he had done, or so he said. But his confession soon followed.

When he died in November 2007, Straffen was Britain's longest-serving prisoner and the press made the most of it. He died in the health care unit at H M P Frankland.

In prison, a person finds strategies of survival if he has a sense of reality and a perception of himself as a person within a known community, But if he has, as Shakespeare said of King Lear, 'Ever but slenderly known himself' then the experience of life inside will be a timeless frame of routine experience in which the fantasy or the dark imagination wallowing inside will fill the vacuum. Robert Douglas saw a shell of a man, and yet he was enjoying disturbing the little birds. Something in him wanted to destroy what was pure, defenceless and innocent, much as small boys swat flies or stand on insects.

But even with this in mind, the fact is that we are still talking about horrendous murders in the Straffen story. His tale begins with him being taken to a Child Guidance Clinic for truancy and petty theft in 1938 when he was in court for the first time and given probation. It became clear to professionals that he had no moral sense, and he was analysed by a psychiatrist. That is when the term 'mental defective' was applied to him. But he was still at school up to the age of sixteen and at that time, was assessed as having an IQ of just sixty-four. He tried to do normal work back home in Bath but he was an isolated figure, stealing from houses and being alienated from human society.

In July 1947 he was arrested. A girl had been attacked and the assailant had grabbed her, saying: 'What would you do if I killed you? I have done it before.' It was clear that he could not be allowed to live in society and so he was sent to what was then called a 'colony'. In the fifties, I can recall the shiver of fear that passed through myself and family or friends when a certain phrase was spoken: 'They'll send you to an *institution*'. That word, coined in the Victorian period, has a resonance through the British psyche. Children who were 'strange' or 'retarded' – the words used at the time – could be taken away and never come out to play or sit in school again. Such was the fate of John Straffen.

At court in Bath, all Straffen could say to account for what he had done with Cicely was: 'She was picking flowers and I told her there would be plenty higher up. I lifted her over the wall. She never screamed even when I squeezed her neck, so I bashed her head against the wall.' But there had been further explanation of exactly what had happened when he had spoken to a police officer.

At Taunton, Straffen was found unfit to plead. He was ordered to be detained at Her Majesty's pleasure and so an explanation was needed. Dr Peter Parkes, medical officer at H M P Horsfield, said that Straffen had been in custody as a mental defective and had been released on licence. He described Straffen as feeble minded, and Mr Justice Oliver told the court: 'You might as well try a baby in arms. If a man cannot understand what is going on, he cannot be tried.'

Straffen's destination was Broadmoor, and so he made the escape. That was to be the start of a furore about security at that special secure hospital. After the body of Linda Bowyer was discovered Straffen was found at Crowthorne and arrested. He said simply: 'I did not kill her. That's a frame-up that is.' He was sent on remand to Brixton prison, but there followed a massive protest when it became widely reported that he had escaped from Broadmoor to kill again. In early May 1952 there was a protest meeting at Crowthorne, presided over by the chairman of the parish council. The MP was there too. A resolution was passed in which the parishioners expressed 'horror and alarm' at the escape. They asked for a system of public warning to be put in place and that there should be such a discipline in place in Broadmoor that escapes would be impossible. They also wanted the Home Office to be put in control of the institution.

There followed Straffen's long prison life. As the years rolled by, there were occasional reports of him being moved, as in 1966 when he was transferred from Horfield prison in Bristol to Parkhurst on the Isle of Wight, where there was a new security wing. There had been an escape attempt by a group of prisoners at Wandsworth and they had wanted to take Straffen with them. The locals wanted him moved and he went first to Cardiff and then to Horfield.

Straffen went to Parkhurst - followed shortly by six of the Great Train Robbers. That was in 1966, just before he was moved yet again, to Durham, where Robert Douglas met him. Successive Home Secretaries consistently refused to free Straffen and in 1994 a special list was compiled of life-term prisoners who must never see the outside world again: Straffen was on that list. In 2002 his application to be considered by the Criminal Cases Review Commission was refused.

We are left with a recurring problem about insanity and the law. What does society do with such people – the ones who are always going to be dangerous to the public? Some will be occupied in education and forms of self-development. They may be quite capable of study and conversation, and of genuine learning processes. Yet there are others, like Straffen, who are destined to be locked in and observed, constantly supervised and checked. They live in a static condition, isolated and shut into their dark imaginations. For some, Straffen's death was merely a desirable cut in the expenses of keeping such a dangerous man away from his prey. For others it was another reminder that we are powerless to affect, change or cure the sick minds of those beyond therapy and outside workable understanding.

That issue will recur in my historical narrative. The various legal defences such as insanity and provocation, and later the idea of diminished responsibility, do not end with the decision of the court and the sentence; they continue as major factors in modern sentence planning, care and efforts towards rehabilitation.

Finally, *suppression of dissidents*. One of the most important elements in Victorian prison history was the trouble caused by the Chartist prisoners, notably by William Martin. What has become known as the Sheffield Plot of 1840 involved Samuel Holberry, William Martin, Thomas Booker and others, devising an attempted coup in Sheffield in which they planned to seize the town hall and the Fortune Inn, set fire to the magistrate's court, and then, linking with other Chartists, form an insurrection also in Nottingham and Rotherham. Their plot was betrayed by James Allen, and Lord Howard the Lord Lieutenant, took immediate action. At York Assizes on 22 March 1840, Holberry was sentenced to four years at Northallerton for seditious conspiracy 'and at the expiration of that period to be bound himself in £50 and to find two sureties in ten shillings each, to keep the peace towards his Majesty's subjects.' He was leniently treated, for under an Act of 1351 he could have had life imprisonment.

The Chartists wanted electoral reform and mainly worked for votes for working men, along with the reform or electoral districts. In the years around 1840, the 'Physical Force' arm of that movement was accelerating and the Sheffield men were out to take extreme measures. William Martin was given a sentence of one year at Northallerton and he became such a problem that the issue reached Parliament. His charge was 'seditious language' and his behaviour in court tells us a great deal about the man. *The Times* reported:

> 'On sentence being passed, he struck his hand on the front of the dock, saying, "Well that will produce a revolution, if anything will." He begged his Lordship not to send him to Northallerton, but to let him remain in the castle at York, saying that he was very comfortable, and having been seven months confined already was quite at home.'[6]

That was a certain way to open up the Northallerton sojourn, as the judges came down hard on Chartists and they would have had no consideration for these radicals' comfort. To Northallerton Martin went, and there he was to stir things up. In court he had already stressed his Irish connections and made reference to Irish issues, entering into 'a long harangue' on 'Orangemen, the King of Hanover and Rathcormac.'

Martin refused to work on the treadmill as he had not been sentenced to hard labour and so such a punishment did not fall into that category. He was put into the refractory cell for that refusal, but his case was supported by the Secretary of State, Lord Normanby, who wrote: ' ... the prisoner, who was not sentenced to hard labour, cannot legally be placed upon the wheel against his consent... and that if he should refuse to labour upon the wheel, it would be illegal for the gaoler to place him in solitary confinement.' But a visiting magistrate argued against this by quoting one of Peel's recent Gaol Acts which allowed for the work done on a treadmill to be defined as either hard labour or as 'employment for those who are required by law to work for their maintenance...'

Martin, as far as we know, was compelled to work on the mill, and he claimed savage treatment at the hands of the Northallerton staff:

> 'One morning as soon as I had left my cell, the Governor's son… took me by the collar and dragged me from the place where I stood and threw me with violence against the wall, and on the following day he told me I must expect different treatment from what I received in York and he added that men had been reduced to mere skeletons when their term of imprisonment expired and that it should be the case with me…'

These examples illustrate that it is possible to define reasons for imprisonment within a given social and political context. But at the heart of this issue is the fact that over the centuries, imprisonment has related integrally to a criminal justice system, and that is turn is created by changing notions of law.

MORALITY, LAW AND PENOLOGY

The centre of this debate is the relation between a prison system, ideas of punishment, and the interplay between legal structures and moral definition. If a legal system is rigid and maintained as a code of immovable laws to be applied, then prison is a clear logical destination for the person charged and sentenced in the court. The illogicalities and injustices apparent in rigid systems are apparent with hindsight, but also at the time of course. Examples are provided by the crime of blasphemy, for instance. In 1697 Thomas Aikenhead, a young Edinburgh student, was imprisoned and then executed for blasphemy after preaching his unacceptable opinions in public, outside the Tron Church. The Blasphemy Act of 1661 stated that the death penalty awaited anyone who 'Not being distracted in his wits, shall rail upon or curse God, or any of the persons in the Blessed Trinity.' In 2004, George Rosie wrote of the case: 'His trial was a mockery, his execution was a piece of judicial murder.'[8]

In such cases, morality clearly informs and sustains the instruments of the law. Yet in most punishment there is a dialogue within the law machine that balances retribution with human knowledge, social and familial factors and so on. This is all based on the creation of law, so that the body of the legislature and the criminal codes across cultures reflect both fundamental belief and passing moral stricture.

At the heart of punishment and the deprivation of liberty there is this interplay of the letter of the law and its interpretation, which is why courts and judges exist. A useful metaphor for this is found in Judaism. The great rabbi Moses Maimonides (1138- 1204) whose work, the *Mishneh Torah* was, as Norman Solomon explains, 'A systematic digest of the whole range of Jewish law.' But the Torah has as its complement the *halakha* – a space for commentary and debate on the words of written law. The dialogue between the two has been not only the source of much Jewish thought on law and morality, but also it has been a rich source for Jewish literature in general.

Punishment and its causation within a criminal justice system is very much like that use of *Torah* and *Halakha*. In English law, a parallel might be the interplay of the heritage of common law and a criminal statute at any given time at a trial. In other words, many societies have had that kind of structure in which prison has its place, but there have been (and still are) many exceptions. It is not difficult to find examples of prison as a strict, inflexible institution, created to deal with a problem and operating like a well-oiled machine, a process as relentless as the mechanical age which arrived with the sequence of industrial revolutions in the West. Yet, even long before that, examples abound of tyrants simply hurling people into dark dungeons. Prison as oblivion has a long history, from the *oubliettes* in castles to the Black Hole of Calcutta.

Nothing can possibly explain, for example, this policy of imprisonment in Mongolia as reported in 1914 after a Mrs Bulstrode had visited Urga. 'Mrs Bulstrode is probably the only white woman who has ever penetrated beyond the spiked palisade of the outer compound of Urga prison.' She went into a compound and saw five dungeons, inside of which were versions of imprisonment far beyond the most inhumane concoctions of any European mind:

> 'Upon entering the first dungeon we could see nobody – only a number of coffin-like, iron-bound boxes on low trestles, each with a hole about the size of a man's head on the side. The prisoners, we were told, were inside the coffins. One or two of them had been inside for as long as twenty years...'

With these considerations in mind, my global history will aspire to recount the dialogue between retribution and rehabilitation and between incapacitation and punishment across the centuries. However, there is more to the very concept of prison from the time of its emergence as part of an organised state system, and that relates to its invention within the western consolidation of modernity. From the Enlightenment to the postmodern neo-utilitarian notion of a prison, there is good reason for expressing the view that the condition of the prison we have now needs to be revised.

It is not difficult to find examples of the large-scale absurdity and unreason that exists in prisons across the world today. In 2008, for instance, the *San Francisco Chronicle* reported on the statistics for San Quentin where the capacity then was 1,152 and of these 674 inmates were living on death row. Since the death penalty was reinstated in California in 1977, fourteen prisoners had been executed. The result of these facts was that the accountants began to see the wastage and the escalating costs as a crisis. The *Chronicle* reported that a plan to build new housing for the death row inmates would cost almost $40m. The main feature on this stated that 'California's prison system is already a big-ticket item, representing about ten per cent of roughly $100 billion general fund spending.'[11]

That is one example of how the notions of the penitentiary, a product of the Enlightenment (first conceived in genesis as the *panopticon* by the brothers Bentham) began within a rational measure for observation and containment, have become absurd and irrational with vast amounts of money used to maintain people who are (eventually) to be killed by the state.

The madness and absurdity of such systems then spreads elsewhere across the world, reflecting the pattern across the span of history. Vivien Stern pointed out the ludicrous creation of a top security prison on the island of Aruba in the Caribbean, a part of the Kingdom of the Netherlands. She wrote: 'Who decided to build a top security prison in a country where most crime is non-violent and petty and where a long sentence is regarded as one of eight months or more?'[12]

My global history will trace the origins of what has undoubtedly been a succession of experiment and failure in all areas of penology from prisons created by local tyrants to the provisions of incarceration by huge empires and powerful states.

If we ask what underpins everything regarding imprisonment since there was something we could call a 'system' then it is arguably the variations on the extent to which prison is used as more than the mere incapacitation created by the withdrawal of free movement. The major part of prison history in all societies except a very few enlightened exceptions demonstrates the tendency for a stretch in prison to have various degrees of further punishment. Perhaps this is most clearly seen in the creation of the 'top security wing' which in earlier days had the equivalent concept of 'solitary' or of a number of dungeon-like places. In these hermetically-sealed prisons within prisons, the inmates, as Stanley Cohen and Laurie Taylor[13] have shown, lose the community of friendship in most cases. They conclude that 'In the security wing one cannot have someone to talk to at work, someone to laugh with at leisure, for the audience is always the same and the choice of companions the same.. There is little role segregation, little opportunity for the presentation of different selves in different contexts.' In other words, things are very much the same for many prisoners as they were in the huge new Victorian penitentiaries when work was done in a cell, in isolation, for many prisoners in the first phase of their sentence regime.

This is simply one extreme example of perhaps hundreds of different secondary elements in a given punishment, accrued on top of the lack of liberty and the physical constraints of space and movement. In one sense, the history of organised prisons, as delineated by Michel Foucault (discussed in chapter 5) is made complex and multi-layered by this dilemma as to what should actually compose and define a prison sentence.

The concept of prison immediately opens up a chain of other theoretical and intellectual ideas, all integrated yet carrying dissent in their very nature: justice, liberty, power and society. Punishment in all its forms enlightens the criminal code it springs from, and the concept of law always had some kind of penalty and moral transgression bound into it. The problems all came when those in charge began to see that law of necessity had to be always generated, adapted and sometimes abolished as moral structures and political exigency made statutes into often frightening edifices that could have within them the most inhuman and unreasonable lines of thought. One of the most recent developments in Britain in this respect has been the creation of the Supreme Court to replace the decision-making of the House of Lords. This is an institution made specifically to temper political dictates with the voice of humanity and reason, to set by the side of the Human Rights Act and the law-making of Parliament a panel of judges who make intellectual decisions about cases before them, and these cases reflect some of the deepest concerns of the citizen in the confusions of modernity.

In previous ages, such checks and measures of restraint and common sense were never even a distant thought in governmental contexts; they were in the province of the philosophers and social thinkers. Such contrasts and fundamental notions of liberty and human rights set against the shifting power bases over time form the first step in my history.

Finally, there is the constant threat to the historian of being centred on the West only, and on a European-focused basis of writing and thought. A global history has to attempt the task of trying to include reference and discussion of numerous prison systems, and so my material will be necessarily limited to summaries at times, but I have weighted the subjects so that virtually every major development in prison history will have a part here. With that in mind, I have included contrasts of West with East wherever relevant, and included discussions of prison within Islamic jurisprudence, particularly in the account of prisons within empires and in the chapters dealing with the last century.

Notes and references

1 Quoted in Anthony Stokes, *Pit of Shame* (Winchester, 2007) , p. 79.
2 Philip Priestley, *Victorian Prison Lives* (London, 1999), p. 114.
3 'Living Death in Prison', *Daily Citizen*,11.4. 1914.
4 J B Bury, *History of Greece* (London, 1966), p. 581.
5 See Robert Douglas, At Her Majesty's Pleasure.
6 *The Times* October 24 1840 p.6.
7 Ibid.
8 George Rosie, *Curious Scotland* (London, 2004), p.64.
9 Norman Solomon, *Judaism: A Very Short Introduction* (Oxford, 1996), p. 43.
10 *Daily News and Leader* 14. 2. 1914.
11 *San Francisco Chronicle* July 30 2008.
12 Vivien Stern, *A Sin Against the Future* (London, 1998) p. 13.
13 Stanley Cohen and Laurie Taylor, 'The Closed World of the Security Wing' in Jewkes and Letherby, *Criminology: A Reader* (London, 2008) pp. 335-6.

Chapter 1

The First Dark Places

From the first time that human groups formed communal rules there were rule-breakers and there had to be regulatory measures to strive for conformity and cohesion in the society so formed. Laws, sometimes termed 'natural' always formed the bedrock of social identity and purpose. Naturally, security needs conformity to succeed. But the issues surrounding imprisonment concern an amalgam of transgressions, from nay-saying individuals to anarchists and dangerous rebels, and from small-time pilferers to terrorists. Those extremes all lie within the scope of what may emerge when a person develops individuality which may be seen to endanger the social norms, as the Russian poet Joseph Brodsky put it in 2002: 'A man who sets out to create his own independent world within himself is bound sooner or later to become a foreign body in society, and then he becomes subject to all the physical laws of pressure, compression and extrusion.'[1]

The early civilisations mostly had such fragmented states, small potentates and federations that legal systems came and went, were often pragmatic, and individual liberty and human rights were concepts well off the radar of governmental operations. The nations with the first codes of law clearly had some kind of penal provision, as we know from Mesopotamian civilisation, and from the Bible. There are references to prisons in Egypt around 2,000 BC, and in the story of Joseph in the Bible, he was imprisoned in the 'Great prison' at Thebes. There were prison officials, and in most cases the confinement was without a termination date. Even as early as 3,000 BC there is the earliest known legal system, the code of Hammurabi in Babylon, and a term used in that empire for a prison, *Bit kili*, appears to have been a broad term for all kinds of inmates and offences.

ATHENIANS IN CHAINS

However, in spite of the tendency for confinement in many cases to be related more to slaves than prisoners for crime, there are examples of legal concepts including justice and the right to trial. A much celebrated example is in Athens, where the great lawmaker and poet, Solon, revised and devised laws from the time he was archon in 594 BC, the archons being a group of nine appointed high officials in the city in the sixth century. Solon devised laws to free the wretched *hektemoroi*, who were men enslaved for debt. These new laws prevented imprisonment and enslavement for debt. At the centre of his reforms was the notion of *seisachtheia* – a 'shaking off of burdens'. Most important of the measures he created was the availability of private prosecutions in court. Before, there had only been public actions.

Previously, the laws of Draco had been in power. In c.620 he formalised law for the first time in written form, and penalties were brutal and extreme. He was clear in his view that even small offences merited a death penalty, and it was said that he wrote his laws in blood, not ink. Certainly, in terms of Athenian imprisonment, we have two words is use in the literature – *desmoterion* and *phylake*. The former term literally indicates a 'place of chains' although both words are used in the same way. There were long prison terms prescribed, and a group known as The Eleven were responsible for the penal provision.

Solon's reforms may have been enlightened, but the applications of harsh punishment was always there, as there were stocks, for example, and men could be placed there for several days. Imperial Athens being a hotbed of intellectual political theory and philosophy, meant naturally, all aspects of the law would be debated and discussed. In Plato, as with much else, we have a theory of imprisonment which anticipates later categorisation of prisons and prisoners. He formulated three varieties: one for general offenders, one for serious crime but with a stress on rehabilitation, and one for those who were past reclamation. The last group were isolated with no visitors and were positioned in isolated locations. Much of this is not too far away from the 1877 nationalisation ideas in Britain when the modern system was adopted in its first form.[2]

There are other insights into the nature and use of prison in the Athenian state. During the expansion of the Athenian empire, there was an expedition to Sicily where a colony was to be established, and the fleet was to be led by Nicias. The charismatic figure, Alcibiades, was in full support of this and was appointed to assist Nicias. But just before the departure of the fleet, some square stones which stood at the entrances of temples, known as the hermae, were mutilated. Alcibiades's enemies pointed the finger of blame at him. He was charged, but the trial was delayed until his return from the expedition. He and others were accused of impiety and although Alcibiades was pardoned, a number of arrests led to several men being imprisoned, and they were all tried and put to death. This is an insight into political and moral trials, matters related to important ideological and state affairs. The mechanism of trial and prison led inevitably to death. Historians have argued that all this was set up by Corinth as they stood to gain by hindering the expedition, with their vested interest in the silver mines of Syracuse. Prison in this case, as in others such as the famous example of Socrates, was an antechamber to death. The *desmoterion* where they were chained must have been a horrendous place.[3]

In the Jewish society as evident in the Bible, imprisonment appears to have similar functions to that of Greece, in that physical punishment including whipping and the use of stocks is referred to. The prophet Jeremiah is confined, and the references to this provide some kind of insight into provision. Jeremiah is confined first in 'the Upper Gate of Benjamin' and then 'in the court of the guardhouse attached to the royal palace.' These locations suggest that perhaps there was no prison in the sense of a central and spacious set of dungeons with staff and provisions. Yet there may have been other establishments, as is hinted in this statement from the *Book of Ezra*: 'Whoever will not obey the law of your God and the law of the King, let judgement be rigorously executed on him, be it death, banishment, confiscation of property or imprisonment.' This is further elaborated by Christopher Marshall in his study of prison in the Bible, when he adds: 'In the ancient world prisons were usually underground dungeons or wells, or pits in the ground… Jeremiah was put in a cistern house. When he was released for interrogation, he begged not to be returned to his cell fearing he would die there.'[4]

ROME AND IMPRISONMENT

As in every other aspect of regimentation and order, Roman civilisation generated laws, and forced confinement was part of the social fabric, even down to the household cell, the *ergastulum*, in which a paterfamilias could hold slaves or even family members who crossed the moral line or who did criminal acts. From the earliest period of Roman history, the Twelve Tables were conceived and applied. These embody the earliest form of Roman law, emerging from class struggle between the patricians and the plebeians. The latter had been left out of law-making and knew nothing of the law, which was the preserve of the rich, but by 450 BC, with the last created law by the committee – the *comitia centuriata* - the laws were formed, based mainly on ancient custom. The law embodied in the Twelve Tables has not come down to us except by way of other sources, but as C. F. Kolbert has noted: ' ...the Twelve Tables continued to be held in great reverence, and Cicero recorded that in his younger days schoolboys had to learn them by heart at school. Such rules as we know are simple, and concerned procedure rather than substantive law... a simple idea of procedure was what the common man most needed to know...'[5]

In everyday law decisions, the magistrates (*tresviri capitalis*) held the power of imprisonment, but there were also courts held in the provinces in the Imperial era, and courts held by the army. It appears that prisons were labour camps and that the chained slaves and prisoners were amalgamated. From the historian Livy in his work on the Carthaginian War it is known that there were quarry-prisons. This passage explains their operation:

'At Rome watchmen patrolled the streets, the minor magistrates were ordered to make inspections, and the three officials in charge of the quarry-prisons to increase their vigilance... the hostages [the Carthaginians] kept should be in close custody,with no opportunity to come out into public places, the prisoners to be loaded with chains of not less than ten pounds weight...'[6]

The Roman prison from that time down to the Imperial years was in the Capitoline Hill, where there was a quarry and within that area there was a prison called the Mamertine prison. The prisons were called *latumiae*, which primarily means 'quarry.' One interesting feature of the prison, the Mamertine, is that it was close to the forum, so that the magistrates in their work clearly knew the destination of criminals, and the common phrase, 'send him down' would have had a resonance related to the geography of the prison and the court.

Roman law, in the form it took during the reign of the later emperors, and known as the *Corpus Iuris Civilis*, was to include the inquisitorial procedure at trial, influential on the legal systems of Europe and America until the later eighteenth century, when adversarial trial slowly began to exist. In other words, the nature of the trial was intended to assume that there was guilt and the Roman in court (as with the Athenian) was expected to appear as a shadow of his former self, as he had not taken the option of self-imposed exile for the sake of honour. Even with the growth of trial rhetoric and persuasion, as demonstrated by the lawyer Cicero, the emphasis was on assumed guilt and witnesses in place to certify that culpability. As Sadakat Kadri expressed the situation: 'As in Athens, citizens facing a capital charge had the choice of departure or submission ... justice in the empire was a tool rather than an ideal, wielded by magistrates whose role was to police an empire rather than to honour a tradition.'[7] The advent of a prison sentence invariably meant slave labour and torture.

There were several prisons on record, including the *alba fucens* and the *Tullianum*. Interestingly, there were departmental elements to a Roman prison, with areas for specific penal applications of punishments. The worst was the very innermost hellish and dark cell, and there are references in the Theodosian Code of the later empire concerning the necessary squalid conditions purposely provided some particular offences. Yet that code (of AD 320) does have an element of clemency and humanity, stating that torture must be tempered by other aspects which at times lighten the burden. This is supported by something explained by St Augustine who wrote that some citizens in prison were guarded by specially appointed officials rather than by the usual gaolers.

Archaeology has also added to our knowledge of punishment in the Roman empire. This work on so-called 'deviant burials' has helped in our understanding of the fate of prisoners of war. The deaths were usually by decapitation or from multiple blows with many cut from front to back, and remains show signs of defleshing. In the graves the heads were often placed between the legs. In fact, the custom the Romans had of 'punishment after death' is evident in these finds. A prisoner could not only be executed and no more. There could be further humiliation:

> 'It could run to the full panoply of damnation memoriae, whereby the memory of the deceased was defiled by mutilation of facial features on statues and other images, the throwing of damaged statues into rivers and the eradication of written works. The aim was to spoil the individual's afterlife by destroying their memory...'[8]

The keynote of ancient justice and punishment in its various forms was that of oppression, not of justice. There is little evidence of a humanitarian concern for rights and understanding of motives in offences and transgressions.

THE MIDDLE AGES ACROSS EUROPE
The other code of law to be applied widely as the early Middle Ages developed was the ecclesiastical law. Both the Roman and the Ecclesiastical (or canon) law systems were to have a massive and widespread effect on prisons and penal thought in the centuries before human rights and adversarial trial emerged. Edward Peters explains the development and application of the ecclesiastical law: 'Only from the ninth century on, chiefly under the influence of Charlemagne (747-814) and his successors, was there an effective movement to shift from the personality to the territoriality of law, that is, to make a single legal system applicable to all inhabitants of a territory regardless of their political origin and make ecclesiastical law effectively binding on Christians everywhere.'[9]

The impact and influence of the church in this respect may be seen in a story from Russia, specifically in Kievan Rus, written in 996. Rus had been converted to Christianity; Vladimir placed his sons in various towns and consolidated power, but the bishops had great power. The Rus clergy knew and used canon law. Vladimir, on gaining power, gave a tenth of his income to the church, and he had to establish a system of justice. The chronicle of the time relates that the Kievan bishops went to Vladimir and asked about the epidemic of murders in the state. He had not punished, he said, because he was 'afraid of sinning'

As Daniel Kaiser explains, the result of the bishops' influence was the return to what the Germanic races had adopted as punishment for centuries – the 'bloodwite' – a blood price to be paid for homicides committed, and it was against the Byzantine law (Roman in origin). Said Kaiser: 'In this case, at least, there are no grounds for assuming that these revenge statutes reflected Byzantine law, where long before homicides had fallen under the authority of the state. Indeed, it was precisely this Byzantine preference for afflictive sanctions which gave rise to the chronicle's account of the bishop' interference with Vladimir's judiciary.'[10]

In other words, in the massive areas in which Christianity extended its legal influence, there was an axis of interchanged notions of punishment, situated between 'blood price' and revenge and imprisonment or torture. This led to many of the early prisons in Europe and Russia being dungeons or cells either held by princes or bishops. Consequently, before established legal codes developed from common law in the Middle Ages, there were prisons privately held and controlled by churchmen, usually with their own gallows. Of course, they had their own courts as well.

In England the ecclesiastic courts began in the tenth century with a law that stated: 'The bishop of the shire and the aldermen in the hundred courts expound both things, as well as the law of God, as the secular law.' Later, after the sixteenth-century Reformation the practice developed whereby courts were held by the bishop, the dean and chapter, and by the archdeacon. The latter held the court for the diocese and so had the most business to do. The bishop of each diocese would have a 'visitation' in his first year in office and then every three years following. For the archdeacons, their courts would be annual, but would be suspended if the bishop arrived for a visitation. The hearing would be presided over by a chancellor, and the final decision was made by an appointed person such as a lawyer- the official principal.

In addition to these courts, there were also 'peculiars' – locations which were beyond the jurisdiction of the bishop, and which could be held under the guidance of a wide assortment of bodies and individuals. Records for the peculiars are not necessarily substantial or even complete in sequences or collections, but Anne Tarver has researched the Lichfield courts and has shown that there are very useful records there.

The records of these church courts are called Act Books, but these may also be termed Courts Books. A clerk would be in the position of the registrar to such courts, and the work he did would be the source of the records, hence the scanty and unpredictable nature of these archives.

Later, the term 'consistory court' came into use. The word was used of all the church courts except for the Court of Arches. This Lambeth court was the highest court and acted as an appeal court in fact. The consistory court and archdeacons' courts would be held on sacred ground, within the church establishment. The placing of the court furniture would be such that the hierarchy of those present would be paramount, so that there would be a high seat for the archdeacon for example, and the seating for those involved would have a boundary structure, making a tight, well-defined court area. There was plenty of business in the courts – in 1575 alone the Archbishop of York in his visitations across his diocese brought 1,200 defendants into the courts.

In the early Medieval years, the canon law had to be rationalised and centralised, and a formative moment in this was when Gratian produced his *Concordance of Discordant Canons*, known generally as the *Decretum*, in 1140. This was the basis of the laws following, and the formations of the canon law were then verified and applied in all the states of Europe through to the period of the Reformation.

Within clerical organisation there were a range of prisons, including those held by monastic orders for punishment of their own members, and also there were prisons used for the punishment and discipline of members of the clergy for extremely serious transgressions. Monks were said to be kept in *murus largus* – close confinement. There were also diocesan prisons for the confinement of recalcitrant clergy. But most infamous, and therefore most subject to myth, were the prison of the Inquisition. From c.1220 there was the creation of the office of the inquisitor of heretical depravity, and so began the long period of inquisition of heretics when prisons were necessary for this process because people had to be held in confinement over the period of interrogation. At times over the following centuries, men in power acted with a measure of humanity and checked some of these prisons, notably Pope Clement V, who had inspections done in the prisons of the South of France.

There were Episcopal inquisitions and papal inquisitions, and particular religious movements and bodies obviously attracted the attention of the inquisitors. The Waldensians and Cathars in the South of France were the subject of intransigent inquisition, and there was a range of punishments in the armoury, including pilgrimage, public recantation and of course, imprisonment. A well-known example of this is the actions against the Knights Templars, whose members were tried across Europe between 1307 and 1314. Periods of detention varied, but in cases such as that of the Languedocian inquisitor, Bernard Gui, long sentences were favoured, and some Templars spent as long as 4 years in prison. Thomas Kramer has researched some procedures and gives examples such as this from France:

> 'The average length of time between the detention of a suspect, his confession and absolution is given in the register of Jacques Fournier as twenty-four weeks. At the time of their first deposition in front of the inquisitor, the Templars of Ales had spent nearly three years continuously in prison. Their second statement followed again one year later.'[11]

Torture was used of course, as the Templars had sworn an oath of secrecy. In the same essay, Kaiser estimates the deaths from torture. 'The effects of torture and imprisonment become clear when one compares the number of the interrogated. In the thirteen months of imprisonment, three of the thirty-two Templars disappeared from the protocols...'[12] Seven more brother knights had their names expunged (and so had died) in the year following this previous count of three.

The instance of the Templars affords an opportunity to see the church and state in opposition regarding penal sentences and torture. In December 1309 King Edward II met papal inquisitors to ratify torture of some knights. The whole idea was against English common law. The meeting at Lambeth was to result in Edward's assent, and he gave it very reluctantly, appointing a certain William de Dene to supervise the torture. This was followed by a request from the inquisitors to have some knights placed in solitary confinement and again he did so, along with permission to use torture. But he was not pleased, despite the fact that ecclesiastical law sanctioned both torture and solitary confinement.

To summarise: before any general prison systems were in place across Europe, the powers of both Roman law and ecclesiastical law were influential in the use of imprisonment. What emerged across Europe was a common learned law: a mix of Roman and local sources and practices. Imprisonment was part of the applied criminal code allied to that practice.

CITY STATES: THE ITALIAN EXAMPLE

It is possible to glean an interesting and informative example of how prisons were used in the city states across Europe in the centuries before the advent of modernity, in its first configurations, in the movements for unification in the nineteenth century, and before the impact of Enlightenment thought in the previous century, by studying Venice. There was a range of prison of different categories and government. At the hub of the justice establishment was the institution called the Council of Ten, created in 1310. The members of this group wore black clothes and met in secret. As part of their reach into the city's less salubrious parts, they employed secret agents, and when people were brought to trial there was no examination of witnesses. Peter Ackroyd explains how this group, and their prison, functioned:

'The examinations of the accused were generally conducted in darkness, and from the room of the three leaders of the council was a staircase leading directly to the dungeons and the chambers of torture. Its verdicts did not permit any appeal. Banishment or death, by strangulation or by drowning followed very quickly.'[13]

In the fourteenth century, there were many prisons, the largest and most fearsome being the two known as the 'Wells' and the

'Leads'. The former was on the lower level of the building on the Rio della Paglia, and the latter was the upper story (the leads referring to the roofs). During the wars with France in the late eighteenth century, one prisoner was found by the invading French forces, and it was discovered that he had been in his cell for sixteen years, having never seen daylight in that period.

Both church and state had legal power, as already discussed, and in Venice, as in other states, the powerful class intermixed secular and clergy. Because it was so normal for the priests to administrate and even to wage war at times, naturally prisons and torture would be a normal part of their structures of control and organisation. Recent research has shown that there were wider issues which influenced attitudes to prisons in the European states, mainly the shift from expulsion to confinement of various dissenting and minority groups. To effect this, states needed to improve prisons in terms of categorising prisoners and by making them less detrimental to health and life.

A good example of what could be done is illustrated by Siena in 1327, where the Council were told that recently more than sixty people had died in the city prison through illness and neglect. Those concerned wanted a new prison where categorisation could be done, and they succeeded. As G. Geltner has argued in a survey of medieval prisons, such measures were part of this move to deal with deviant groups in less deadly ways:

> 'Local governments developed mechanisms for maintaining social order in a new key. Rather than physically annihilate the presence of religious and social deviants, various regimes created or annexed marginalising institutions such as leper-houses, brothels, hospitals and Jewish quarters. The central, municipally run prison was a later but equally ubiquitous expression of such attitudes to social control.'[14]

Geltner's work on medieval prisons has shown that what was really happening, different from established views, was that prisons in this period show that deviants were 'contained and maintained'.[15] This work also shows that previous attitudes regarding the domination of the church and of monastic orders in terms of the development of the prison were overstated, and the changes effected by city states underestimated.

What happened in most places, as European examples show, is that local and city prisons were multiple, varied and never quite the same. The Medieval period was before what J. R. and William McNeill refer to as the 'First Worldwide Web' when mass communication and the 'shrinkage' of the globe had not occurred. Alliances and internecine wars, along with such matters as fears related to populations on the move through war or poverty and starvation, dealt with crime through panic and fear, with *ad hoc*measures often being extreme and inhuman. It makes sense that when the city states consolidated the notions of citizenship and social conformity, they had to deal with deviance in ways that would not utterly deracinate the sub-groups concerned. The reasons for this were surely practical: the deviants were also the main source of cheap labour supply and cannon-fodder. In England and in France and German states, one action taken in court trials was to send a culprit into the ranks of the army rather than to prison.

Medieval society in all places had to cope with extreme economic pressures, from starvation after bad harvests to the arrival of the plague. Add to that the frequency and savagery of war and it becomes clear why prison was not necessarily the best option in criminal justice systems. In the thirteenth-century court rolls for manors and for towns, there are frequent decisions of fines rather than imprisonment in the court decisions. Fines were very useful for sovereigns in need of money for warfare.

Notes and references

1 See Cynthia Haven, *Conversations with Joseph Brodsky* p. 22.

2 For more on this, see Edward M Peters: 'Prison Before the prison' in *The Oxford History of the Prison* pp. 6-8.

3 For a full account of this trial and judgement, see J B Bury, *History of Greece* (London, 1966) pp. 466-468.

4 Christopher Marshall, 'Prison, Prisoners and the Bible' on www.restorativejustice. org p. 5.

5 C.F. Colbert, *Justinian: The Digest of Roman Law* (London, 1979), p. 13.

6 Quoted by Peters, above 2 p. 17.

7 Sadakat Kadri, *The Trial* (London, 2006), p. 13.

8 Alison Taylor: 'The Deviant Dead' *Current Archaeology* 24 July, 2010 p. 25.

9 See Peters (ref.2) p. 22.

10 Daniel H Kaiser, 'Reconsidering Crime and Punishment in Kievan Rus' *Russian History* Vol.7 part 3 1980 pp. 283-293 p. 287.

11 Thomas Kramer, 'Terror, Torture and the Truth: The Testimonies of the Templars Revisited' in *The Debate on the Trial of the Templars* (Farnham, 2010), p. 81. This collection of essays by scholars provides a widely referenced and closely detailed account of the use of trial and imprisonment in the eradication of the Templars across Europe.

12 Ibid. p. 83

13 Peter Ackroyd, *Venice* (London, 2010) pp. 97-98.

14 G. Gertner, *The Medieval Prison* (Princeton, 2010), p. 11.

15 Ibid. p. 13.

Chapter 2

Judgement and Trial

It is useful to recall here that prison is simply one of a number of options defined as punishment, in all societies and at all times. Segregating deviant populations in states and communities was not high on the list in societies such as the Normans, Vikings, Kievan Rus, Celts, Romans and Greeks who all saw that infringement of laws carried moral and dissenting elements, and chose a punishment from a number of options such as mutilation, banishment, branding, whipping , shaming and of course, judicial execution.

The reasons for this are not hard to find: dealing with offences without any concomitant burden of expense or continuing maintenance is much to be desired if the society and its power relations are to continue unimpeded. In addition, as mentioned briefly in the last chapter, there was the smart notion of using transgressors of all kinds to work as slaves, as in the Roman civilisation, and in the French society up to the early nineteenth century. Feudal and despotic systems, in short, saw offenders as sources of finance, labour or opposition to be swiftly eradicated.

The formation of a court is almost everywhere evident within the criminal justice systems across the globe as they operated in isolation. Clearly, where certain people expanded and took their punitive systems with them, some forms of imprisonment began to be evident, most obviously in Rome and Greece, where all central processes and protocols were replicated in conquered cultures. In early Russia, before the Romanovs, the church and state could use confinement before trial, just as the Germanic people had the idea of a common law, or the late Roman Empire and the Carolingian Empire had their courts and the practice of using some kind of dungeon before trial. In England there is a very clear example of what happened when an absolute ruler went above and beyond the law in order to have a court that would deal with anyone in opposition - a court linked organically to a specific prison.

COURTS AND CRIMINAL PROCESS

The Court of Star Chamber was the institution in question and its victims were usually sent on to rot away in prison. This was supposedly created to deal with 'unlawful combinations, riots and assemblies and offences of sheriffs and jurors' but was later extended to 'offences against royal proclamations'. In other words, it began in a statute of Henry VII in 1487 and continued until it was abolished in 1640. In its later phase it was used to cut out the work of lower courts and to put the powerful gentry in front of the judges with speed, and to deal with them by oppression. Most notoriously, Cardinal Wolsey used it to bring to trial opponents of the policies of Henry VIII.

Under Charles I the court was also widely used as a means of crushing dissent, as is well indicated by the case of John Lilburne, the Leveller leader who was flogged, pilloried and imprisoned for distributing anti-episcopal literature.

Yet there had been the development of the assize courts and the circuit judges from the mid-twelfth century, and these provided the strength and central regal authority of he Angevin empire, and the concept of gaol delivery and *oyez* and *terminer* as powers give to the travelling justices by royal permission. This was the central system of the criminal law, and local gaols began to be used to house those awaiting trial for felonies at one of the two annual assizes. That system, of quarter sessions (from the magistrates' arrival on the scene in the mid fourteenth century) and then assizes, meant that prison now had a definite purpose, but it was never uniform and well regulated. It was a system subject to horrendous abuse of course, and the gaol fever tended to remove a high proportion of prisoners awaiting trial before the assizes happened. There was no regulation of bail until Sir Robert Peel was Home Secretary in 1822, and indeed, the 1689 Bill of Rights had noted that 'Excessive bail hath been required of persons committed in criminal cases to elude the benefit of the laws made for the liberty of the subject' which hints at a large scale of abuses of that system.[1] Consequently, under Henry II there was the refinement of the jury of presentment and the beginnings of the Grand Jury, later adopted in the USA. But the ordeal method of trial dominated with execution, mutilation or banishment as punishments in many cases.

This attitude, extending across Europe in various forms, was an extension of regal and imperial power, assimilating common, Roman and /or ecclesiastical law according to pragmatic considerations. If we need a clear example of how uses of imprisonment fit into this scheme then a classic example is the lofty notion of the royal pardon.

In the centuries before the first establishment of prisons as destinations for criminals of all kinds, prison was largely used for debtors and for those who were perceived as enemies of the state – the ideologically unsound, the religious dissenters and the rebels of all hues. Understanding the nature of incarceration in those centuries before the central criminal justice system slotted prison into its place in the structural hierarchy involves some extended consideration of courts, trials and individual liberty. In England there had been Magna Carta of course with its multiple rulings about human rights within the King's realm. It was all hurried and messy, having to be clarified in 1225, but there was nothing there about subjects being placed in prison against what was stated as 'the law of the land.'

At the core of this issue is the concept of habeas corpus, the writ which has been used over the last three centuries in Britain and across the world in her empire to order gaolers and other judiciary persons to bring the accused to trial and stand before a judge. It is a writ of the nature of a prerogative – that is, with the force of the sovereign, so anyone ignoring that command has committed a contempt of the court in question.

What happened was that a specific writ began to be used, something that was habeas corpus in its proto-version, as Paul Halliday had recently studied and explained: 'But many court instruments from the thirteenth century might seem to resemble ancestors of the later habeas corpus in its *ad subjiciendum* form....'[2] This writ was 'less concerned with moving bodies - many writs did that – than with inspecting the thinking and actions of those who confined bodies.'[3]

However, in Britain, as in the medieval empires and states across Europe in the medieval years, a court could be of several varieties, and of course, could stand outside the law as written and defined, or it could be simply an assembly with the potentate in command, with full powers of punishment. Writs seem all very well and very worthy in theory, but in practice, if a person had sufficient power, then a writ such as *ad subjiciendum* could be ignored or deflected. On the positive side, there were established writs, from the twelfth century, such as *mainprise*, designed to command sheriffs to ensure that prisoners appeared in court.

The notion of a royal pardon between the accession of William I and the Tudors was largely something concerned with power rather than with mercy. We like to think that a pardon is some kind of honourable, humane measure taken against a transgressor, and that, as Shakespeare famously said, 'The quality of mercy is not strained.' But in fact, after the Anglo-Saxon and Roman years in Britain, when laws had developed in certain regions in which various Saxon kings had worked out a *wergild* – a 'worth money' for crimes, the pardon became a concept that would on the one hand increase the prestige and status of a monarch, and on the other hand provide a touch of 'PR' as mercy was shown openly and with great pomp and ceremony.

We must first consider the partner of the pardon and the reprieve – capital punishment. In the Saxon centuries there was hanging as a standard punishment for such offences as murder and cowardice, but there was also a variety of other punishments. But to take a man's life was as often related to religious and moral concepts as much as to a strict criminal code. In the medieval period, outlawry was a common option in the courts, but that really meant a death penalty as the culprit would be hounded and hunted down, killed, and all his property taken from him. The old phrase relating to this is far from the world of Robin Hood – the outlaw should be treated 'like the head of a wolf.'

In the earliest times of Celtic Britain, the tribes existing before the Roman conquest clearly had capital punishment, but with the Saxons, the concept of punishment, tied to the wergild, meant that there was a sliding scale, so that the notion of *manbot* was created. This referred to slaves, so that a slave had value. The *wergild* and the *manbot* meant that, for instance, the money paid in compensation for a tooth being knocked out was one shilling in c.600 according to the laws of Ethelbert of Kent. If a person could not pay the *bot*, the results were dire. It was possible that the offender could lose all his land, or be outlawed, or even be ordered to pay the King a fine called a *wite* – the same concept as understood across Europe, embracing the Scandinavian and Rus cultures.

There is no mercy in any of this, merely a money motive and an eye to profit in actions of grievous bodily harm. It took changes in the nature of kingship to bring about developments in the criminal justice system of course, and before the creation of a national state around AD 900. Therefore, King Edward the Elder's reign saw the beginnings of more definite engagement with the justice system from the sovereign. In the middle years of the tenth century Edward ruled that if someone forced their way into another person's home then that transgressor was breaking the custom of royal protection. That offender would be deemed to be *botleas* – having no status to provide compensation. The result was it was the King's decision what would happen to that offender; whether he would live or die in effect.

Not long before the Norman Conquest, then, the status of the king as someone who could act by giving a pardon was established. Although death by hanging would be the obvious result, the king could also elect to substitute other forms of punishment such as maiming and mutilation or even drowning or stoning. Perhaps the most astonishing and impressive document in this context before 1066 is a law of King Cnut of 1023 with the following decrees:

'If anyone eagerly wishes to turn from wrongdoing back to right behaviour, one is to be merciful to him very readily , as best one can, for the fear of God. And let us always help quickest those who need it most. The weak man must always be judged and prescribed for more leniently than the strong, for the love of God. For we know full well that the feeble cannot bear a burden like the strong... For we know that we must moderate and distinguish reasonably between age and youth, wealth and poverty, freedom and slavery, health and sickness..... Also in many a deed when a man acts under compulsion, he is then more entitled to clemency in that he did what he did out of necessity... and if anyone acts unintentionally, he is not entirely like one who does it intentionally...'[4]

The last sentence and the penultimate one contain the kernel of all the major issues concerning pardons in the medieval centuries. At the centre was the problem of what to do about the unintentional slayer. A cursory glance at the court records of manors and bishoprics over the thirteenth century, for instance, makes it clear that those with ecclesiastical power and those with the administration of the *eyre* – the circuit court established in 1176 who were supposed (by Magna Carta) to go into every county once every year which preceded the assizes – could hang felons at their local gallows. Publications of county records societies today show thousands of cases of forced entry, assault, murder and rape for which there was merely a fine or an acquittal. Therefore, it is clear that Cnut was ahead of his time, but later, with the reforms of the fourteenth century and the creation of assize courts, the king emerged as an entity linked profoundly with the notion of a pardon.

Even in the fourteenth century there was no dependable outcome of a trial. A general issue of a pardon could be done if the king needed soldiers and the offender could go and fight on campaign. Sometimes the king needed money and would therefore benefit from a large fine rather than having a man hanged. There was no financial benefit in giving a royal pardon. By the reign of Henry I hanging was generally established, after his father, William the Conqueror, had decreed that 'no-one would be killed or hanged for any cause.' Henry's reign saw such events as the mass hanging in 1124 of forty-four thieves in Leicestershire. Death at that time was the punishment for treason, burglary, arson, robbery, theft and homicide.

The contrast between the Anglo-Saxon world and the later medieval years then, is seen in this contrast. In the seventh century under Ethelbert, a murderer might pay a hundred shillings, but for grievous bodily harm the *wergild* was only twenty shillings. There was compensation demanded by the church courts as well if offences were done on holy days for instance. In other words, the Saxon saw offences as transgressions against the community and saw reparation in terms of wealth. By c.1100, there was more chance of a hanging and so there were more appeals for pardon.

Clearly, before the later kings' reigns in which the assizes began to have more power, the situation was one in which the local power-base had immense control and influence: that is to say the church and the manor. When justices of the peace were created in 1361, there was a markedly more streamlined approach to the administration of justice and offenders and more notice taken of gaols and the need for gaol delivery at certain times of the year. In most cases the early medieval prisons of local barons were places where one could expect to languish and then die before a court appearance appeared.

In the centuries before the assizes, then, established in the reign of Henry II, and the beginnings of the idea of the grand jury in the 1166 Assize of Clarendon, the barbarity in penal thinking was clearly a deterrent to the seasoned villain and a horror for the everyday citizen who found himself in trouble with the law. A man with no legal process behind him would stand with his accuser and there would be an ordeal which could be cold water, hot water or of fire. In the first of these, the accused was tied and thrown into deep water. If he sank he was classified as innocent. In the second, the accused had to put his hand into boiling water to grasp a stone. If his hand had healed three days later he was cleared of the charge. In the final ordeal, fire, the accused had to hold a hot iron bar and keep hold as he took nine paces. Again, healing had to take place in three days for him to be cleared.

HOMICIDE, PARDONS AND ASSIZES

To summarise all this criminal justice chaos in the centuries before the Tudors, there was always uncertainty at trial. Outlawry and fines were common, as were acquittals, but if a punishment was given, the consequences were never anticipated as if there was a codification of sentences and a regular ruling. For instance, in a case from 1282 from the Yorkshire *eyre*, there were four prisoners who had been gaoled in 1279. After three years in prison, two men were judged to have killed by accident and were released and then pardoned; the two others who had clearly killed in self-defence were never pardoned.

In countless cases of homicide in the medieval centuries, there is evidence of confusion and miscarriage of justice in all areas. A story that illustrates this is from 1290 in which John de Oklesthorp was bailed after a verdict of killing in self defence. What happened was that John and his friend Hugh were bailiffs and had seized a cart and horse from Robert Turpin, who had followed then wielding an axe, and had been shot with an arrow by John. As the bailiffs grappled with Robert the arrow was forced deeper into his chest and he died. The evidence showed that John pushed the arrows into the chest (and he had fired the shot). Yet John was pardoned and Hugh was hanged. There is not sound reason why John was pardoned.[5]

But nevertheless, in the twelfth and thirteenth century there were all kinds of measures taken to reform and modernise the penal and criminal justice system. Specialist historians of the subject of pardons have demonstrated effectively that royal pardons were created to play a principal part in these reforms. But Cnut's wise words about killings done 'unintentionally' was never going to be clear-cut in the courts, and those who might be termed 'excusable slayers' would never have been confident of a fair outcome after legal process in these years. The prospect of serving the king against the Scots or the Irish must have seemed much brighter than outlawry or taking your chance in a court.

In the Tudor period, the nature of the royal pardon was to change radically. Although on the surface, and with the images of popular culture in mind, the Tudor dynasty appears to be one of mass slaughter sanctioned by the sovereign and state and there is ample evidence that the royal pardon really came into its own in this century. Cynthia Herrup's influential book, *The Common Peace* (1987) has shown that pardons were used with a sense of *Realpolitik* and pragmatism, and were part of a process of creating the kinds of citizens the Tudor enterprise wanted – people who could be formed and moulded into subservience.

Anyone in Tudor Britain must have been aware how easy it was to slip into a category of behaviour which could be termed 'treasonable.' Historians of the period have often pointed out the similarity between Tudor policy and the Soviet oppression under Stalin. A trial for treason was the surest way for the state to bring down anyone who was deemed to be unacceptable in beliefs or actions. One foreign visitor to England in 1558, Etienne Perlin, noted in *Description des Royaulmes D'Angleterre* that 'a man cannot be certain from one day to the next who might be closest to the King's confidence and who degraded, stripped of his possessions and imprisoned awaiting the death of a traitor.' Perhaps the defining statute in this respect was in 1534 when a Treason Act elaborated on the old, basic definition of treason as 'compassing or imagining the King's death' and 'levying war against the king in his realm' or 'adhering to the king's enemies in his realm, giving them aid and comfort here and elsewhere' (Treason Act 1351). The 1534 Act added the words, 'Those who maliciously wish, will or desire, by words or writing, or by craft imagine the King's death.'

Bearing in mind the frequent uprisings and revolts of the sixteenth century, notably the 1536 Pilgrimage of Grace and the 1569 rising of the Northern Earls, it is plain to see why there was so much repression. Clearly, the religious ferment made matters worse, and there is paranoia in much of Henry VIII's actions of repression, and again with Elizabeth's tough actions on plotters. But the state was so extreme and terrifying that a man who wrote to Lady Lisle in 1535 could say: 'It is rumoured that a person should be committed to the Tower for saying that this month will be rainy and full of wet, next month death and the third, war.'

In this context, as Cynthia Herrup has shown, the royal pardon was such a stunningly effective public relations exercise that the Tudor monarchs, mostly experts in 'spin', cultivated its use. She notes that Henry VII for instance, issued five general pardons in his reign and over 1,600 people were saved. The patent rolls for 1485-1603, covering the whole dynasty, show almost 14,000 people who were given grants of mercy. Herrup has made a convincing case for the view that the Tudors saw the value in demonstrating mercy as a way to persuade people that a trial was to be preferred to outlawry. After all, this was the age of the 'sturdy beggar' and the massive problems of the parish labour troubles when legislation on apprentices, masters and servants, and poor houses was created.[6] It was also the age which made the house of correction. In short, there was repression, but there was also a clever dissemination of an ideology that gave a semblance of a beneficent state and an enlightened monarch. Although Henry VIII was the man who promised pardon to the leaders of the Pilgrimage of Grace and then saw dozens of them hanged both in London and in the north, he was also the man who revelled in demonstrating his capacity for mercy.

Mary was the same. In the aftermath of the Wyatt revolt, she showed the same public image. Sir Thomas Wyatt was a poet and courtier and had land in Kent. When Queen Mary was to marry

Philip of Spain, it was all too much for him and later he took part in what he thought was a general revolt across the land, but in effect it was merely a Kent uprising. He failed and was hanged on Tower Hill in April 1554 when over four hundred of Wyatt's followers were brought from Kent to the London prisons, strapped together like animals going to the slaughter. In the courtyard at Westminster they all knelt and begged for mercy and Queen Mary graciously gave her pardon.

It has been estimated that in Henry VIII's reign, 72,000 people were executed. But again, it was clear from early in his reign that if there were to be pardons, then he would have the monopoly. In a statute of 1536 we have these words:

> 'No person or persons of what estate or degree so ever they be of shall have any power or auctorities to pardon or remit any treasons, murders, manslaughters or any kyndes of felonyes... but that the Kings highness, his heirs and successors ... Kings of this realm shall have the whole and sole power and auctorities thereof united and knit to the imperial crown of the realm....'[7]

In this same period, the famous lawyer Sir Edward Coke stated that the pardon only applied to public offences which had been prosecuted by the crown. He also said the royal pardon could negate the death penalty but that the King could not change the form of the execution. This was important because the different methods of execution given to people of different rank or whose crimes were in law to be punished by a specific form of execution had to relate to the written law and the sovereign could not interfere with such procedures.

Paradoxically then, the Tudors learned the value of a pardon as a powerful tool to promote conformity and adherence to the state. There could be as many secret executions as a sovereign desired, but if pardons were public, then they would have the attention of the London mob and the word would be passed around that the King or Queen was munificent and a good Christian prince. The iconic words were created: *'Now know ye that We in consideration of some circumstances humbly represented to Us, are graciously pleased to extend Our Grace and Mercy unto the said......*[8]

There were also the more routine pardons and reprieves in the Tudor courts, notably the concept of the 'pleading the belly' appeal in court. The thinking here was the chid in the womb could not be considered guilty and so should not hang. The notion was that the reprieve was temporary with the mother supposedly being hanged after the birth of the child. But, as James Sharpe has shown in his book, *Crime In Early Modern England*, it was common for these mothers to be fully pardoned. He points out that in the Home circuit of assizes between 1558 and 1625, 'nearly half of the women convicted of a felony claimed to be pregnant and over a third (38 per cent) were successful in their claim.'[9] The procedure was that a group of matrons would examine the woman in court who claimed to be pregnant. These were wives and midwives, arbiters of the female body, and of course, they would have a whole panoply of various bits of knowledge with which to examine the women.

Pardon in Tudor England was of course also related to people with wealth and a certain 'high degree' with the everyday villain or rogue ending up with a date on the scaffold or languishing forgotten in a hellish prison. The only other possibility of a reprieve would come from the 'benefit of clergy' – a simple test of literacy based on being able to recite a passage from the Bible.

Between the Tudors and the arrival of the Hanoverians in the eighteenth century, little changed in this context with the escapes from the rope open to felons consisting of pardons, benefit of clergy or 'pleading the belly.' But generally the hangman was busy and the sixteenth to eighteen centuries, before the creation of the Home Office and the Home Secretary, were years of savagery in the criminal justice system. Throughout the Georgian period, various murder acts created more and more capital crimes. In terms of pardons and reprieves the watershed came in 1782 when the Home Office became central to the whole business of reprieves and respites.

The court as an institution was crucially important to the developments of prisons across the world. A court could be created and convened for a specific purpose, as with the Star Chamber. Courts also existed for military purposes, for ecclesiastical and for *ad hoc* reasons in the event of rebellion or civil war. After all, even in kingdoms, a court could have the sovereign sit waiting for judgement, as was the case with Henry VIII when he wanted a divorce from Catherine of Aragon and had to sit before the bench in the Cardinals' Court at Blackfriars. The pardon, first royal and later state controlled (as a *respite*) was linked specifically to courts or gatherings for decisions, as was the case with the Recorder's Court of London in the Regency which decided who would hang and who would be reprieved.

Even with habeas corpus and other writs, and despite the presence of the church, a court could be often no more than an antechamber to a prison cell, and in the medieval and Renaissance centuries, as the use of pardons shows, prison became a limbo, something to be manipulated by sovereigns. In fact, until the advent of the regulated local gaol, prisons were primarily places where debtors and political prisoners existed 'outside time' – unable to participate in life, classified as non-citizens and non-persons who were subject to laws and powers which were ultimately subject to the sovereign, either by process of the criminal law or by the direct wishes of the power-base for profit (ransom) or for political reasons.

This can clearly be seen in famous instances across Europe in this period such as Richard I held for ransom, or Walter Raleigh kept in the Tower and later in Dover Castle after being tried at Winchester for treason. In Raleigh's case, we may discern a pattern: high-class and celebrity prisoners were an embarrassment (Mary, Queen of Scots perhaps the most widely studied of these) and their limbo could be prolonged indefinitely.

DEALING WITH DISSIDENTS AND DEBT

The horrendous narrative of the Tudor Catholic recusants provides a typology for the pre-utilitarian prison with Henry VIII purposely creating various types of gaols for these unfortunates. In October 1540 he visited Hull to inspect the fortifications and directed that blockhouses were to be built there, using stone from a number of priories and churches. The result was two terrible blockhouses to which recusants from across the north were to be sent to be held until trial. But for many there was no trial. For others the only exit was in a coffin.

The blockhouses are of particular interest here, notably for their conception and structure, as described by Francis Hall:

'The blockhouses were planned as a trefoil, and resembled the ordinary playing card. The entrance was arranged in the square or flat part of the structure, and communicated with an open courtyard... The blockhouses were of two storeys, with walls fifteen feet in thickness. Circular staircases of stone built within the walls provided means of communication between the upper and lower floors of both castle and blockhouse.'[10]

These were used as destinations for recusants under the terrible penal laws, and the result was, as Hall explains, an example of the worst excesses of pain inflicted on man by man: 'Light and ventilation there was none, neither were the ordinary necessities and conveniences of life provided. At spring tides many of the floors were flooded and the number of prisoners who died there is positively appalling.'[11]

Exactly the same use of prison may be seen in the French *Ancien Regime*, and again in the following Revolution, as may be seen in the case of the Swiss Guards. There was never even the faintest whiff of the human rights thinking as existed in habeas corpus:

'A number of Swiss Guards had been in detention since 10 August. Maillard proposed that examining them would be a waste of time; they must be guilty de facto. The tribunal agreed with one voice – "To La Force" – the prison close by the Bastille. Proceedings at the tribunal were brief. Prisoners were stripped of wallets, jewellery, watches, and brought in one by one for judgement. Once condemned, in a travesty of mock-execution with the words "Let him go" the prisoner was shoved down the steps to where his executioners waited at the bottom. One hundred and nineteen victims were dispatched in under two hours.'[12]

The overall picture of the uses of imprisonment between the early medieval period and the Reformation was that of confinement and incapacitation. For dissenters and rebels and those who were a thorn in the side of authority, the reasons were clear-cut. When we turn to the question of debtors in prison, a different perspective is needed. It is clear that in some states, notably France, debtors were mixed with other categories of prisoner without any thought. Debtors were, in most countries, treated humanely, with certain degrees of freedom allowed. Towns in the German states had them, as at Dinkelsbuhl, where it was a distinctly separate place. This was also the case in Islamic fortresses and towns, where distinctions were made between the 'jubb' or pit for robbers and political prisoners, as opposed to debtors' prisons which were ruled by the thought that 'Prisoners should not be confined without a complainant and even conjugal relations might be permitted.'[13] This is in sharp contrast to the French issuing of *lettres de cachet* which would enable individuals to have debtors thrown into common gaols. In Islamic classical law, the conduct of the judges (*adals-al-qadi*) governed the more enlightened thinking.

Although in Britain and Europe the debtors' prison became somewhere in which a person might continue 'normal' life by having visitors and being able to buy food and drink, there were terrible abuses. The thought behind the establishment of the debtors' prisons was that debtors could be placed in a condition in which they could not create further debt, and a long-term method could be worked out through which repayment could be made. But then, there were people who owed money to the Crown, so specific prisons were made for them, as in the case of the Fleet prison in London, which was created just after the Norman conquest of 1066; this first prison decayed, and so did the second version, the third being built after the rebellion of 1381. Debtors to the Crown or to private individuals became the most numerous class of prisoners as time went on.

By the seventeenth century the gaols and bridewells across the land had become places where all kinds of people were crammed together beyond society and left to rot. Only the wealthy, fallen foul of creditors, could enjoy a reasonably comfortable life behind the prison walls, because they could buy food and drink from the traders who came into the prisons. Generally, dumped into gaols were felons, debtors, small-time thieves, prostitutes, beggars and invalids. They were the last residence of what the society considered to be trash.

On 2 January, 1752 an anonymous prisoner wrote this letter to the *Gentleman's Magazine*:

Mr Urban,

I am an unhappy prisoner now lying in one of the gaols within this kingdom, to which I was committed about 10 months past, on an accusation of felony, though entirely innocent as afterwards appeared on my trial, my poverty and want of friends preventing any person till then from speaking the truth in my favour. But the grievance I complain of is not my commitment for a crime of which I was not guilty, but the tyranny and oppression of the gaoler, for after I had been declared innocent by the jury, and the prosecution found to be on malice and ill-nature, instead of being immediately discharged, I was hurried back to the prison again, there to lie till I could raise 30s to pay the gaoler what he calls his fees. If any situation on earth merits pity or any evil merits the attention of the legislature, surely 'tis the case of unhappy prisoners in my circumstances. I have lain here six months, my family starves, my credit and character ruined and my spirits broken, without any my procuring redress against the unjust prosecutor or any satisfaction for the numerous calamities he has brought upon me. I have heard much talk of the equity of our laws but surely if they have not been defective or abused, I should not now suffer.'[14]

The wretched man, in modern terms had been on remand, guilty of no crime, and yet had been totally ruined in every aspect of his life and health. What we think of as 'remand' at that time was awaiting gaol delivery if at assizes, or some other kind of trial in other courts. There were dozens of different courts across the land in 1750, from manorial to admiralty and from military to assizes.

As the writer pointed out, the basic problem was that gaolers in local gaols rarely had no fee. From the earliest local gaols there had been sporadic fees paid in some prisons, but there was no national or regional system of fees. The gaoler or turnkey had to exist by taking a number of fees from their prisoners. This was known as 'garnish' in the argot of the time, and everyone suffered, perhaps most of all the debtors, as the writer explains as he ends his letter to the editor: 'If gaolers do not have large salaries for the execution of their office, let the public pay them and let not the sufferings of the wretched be increased by their rapine… My companions here are debtors, who though they have either satisfied or been forgiven by their creditors cannot obtain their liberty till Mr Gaoler is paid his fees. Here therefore they languish, many of them with cold and hunger and some with infirmity and disease till death sets them free without fee or reward.'[15]

In other states the thinking behind imprisonment for debt was different. In Germany, for instance, in medieval times a private debtor could be gaoled but there would be a programme of work imposed along with the sentence, rather than there being sheer idleness and atrophy. Later, in the Reformation period, cities and towns had special gaols called *Schuldturmen* – public law debtors' prisons. The sentence then had a *Strafvollzug*, a cycle of work set out to earn the money for repayment.

One of the main complications concerning the contract of a debt was the attitude to usury in the Middle Ages. As Shakespeare makes clear in *The Merchant of Venice*, usury was necessary but generally reviled, and often those who lent money out at exorbitant interest rates were subject to calumny and hatred. But still debts had to be paid; that was recognised. Taking a larger view, it is with the arrival of the global commercial enterprises that debt and borrowing become much larger issues in morality and law.

There have been arguments seeking to explain why medieval prisons in some states were humanely handled, and these arguments provide striking differences from the later developments when regulated and uniform penal systems were in place. Generally on the continent of Europe, as previously noted, the Roman law was still an influence into the later Middle Ages. In German areas this may be observed in the prevalence of brutal tortures and executions rather than long prison terms. In France and Germany there was more fragmentation, and in the former case, national unity under one ruler came later than in England, for instance. Italy provides a fascinating difference, if the theories of G. Gertner are to be accepted. In his *The Medieval Prison: A Social History* he argues that civic identity and urban development influenced the nature of prisons in the major states. What made this difference is related to the transformation of public space and the advancing drama of the law courts.

Gertner even sees the effects of new legal procedures as being formative of new prison administration; he sees the centralised communal regimes of Italian states as creating prisons which aligned with other palazzo, and indeed he writes of a 'tower to palazzo' development. This leads to a confirmation of the common view of the renaissance as a creation of civic organic social cohesion, yet one in which the inhabitants of prisons were still related to the outside events, rather than cast into oblivion. Of course, as in Venice in earlier references, there were still some courts and crimes which worked in nasty and drastic ways, but Gertner sees the general trend as one towards accepting elements of deviance, rather than simply trying to eradicate them.[16]

Looking for patterns and similarities in the versions of prison across the world before the revolution in penological thought in the eighteenth century is a difficult task, but at least there are elements of this thought which provide common ground. Some states saw the value of tempering retributive measures with some humanity; others concentrated on severe punishments for bandits, robbers, pirates and killers, often without prison – and more studied and suitable punishments for other offenders. Categorisation and notions of 'contamination' of first offenders by seasoned criminals was still an irrelevance for most authorities, yet at least before c.1700 there were concepts of such differences as 'social crime' and offences committed through exigency and desperation compared with acts done by professional criminals.

Basically, as legal systems were still at formative stages across the world in the Middle Ages and in Early Modern stages of development, consequently penal systems were the same, except in those exceptional places, such as some Italian city-states, in Arab states and in England, where rapid commercial expansion brought about adventurous initiatives in containing and maintaining marginal groups, criminals amongst them. A landmark in this context, by any criterion, is surely the establishment of the first Bridewell in London, as John Stow, in his *Survey of London* (1598) explains: 'George Baron, being mayor of this city, was sent for to the court at Whitehall, and there at that time the king gave unto him for the commonalty and citizens, to be a workhouse for the poor and idle persons of the city.'[17]

The 'workhouse' and 'house of correction' had arrived. Those four words hinted at virtually every idea linked to incarceration in the time to come, in societies where prisons were not simply antechambers of death. The first Bridewell opened for business in 1555 and the word itself became a generic term for a house of correction. Created by pressures of homeless beggars, people wandering out of their own parish, and rootless ex-soldiers, the Bridewell was largely created from the overall revulsion at the thought of the idle and undeserving poor' as opposed to the real criminal class who were'undeserving'but the construct of a community for work and correction provided a concomitant space for the criminal deviant as well.

Notes and references

1 See Costin and Watson, *The Law and Working of the Constitution* (London, 1952), p. 68.

2 See Paul Halliday, *Habeas Corpus* (Cambridge, Mass. 2010) p. 16.

3 Ibid. p. 17.

4 See Fenton Bresler, *Reprieve* (London, 1978), p. 20-21.

5 For a full discussion of the moral and legal issues around this, see Naomi Hurnad, *The King's Pardon for Homicide before AD 1307* (Oxford, 1969), pp. 150-153.

6 Cynthia Herrup, *The Common Peace: Participation and the Criminal Law in Seventeenth Century England* (Cambridge, 1997), pp. 200-201.

7 Bresler, *Reprieve* (London, 1978), pp. 28-29.

8 For examples, see C H Rolph, *The Queen's Pardon* (London, 1978), preface.

9 James Sharpe, *Crime in Early Modern England 1550-1750* (Harlow, 1999) p. 97.

10 Francis J Hall, *The Blockhouses of Kingston-upon-Hull* (Hull, 1913), p. 4.

11 Ibid. p. 5.

12 Graeme Fife, *The Terror* (London, 2004), p. 70.

13 See Josef W Meri, *Medieval Islamic Civilisation* (London, 2005), p. 642.

14 Anon. *Gentleman's Magazine*, 2 Jan 1752 p. 230.

15 Ibid.

16 For a response and analysis of Gertner's conclusions, see Jonathan Rose, *Reviews in History* at www.history.ac.uk/reviews/review/805.

17 John Stow, *A Survey of London Written in the Year 1598* (Stroud, 2005) p. 333.

Chapter 3

Prison and Imperial Power

THE FIRST WORLDWIDE WEB

The historians J. R. and William McNeill described what they called the first worldwide web in their survey *The Human Web* (2003) and convincingly showed that the first establishment of globalisation was a 'painful, sometimes brutal process'. They argue that 'in the three and a half centuries after 1450 the peoples of the earth increasingly formed a single community.'[1] Before that time, the Ottoman and Mongol empires had expanded, gaining land by conquest while the first tentative steps towards exploration of the furthest regions of the world were hesitantly being taken. Then in 1453 Istanbul was made the centre of the Ottoman empire; the Safavid empire was established in Iran c.1510; later Suleiman the Magnificent expanded the Ottoman empire. Parallel with this, the European powers had gained footholds and colonies in the Americas and the Russian, Chinese and Indian rulers, in states and in new colonies, began to extend worldwide trade.

Naturally, the laws went along with this expansion, so that outposts of empire found themselves having to administrate their new territories according to the jurisprudence back home. In many cultures and societies this was difficult, as the laws behind their regimes were, as with the Islamic for instance, always in process, with the holy *Qu'ran* being a basis for interpretation, just as the Torah was for the Jewish people. Because imperial conquest was a baggage of legal, moral and spiritual principles as well as applied social codes of right behaviour, administrations were subject to abuse and infringements of human rights. Of course, the notion of human rights did not extend to all societies. A check on holy texts suggests laws set in stone, such as the *surat al Imran* in the *Qur'an* where we have: 'Before, as a guidance for the people he [God] sent down the *furqan* [a 'separator' – the *Qur'an* itself]. For those who disbelieve in the signs of God, a terrible chastisement awaits them.' Built into the *Qur'an* was a reference to some kind of incarceration. In *surat al-bara'a* we have: ' … slay the idolaters wherever you find them, and seize them and confine them…'[2] Prisons did exist, as noted in the last chapter, within Islamic communities, mostly for robbers, political enemies and serious criminals awaiting execution.

As far as the European expansion was concerned in those centuries before c.1700, slavery and imprisonment went hand-in-hand of course. A prison sentence, however, as a specific punishment, was always available. The Christian nations took all the usual civic and legal panoply along with the armies of conquest. This new web 'favoured predatory people who lived from the rewards of slaving and invested the proceeds in horses and guns' and 'Perhaps 20 million guns entered Africa in the slave trade.'[3]

Russian expansion had extended into Siberia by 1640 when Cossacks had reached the Pacific and come face to face with the Chinese, establishing a peace treaty there in 1689. Almost every part of the globe had, to some extent, known the arrival of foreign people by c.1700 and when we look at the application of justice and punishment in the new world, it is hard to disagree with the verdict that: 'As human history grew more unified, it grew more unstable and chaotic than ever, a condition with which we still live.'[4]

A practical aspect of the new 'web' was the invention of printing which enabled legal texts and handbooks to be easily disseminated. By the end of the fifteen century, 236 European towns had movable-type print-shops. In 1483, as Richard III fought and died at Bosworth Field, the Cyrillic alphabet was printed in the new manner, and by the mid-sixteenth century, there were presses in Spanish America. Administrators became legislators in the outposts of empire and the centres of the empires generated more repressive laws in order to cope with the growing feature of conquest and power: a steadily increasing gap between rich and poor.

Empires are an extension of a solid base power, and the exercise of power has to have a punitive element; enforced power and control naturally create dissenters and rebels. The criminal justice system is than applied relentlessly to maintain the power base. One of the most alarming and negative aspects of this is that once established, imperial punitive systems and attitudes persisted into the twentieth century, as has been strongly described and analysed for instance, by Gorge Orwell, in his essays, *A Hanging* and *Shooting an Elephant*, in which he has question the nature of imperial power at first hand.'[5]

In focus in this context is the idea of the subaltern – the administrator and representative of empire. In penal history across these first great global empires, the gaols, as with everything else in the new colonies, had to be aligned with the rules of law. The subaltern is a term used for those within this system who are without power – the minions. In postcolonial theory, the subaltern is used to refer to anyone with no access to cultural imperialism. This helps in our understanding of the early great empires, in that it defines the oppressed but also what Gayatri Spivak has called 'a space of difference.'[6]

The creation of prisons within the empires opened up the nature of the oppressed, and in many cases, shone a light of clarity on issues of dissent and political offences. Of course, there were frequent wars and uprisings, so prison punishment opened up many aspects of the law of warfare and human rights as well.

THE EXAMPLE OF INDIA
In 1601 Elizabeth I granted a charter to the East India Company which had been formed in 1599. When it was fully developed, the Company governed a fifth of the population of the world, made more profit than England itself, and as Nick Robins has put very cogently: 'The Company grew to fame and fortune by trading with and then conquering India. And for many Indians, it was the Company's plunder that first de-industrialised their country and then provided the finance that fuelled Britain's own industrial revolution. In essence, the Honourable East India Company found India rich and left it poor.'[7]

Later, after the Battle of Plassey in 1757, the Company was to stop fighting with the Dutch for the Spice Islands and began to control land on the main continent of India. It was to last until the aftermath of the Indian Mutiny of 1857. From the beginning, it was to have its own fighting men, later becoming a major presence in India, alongside the regular army. It also had the power to make ordinances for the government of the lands it occupied, including the right to try and imprison people. The important phrase was that officers out in India who did acts 'contrary or repugnant to the laws of this our realm' would not be tolerated.

There were two major problems with this. The first was the question of exactly who was covered and protected by the laws 'of this realm' and the second was how this would be regulated. In the following two centuries, more powers were given to British administrators in India to judge and punish. By around 1700 they were ruling over native Indians as well. By the mid years of the eighteenth century, a law was passed enabling a system following the English assize practice of gaol delivery to be imposed. In other words, Indians could be arrested and kept for long periods in gaols until there was a court held.

Before the British began to control large areas of the land, and to impose law, there had been Islamic and Hindu legal systems in place with their own penal laws. There were four different categories of offences and different modes of imprisonment used along with these. But criminals as such were not imprisoned, but merely detained until trial, at which sentences involved fines, whipping, mutilation, loss of status and banishment. Fortresses were generally used for detention.

For Indians of high status, there were 'noble prisons' in Mughal India, principally at Gwaliar. A prison at Ranthambore was for the condemned, where they waited two months until execution. Rooms in forts were used also called *Bandhikhanas*. For lower caste prisoners and adulterous women, hard labour was part of the sentence. This set of practices gradually found themselves alongside British legal process. The result was a situation open to all kinds of abuses. There was ostensibly the protection of writs – but the issue of exactly what legal status the native people had in terms of English law was a blurred concept.

In 1774 Britain passed the Regulating Act to try to sort out the problems, but it took the case of Kemaluddin Khan, with Chief Justice Sir Elijah Impey involved, to change things for the better. Common law allowed the use of habeas corpus, and that had not been extended to India at the time. As the justices in India were allowed the same powers as the justices of the King's Bench back home, then, Impey argued, Indian subjects could sue for a habeas corpus writ. Khan had been put in gaol by the Company's council in Calcutta, for debts owed; the first writ of habeas corpus in India was issued, and Khan was subsequently released. The significant outcome of this is that justices had been influential on the powers and judgements of the East India Company.[8]

There had been friction long before this, however, between the Company and individuals. Between 1666 and 1670 Thomas Skinner, a merchant, sued the Company for 'barbarous oppression.' He was an Englishman, so it was not only the native people in the developing empire who had problems with the juggernaut of world power that was 'John Company,' as it came to be known. The Company had ignored, and then played for time, in this action against them, but in 1668 the House of Lords awarded £5,000 damages to Skinner. Clearly, the Company was a threat to the most prestigious institutions in the land.[9]

In the nineteenth century, India and its neighbouring states provided the focus for the 'Great Game' of Asia, in which Britain and Russia continually played gambits in a long series of moves to use espionage and Realpolitik to keep the Indian sub-continent in their dominion or at least in some kind of buffer state alliance. That situation meant that Britain had to rule more tightly, and the Company played a major part in this, as magistrates of the Crown and Collectors (administrators and regional managers) of the Company organised the legal applications of British rule, including the use of gaols.

William Sleeman is arguably more famous for police work than for military exploits, but nevertheless he demonstrated some working methods that would influence all kinds of practitioners in enforcing criminal law. Sleeman was born in Stratton, Cornwall, in 1788. In 1809 he joined the Bengal army and became a lieutenant in 1814. In 1854 he was made Major General. Where his talent lay was in the work of political officer in the Central provinces. His work against the formidable army of murderers known as the ' *Thuggee'* in 1835. These troubles were cause by organised bands of killers who would select travellers as victims and brutally take their lives and rob them. The *Thuggee* moved in large numbers and were difficult to track down. Sleeman managed to find and hang or transport for life over a thousand of these killers, and the reason for his success was the use of 'approvers' – informers. In 1830, for instance, in Jubbulpore there were reports of a band of *Thuggee* active on the roads. There were four approvers in the gang arrested, and the case went to court.

One of Sleeman's most remarkable talents was his skill as a linguist. All political officers had to learn the usual Hindi and sometimes some Arabic, but Sleeman had fluent Hindi. Even before he arrived and even before he was thirty he was, according to one report: 'Probably the only British official ever to have addressed the King of Oudh in correct Urdu and Persian.' He could also get by in Nepali and Gurkhali. So enthusiastic was he for gaining and understanding of India that he wrote a voluminous journal on his time in Oudh and developed a deep interest in the poor land-workers of the country. In this way he could be the eyes and ears of the foreigner in a military capacity when needed, in a wide range of contexts, in the field with the poor or in the salons and messes of his peers and compatriots.

Sleeman represents the typical political officer of the time: someone profoundly located in the civic and economic life of the local community, paternalistic and knowledgeable. He would have had to travel around a massive area that was his responsibility and also act as magistrate. When wars came along, a man like Sleeman would be indispensable to the army in the field, of course. He became political resident in Gwalior between 1843 and 1849. He was a notable success, but incident and danger were never far away from him. In 1851 an attempt was made on his life. But before that crisis, he had done the solid work of report-writing for Lord Dalhousie and it was that kind of labour that made Dalhousie offer Sleeman the Residency of Lucknow. In 1854 he had to retire north to the hills, as he was a sick man. He died in 1856, on board ship, on the way home.

Basically, his success against the *Thuggee* was based on his questioning of captured men who would turn approvers. He was up against far more than a system like the British one, however. Sleeman had to understand and exploit the Islamic courts. His approach was to communicate with men captured who would subvert the enemy, if handled properly, with discretion and patience. The Islamic law did not put stress on witness testimony, so Sleeman, on signing up his agents, made sure that they knew what was needed to overcome the testimony problem. There were conditional pardons for approvers who did the witness statements given in the 'contract' with Sleeman. There was also a small amount of money given to the approvers' dependents. The approvers were questioned in Hindi and then testimony written down in Persian.

Thousands of *Thuggee* were imprisoned, although many were executed, and the British in India created one of the first large-scale cellular gaols in imperial locations. This was in the Andaman Islands, and many of the *Thuggee* were sent there. The Andamans, in the south east of the Bay of Bengal, was first used as a prison by Lieutenant Blair of the East India Company, in 1789. The major penal development was used after the 1857 Mutiny, and those leaders of that attempt at freedom who were not strung across cannon were sent to the Andamans – many of them for life. The first 200 freedom fighters were placed there in 1858. The regime was very hard and punishments severe: an escape attempt in 1868 shows the brutality of the establishment, as 87 of these men were hanged after they failed to escape.

RUSSIA BEFORE THE REVOLUTION

Any reference to the prisons of the Tsarist empire immediately brings to mind two famous writers and their prison experience – Fyodor Dostoievski and Anton Chekhov. The former was exiled to a Siberian prison after taking part in the Decembrist attempted coup of 1825 against Tsar Nicholas I. He was sent there after being led to believe he was to be shot. A hundred of the plotters were sent that immense distance. Previously, the criminal code of Russia, before the eighteenth century, had involved horrendous cruelty, including mutilation and torture. Exile to Siberia was seen as a more humane sentence than that. However, the journey to Siberia was extremely arduous. The convicts had to get there on their own. Dostoievski wrote about his journey through the Urals on his way east: 'The horses and sledges sank in the snow-drifts. A blizzard was raging. It was at night and we had to leave our sledges and wait until they were dragged out of the snow... It was the border between Europe and Asia, in front of us was Siberia and our mysterious future...'[10]

Once there, he wrote *Memoirs from the House of the Dead* (1862) and he describes the Siberian camp he awoke to find:'You would look through a chink in the stockade at God's blessed daylight… you saw only a glimpse of sky and the earthen rampart, overgrown with weeds, with the sentries pacing back and forth, day and night, and you would think that years would come again in just the same way…'[11]

Siberia was useful to the Tsar for purposes of settlement of course; such a vast territory had to be filled, and the far east was not the most enticing part of the empire. Peter I's city of St Petersburg had its prisons, notably the Peter and Paul fortress, built in 1703. Later, in the 1870s, the Trubetskoy Bastion was built there and was to become one of the most notorious Russian prisons. But there were ordinary gaols in the Russian state long before that, and we have a rare insight into the Russian penological establishment from the great prison reformer John Howard who made two journeys there to inspect the prisons. The first, in 1781, was what one biographer has described as'a glittering tapestry of aristocratic enjoyment… everything western, French or English particularly, was fervently admired.'[12] But that was not for Howard. He was there to find out for himself if the system was more humane than the British; after all, there was no capital punishment there. Yet there were surprises and shocks in store for him.

Tsarist Russia in the centuries of the first worldwide web was a state existing on serfdom: slavery was essential to the fabric of life, and was not to be abolished until 1861. Howard saw for himself the prisons in a place where, in one sense, the whole structure was, as has often been said,'a great prison' or'a prison of countries.'What he saw was a system with cruel corporal punishment, most barbarously expressed in the use of the knout, which he described:

'The knout whip is fixed to a wooden handle a foot long, and consists of several thongs about two feet in length twisted together, to the end of which is fastened a single tough thong of a foot and a half, tapering to a point, and capable of being changed by the executioner, when too much softened by the blood of the criminal.'[13]

The use of the knout caused death in some cases. It was also applied to women. Howard saw the knout used on a man and a woman, she receiving twenty-five strokes and the man, sixty strokes.

The penal system was guarded by the army rather than by professional gaolers. There was a method of categorization, and debtors were housed separately. As with most places, there was a place of detention for those awaiting trial. In Moscow Howard visited the Kaluska Ostrog where he saw two wooden cages where 'men were chained by the neck to the wall, with irons on their legs' and at Riga he saw what happened to those who committed the most serious crimes: 'I saw two Russians sent hither about four years ago; they had a guard at the door and had never been out of the room, and are heavily ironed both hands and feet; they are never spoken to, nor is their crime known.' They had been mutilated, a cut in the nostril showing that they were lifers.[14]

Before this era, in the centuries after the reign of Ivan III, when he had created the single code, the *Sudebnik*, of 1497, there was a general picture in which the powerful lords, the Boyars, had their own laws, and the Tsar his laws. But at grass roots level, there was a handbook called the *Domostroi*, covering all areas of the social hierarchy, and punishment was integrated into that. The historian Geoffrey Hosking explains the basis of this: 'Villages tended to improvise their own arrangements to share risk, by mutual action to discourage deviant behaviour, and to punish it and minimise effects when it took place.'[15]

There had always been local and regional moral regulation in the peasantry, with conformity and right behaviour always valued and encouraged. Penal punishment in that context was slower to conform to developments in Europe for several reasons. There had been advances in health care in Europe which had not had an impact on Russia. There was a priority on forced labour under the Tsars, and there was a slower growth of what might be called civic society. The vastness of the land was always going to create obstacles to all kinds of progress, and change was slow in all areas. But in the nineteenth century, with the arrival of more dissent and open rebellion, prison attained a new status. Under Alexander II (Tsar 1855-1881) there were radical reforms of the law; the serfs were emancipated in 1861 and bodies called *Zemstva* were set up to run local government. The court system was overhauled, the equivalents of the British Justices of the Peace were created, and judges for the high courts were better trained and qualified. This judicial reform took place mainly in 1864 and for the first time there was a mechanism to take on whimsical authority and also the entrenched habit of having collective responsibility and no place for the individual.

The formation of new investigative lawyers in place of the police in criminal investigations was an important part of this. Most impressive and innovative was the establishment of advocates – defence lawyers. There was still Siberia and exile and there were many enemies of the state. Amongst the writers and intellectual there was (and still is) a high level of esteem, so that their views and opinions were respected. But the middle years of the century saw the acceleration of oppositional groups, so the prisons were busy.

Representative of the need for more prison space after the 1861 liberation and the later legal reforms is the Kresty prison in St Petersburg. This is still in use today, and its history goes back to the first decades of the eighteenth century. In the 1860s it was enlarged, to accommodate over 700 inmates. Then enter Anthony Tomishko, prison-builder specialist, who created model prisons for the Alexandrine regime, including the Uyezd prison. He was one of the many designers who felt the influence of the Philadelphia system (discussed in the next chapter). Through him the panopticon system entered Russian penal regimes. Kresty was completed in 1890 and was a beacon for the modern age, even having electric lighting. It was designed with a nod of appreciation and influence to the Enlightenment, and John Howard in particular – a statue to the great reformer being included in the new site. Both criminal and political prisoners were housed there. Tomishko was very successful, and his work extended to the design of the lower palace at Alexandria Park for Tsar Nicholas II.

CHINA: PUNISHMENT 'EXACTLY RIGHT.

For Europeans through history, Chinese prisons and punishments have been synonymous with terrible physical torture and brutality. Typical of the way in which such matters were reported in the nineteenth century is this item from 1827:

'The following extract from a book recently published will give our readers some idea of the manner in which criminals are treated in China. An "unjust" judge is beheaded. He who in time of war is guilty of embezzlement or of malpractices with respect to the supply of troops, is strangled... the stealing of a small sum is punished with a severe bastinado... .[16]

Three years later, *The Standard* was even more direct on the subject:

'In their punishment the Chinese exhibit a degree of cruelty and a refinement in torture that is truly horrible. Torture is allowed by law in China to obtain the truth from witnesses... None of their punishments is more unmercifully executed than whipping... It was our misfortune to witness this punishment on the persons of three malefactors convicted of theft. Their arms were bound behind them with a cord extremely tight, and an executioner beat them severely to the accompaniment of a gong. They were very fatigued and one of them had undergone the punishment for several days...'[17]

Such was the fascination with this subject that ornaments were made on the theme, as one advert from 1844 shows: '... a figure, exhibited for the first time, showing curious Chinese punishments.' In fact, such was the relish with which the English press reported such things that 'an outside barbarian' wrote to the *Daily News* in 1857 to complain that 'crude notices about Chinese cruelties in the papers' were distorting the truth. The writer had a point as the origins of such matters explain what was really happening in the Chinese penal system.

The origins of Chinese thinking on punishments, including imprisonment, reach far back in time. The Chinese character for punishment is 'xing' and that is a mix of two concepts – literally meaning 'to cut a throat' but also with a part-construct meaning 'law.' The etymology goes deeper also, because 'xing' implies a penal treatment which will 'trim' a person: a sense of reform being in the punishment. A crime is 'zui' and that word has a straight meaning of 'to transgress in the law.'

Punishment did indeed become central in Chinese civilization from earliest times, but it is not so seemingly brutal as the Victorian reports show. In the time of Confucius (550-479 BC) there was a considerable amount of theorising about punishment and the great philosopher himself said: 'Guide them by edicts, keep them in line with punishments [xing] and the common people will stay out of trouble and will have a sense of shame. Guide them by virtue, keep them in line within the rites and they will, as well as having a sense of shame, reform themselves.'[18]

As time went on, punishment was seen as having to be 'exactly right' and eventually there were written rules, called 'fa' which set down 'right behaviour.' The notion of punishment went far beyond fear and retribution. As Klaus Muhlhahn explains: 'Punishments were meted out not only with the intention to correct evil, but also to preserve the harmony and balance that transcend the human world.'[19]

A formative event in the Chinese penal system was the printing of codified laws in 624, during the Tang dynasty, and then much later, in 1740 when the Qing Code was created. These specified five punishments for crimes: beating with a light stick; beating with a heavy stick; penal servitude, exile for life, and death. After that, the criminal justice system put in place a magistrate in every *yamen* (area of administration) and he had charge of a gaol for those awaiting trial. Restraints were used, and these certainly contributed to the western view of Chinese barbarity. Objects called *canques* were used. These were large wooden blocks weighing 32lb (later, after 1820, weighing 54lb) put around the collars of criminals.

Penal servitude meant a period in prison of between one and three years, but there was a general guideline about leniency for very young or very old prisoners. The object, stated in the codified laws, was to 'enslave and disgrace.' By the Qing Code, the point about punishment was that it should be in line with the situation at the time and with the morale of the community, hence the severe punishments for leaders and people in positions of power, as reported by the English press with extreme revulsion. In fact, when it came to the death sentence, the Chinese approach was more humane than the British. In London in c.1800 for instance, a man sentenced to hang would be hanged within four days, whereas in China, a person awaiting death would have a period of months to wait, to give time for his case to be reviewed.

These examples from great empires throughout the burgeoning of the 'worldwide web' and into the nineteenth century when so many technological inventions began to be applied, and then to streamline global communication, show that up to and beyond the European Enlightenment, there were massive differences in various penal systems, and the use of prisons varied greatly. It is necessary to retrace steps to the Enlightenment and the age of the panopticon now, to understand the revolution in penology that was happening alongside these empires across the globe.

Notes and references

1 J R and William McNeill, *The Human Web* (New York, 2003), p. 155.

2 See Norman Calder et alia, *Classical Islam* (London, 2003), pp.10-12.

3 J R and William McNeill op.cit. note 3 p, 171.

4 Ibid. p. 178.

5 See in particular Inside the Whale (London, 1957), p. 92. 'It was a tiny incident in itself, but it gave me a better glimpse than I had had before of the real nature of imperialism...' He understands how repression by a legal code involves moral imperatives rested on the subaltern's shoulders – the other people he has working for him, from the native community. That is, Orwell does shoot the elephant, by pressure, and a man is hanged, but not by Orwell.

6 Gayatri Spivak, in *Ariel* Vol. 23, number 3 1992 p. 30.

7 Nick Robins, 'Loot: in search of the East India Company, the world's first transnational corporation' *Environment & Urbanization* Vol. 14 No. 1 April 2002 p. 79.

8 For a full account of this, see Paul D Halliday, *Habeas Corpus* (Cambridge, Mass., 2010) pp. 286-289.

9 See Skinner v The East India Company, discussed in W C Costin and J Steven Watson, *The Law and Working of the Constitution* (London, 1952), pp. 157-161.

10 Fyodor Dostoievski, 'A Nightmare World' in p. 177.

11 Fyodor Dostoievskl, *Memoirs from the House of the Dead* (London, 2001) pp. 6-7.

12 D L Howard, *John Howard, Prison Reformer* (London, 1958).

13 John Howard, *The State of the Prisons* (Dent, 1929), p. 76.

14 Ibid, p. 82.

15 Geoffrey Hosking, *Russia and the Russians* (London, 2002), p.98.

16 See 'Chinese punishments' *North Wales Chronicle* Nov. 1 1827 issue 5.

17 *The Standard*, April 16, 1828.

18 Quoted in Klaus Muhlhahn, *Criminal Justice in China: A History* (Newhaven, 2009), p. 17.

19 Ibid. p. 22.

Chapter 4

Europe: From Dungeons to Houses of Correction

The years spanning the late-seventeenth and eighteenth centuries are thought of as the Enlightenment. This term has been a slippery one to define, but essentially, it was a period when the nature of man as an individual and in society was examined from new perspectives; philosophy and natural science moved centre-stage, the arts and literature took on the big social questions and the human species and how its members interacted became something with endlessly curious enquiries aimed at it. Improvement was a desired objective, but many areas of life were late on the list of aspects of life to be changed for the better, and the criminal justice systems across the world fell into that category. Not until the early years of the nineteenth century did any real reform take place.

However, there is no doubt that the eighteenth century generated a glut of writings on penal issues. Bentham and his brother conceived of the penitentiary (see chapter 6); Cesare Beccaria prsoduced his monumental work, *On Crimes and Punishments* in 1764, and John Howard surveyed and reported on gaols from London to Moscow, and from Italy to Ireland. There were several attempts to place the theory of incarceration in line with such illusive notions as goodness, morality and religious precepts. Art and philosophy were turning the microscope on man as a phenomenon, in all his complexity and with all the contradictions that Shakespeare had expressed so powerfully in *Hamlet* for instance, in which the Prince reflects on the capacity for evil in a creature who has been made by a beneficent creator. In other words, the problems of evil and of different modes of transgression were examined at length. Even men in the criminal justice system and in the ranks of the writers and radicals of the time chose prisons as subjects for enquiry and reflection, as in Henry Fielding's *Tom Jones* (1749) and William Godwin's *Caleb Williams* (1794).

BRITAIN'S GAOLS

The gaols were limbos of neglect, with a range of punishments in the tough regimes maintained by the tyrants who held the keys and the food supplies. A few humanitarians occasionally tried to change things, but one additional problem was that offices and responsibilities of all kinds were up for sale in an age of nepotism and corruption. The Georgian period and regency were times in which sinecures were bought and sold as a matter of everyday business. A publication called *The Red Book* listed these offices and their value. A typical example was the Wardenship of the Cinque Ports, which paid £1,000 a year. A celebrated case was that of Ashley Cowper, younger brother of William Cowper, who was a barrister in 1723. Also a Mason and a member of the Horn Lodge, Ashley acquired the post of Clerk to the Parliaments, a very well-paid and esteemed post. The post was in fact bought for him by his father, who just happened to be Judge Spence Cowper.

There was no investigation into nepotism and sinecures until 1780. The situation was that the law courts, the established church, part of the army and the royal household, contained many positions in which the occupants did very little for the money they received. In some of these the offices were bought and sold according to circumstances, and naturally, the actual management of establishments could be left to lower-level persons who found that the worst and most arduous tasks were delegated to them.

In the management of prison, this was a very dangerous and destructive practice, particularly as the man who bought the governorship could stay away from the prison as often as he liked and leave a minion in charge. One of the very worst of these abuses was highlighted in the case of John Huggins, warden of the Fleet prison, who was tried at the Old Bailey in 1729 for the murder of one of his charges, Edward Arne.

Huggins bought the wardenship of the Fleet for the huge sum of £5,000 for himself and his son. Of course he then had to get the investment back, by any means possible. The Fleet was at that time mainly a debtors' prison, and we know what it was like because the great reformer John Howard reported on it. At that time, debtors' prisons had two sides: Common and the Masters. On the latter side lived those who could afford to rent their accommodation, but the Common side, as Howard describes, was horrendous: 'The apartments for the Common-side debtors are only part of the right wing... Besides the cellar there are four floors. On each floor is a room about twenty-four or five feet square, with a fire-place; and on the sides seven closets or cabins to sleep in. Such of the prisoners who swear in court or before a commissioner that they cannot subsist without charity, have the donations which are sent to the prison, and the begging box and grate.'[1]

The grate was the street-level aperture from which they could beg passers-by for alms or even just water. But their situation would have normally been like that of the anonymous writer to the *Gentleman's Magazine* (discussed in my introduction), were it not for the fact that John Huggins and his gang of assistants were sadists. At the basis of the sentence was the table of fees for the gaolers. These included fees for the chaplain, the porter, the chamberlain, the turnkey. Added to these were fees for 'liberty of the house and irons when first coming in' and a dismission fee. The total cost of all these fees was supposed to be under £2 but in fact £3 5s was the sum taken, as increments were applied.

Huggins decided, as he aged, that he would sell his position to a certain Thomas Bambridge, his deputy, along with another scoundrel called Dougal Cuthbert. A barbaric and murderous regime was to follow, and the scandal broke not long after Bambridge took over control. At the centre of the affair was the death of a prisoner, Edward Arne, who had been committed to a horrible den called the 'Strongroom' where he starved and was submitted to infections and diseases so extreme that he lost his wits before dying a miserable death inside the walls. At the trial, the 'Strongroom' was described by a witness called Bigrave:

Solicitor-General: 'What do you know of the building the strong room?'

Bigrave: 'When I came there there was a stable which was converted into a strong room...'
Solicitor-General: 'What sort of a place is it?'
Bigrave: 'It is arched like a wine vault, built of brick and mortar.'
Solicitor-General: 'What are the dimensions?'
Bigrave: 'It is eight feet wide and eleven feet long.'
Solicitor-General: ' How near was the dung-hill to it?'
Bigrave: 'The dunghill was as nigh as to the other part of the court.[2]'

Another witness called Bishop said, referring to Arne: 'When he was brought in he was in good condition of health and in his senses... being put in the strong room in the Fleet would have killed anybody, and that forwarded Arne's death.'

Poor Arne's last days were pitiable. A turnkey called Farringdon gave the most touching account of the man's death:

'...he grew somewhat disordered and from the time he was put in the strong room he altered every day, grew hoarse, and at last could not speak, and he grew weaker and weaker every day; about the beginning of October he lost his voice, he then grew delirious, and ripped open his bed, and crept into the feathers, and one day he came to chapel with excrement and feathers sticking to him like a magpie, beingforced to ease nature in that place... After that I saw the prisoner at the bar looking into the strong room, the door being open, and Arne was lying in the bed ripped open...'[3]

The trial was widely reported and brought into the public eye the lamentable state of the debtors in His Majesty's prisons. The story of Huggins and Bambridge gradually came out in full as witnesses were examined. Huggins had left Bambridge to take over, before actually selling him the office of warden, but Huggins had stayed at home, miles out of London, and had only been to the Fleet twice over a period of nine months. He had left the prison in the control of a cruel, heartless monster who only wanted the profit, and was only too happy to see the prisoners die if they could not pay his fees.

HOUSES OF CORRECTION

Following the first Bridewell, in 1553, the idea of the misfits and offenders, debtors and vagrants of society being shut behind doors and high walls and made to work was attractive to those good citizens who were tired of being robbed and pestered, or who were simply upset and perplexed by the level of social upheaval around them. The quarter sessions around the land were overworked with parish business dealing with sturdy beggars and footpads, bastard children and invalided soldiers. The house of correction, as the name implies, was a place where the deviants could perhaps be placed on the road to moral virtue. But if that did not happen, at least they could work and be productive.

How many people were in the local gaols in the years before any kind of real reform? Who were they and what do their crimes tell us about the society generally? The report of 1818 provides some figures. In that year there were 73,363 prisoners committed, and the number the prisons were capable of holding was 14,925. The courts often tried hard to reduce the committals, as this entry from the Guildhall shows: 'The same day the sessions ended, when 18 convicts received judgements of death; one was ordered to be transported, nine to be imprisoned... eight to be whipped and 25 discharged by proclamation.'

A few examples of the criminals admitted to gaols gives a glimpse of the trajectories of criminals, from life circumstances to offence:

M.M. a girl of 8 years of age, was found in solitary confinement in one of the prisons in the metropolis. She had been committed for one month, on a charge of child-stealing. It appeared the parents had driven the girl into the streets to beg...'

'S.M. aged 18, committed to Cold Bath Fields prison for pawning a watch, which she had taken from a house of ill-fame where she lived'

'J. B. aged 13, having associated with some bad girls, was enticed from her parents in London, after being absent some time taken up at Maidstone, and committed to the Bridewell as a vagrant, being in a destitute condition...'[4]

In the houses of correction matters could be as hard as the local gaols. The late eighteenth century saw several new ones being created, and they were basically businesses, often run by families from the locality. Their regime was a round of hard physical work, some levels of separation, prayer and basic education, with an array of punishments, mainly the use of the 'refractory cell' – a bleak form of solitary confinement.

Typical of these new establishments was Northallerton in North Yorkshire. We know a great deal about the gaol from its inception in the late eighteenth century through to its radical development between 1848 and 1852 as it had to cope with far too many prisoners to accommodate with safety. It can boast that it was the first custom-built gaol in England still in the prison service. That means that if we leave castle prisons out of the reckoning, the foundation for Northallerton gaol in 1783 is significant in the history of penal records.

As with all county local gaols, there were many facilities existing before that date in order that the justices had somewhere to send felons as well as debtors. The site for the prison was on wasteland to the east of Zetland Street, granted by the Bishop of Durham, John Egerton. The proviso was that his bishop's court should be held there as well as the local courts for summary offences and the magistrates' court to deal with felons. One of the town's first historians, Ingledew, explains that the land was low and swampy and contained the town rubbish dump and a pinfold – the area where stray cattle were impounded from the common land.[5]

Dr Neild, writing in 1802, had left us a description of the House of Correction:

'This prison for the North Riding is removed from Thirsk and has been built for about twenty years. The Sessions House under which are the gaolers' apartments adjoins. The whole is nearly enclosed by a boundary wall. The building has a double front and each has a spacious and airy court so that the sexes are completely separate.'[6]

There was a vegetable garden and a wash house. For prisoners there were twelve cells around four yards square divided from each other by a passage two yards wide. It is notable that two of the cells were solitary. This means that the notion of the 'refractory cells' was there from an early date. Often called 'dark cells', these were tiny places which were one of the key elements in the later conception of prisons as places of a punitive regime before the nationalisation of prisons in 1877. Men could be placed in these cells for days or even weeks in a space just 12ft by 5ft 6in wide and 12ft high, or in the worst of all, which was only 7ft by 5ft 6in wide and 11ft high.

The place also had a large workroom (used as a chapel on Sundays) and another workroom of quite a large size. On the upper storey were the cells for women and the 'bell room' where the turnkey lived. There were five cells for women.

By 1800 it had been changed further. There was a courthouse within, a large area outside, and jury rooms and magistrates' rooms were added. It was long overdue. In earlier years there had been sessions held at the Guild Hall (which became the town workhouse by 1800) and then at Vine House from 1720.

The new House of Correction was not ready to receive its first prisoners until 1788. In 1777 the prison reformer, John Howard, had published his seminal work, *The State of the Prisons* and although it happened slowly, there was pressure for reform at the local level. The first prisoners at the new venue were taken there from Thirsk. They were coming to a gaol that was to be a 'going concern' as well as a prison. It was to be controlled by a committee of visiting justices who would inspect and present their reports to the Quarter Sessions. From their minutes we can glean very interesting information, such as this entry from 1788: 'Ordered that sacks be made of Harden [a fabric made from flax or hemp] to be filled with straw for bedding to fit the bedsteads of the different cells according to the pattern already made by Thomas Winspear. That a blanket and rug be provided for each of the beds according to the pattern produced by John Marshall.'[7]

The prisoners in this early period usually arrived in a state of dishevelment, were often diseased and desperately needed new clothes. From the very beginning a standard issue of garments was prepared: men were to wear a jacket, waistcoat, trousers and cap – the order specifying 'the right side to be made of blue kersey stuff and the left side of the same sort of material of a browndrab colour.' The women wore a jacket and petticoat, again mixing blue and drab. Comfort was not the main concern as kersey was a coarse cloth, usually ribbed. Drab was simply undyed cloth used so often that it became a 'colour' in its own right and was used by all kinds of working people.

One of real problems was in health and accommodation. The 1837 report brought to light many aspects of the prison regime which were undoubtedly cruel and severe, though with rather perverted 'good intentions' behind them. For instance, there was no heating in the cells and there was poor drainage and although a surgeon attended the prisoners every day, he struggled to treat the constant problems of rheumatism, lung infections and diarrhoea. There were also periodic bouts of typhus fever. There was also the barbaric practice of the 'dark cells' for misbehaviour. The surgeon told the inspector, 'I do not approve of putting men in the refractory cells in the ground floor in this damp situation. I think the cells should be warmed. I have great difficulties in preserving health.' There was scurvy too, and sometimes dysentery from which people often died.

There is a remarkable example of one prisoner who proved intractable to discipline and refused food, even in the dark cell. This man spent fifteen days in the two sizes of refractory cells over a period between March 25 and May 12 and took no food in the time he was incarcerated. The surgeon reported that the man was 'of a melancholic temperament and... would have starved himself to death if not released.' Everyone did their best to entice the man to eat, including the chaplain, the surgeon, the magistrates and the turnkeys, but all to no avail.

There was also the topic of 'solitary' with the most troublesome inmates placed in the 'refractory cell' where they could be alone in semi-darkness and supposedly reflect on the errors of their ways.

Solitary confinement was central to the running of the gaols. The use of the refractory cell was a threat hanging over the worst prisoners for it conveyed thoughts of starvation diet, darkness and isolation. The germ of this punishment lies in the gradual switch from a constant application of physical punishment to one of deprivation. By the 1820s the notion lay behind the latest concepts of rehabilitation, but in the local gaols which Howard saw, we have a good idea of how the refractory cells were used. The gaol registers at

Maidstone show a typical range of cases. J. Savage was confined to a dark cell for three days 'persuant to the order of the visiting magistrate'. Also confined to dark cell for three days, was Mary Burrell, on the report from the matron that she had used 'improper language respecting the chaplain and for riotous conduct.' At the same gaol in 1821, William Constable and George Merchant were confined in dark cells; Constable for 'assaulting and beating James Styles', Merchant for 'singing in his sleeping cell.'[8]

A survey of some instances of the application of solitary confinement in the years between c.1790 and 1830 shows that it was a controversial topic, but was generally accepted as the most severe punishment except for the lash. Some of the sentences given in court specified solitary rather than the usual gaol regime, as in the case of John Webb in 1828, who was in court for stealing three pewter pots from a pub in St James's. A female servant testified against him, and Webb, from the dock, took off a nailed shoe and violently threw it at her, striking her on the arm. The judge said that such an action deserved 'the heaviest penalty of the law' and that meant imprisonment in Newgate for six months, the whole time to be spent in solitary. This was to be followed by seven years of transportation.

Clearly, solitary confinement, though a regular short-term punishment in local gaols, was a special case in the general actions taken in sentencing. In 1816 William Price was sentenced at the West Sussex quarter sessions to six months solitary confinement on bread and water for stealing a leaden weight. It was also seen as an essential punishment for young criminals, with the attitude that it would deter them from further transgression. In 1831 at the Thames Police Court, an eleven-year-old girl called Isabella Brown was charged with stealing property from her employer in Commercial Road. The girl's mother begged the magistrates to do something to 'check the girl's propensity for pilfering' and the sentence was fourteen days in the house of correction to be in solitary confinement.

THE FATE OF THE INSANE
There is also the question of the insane and what could be done for them apart from dropping them into the hellish confusion of the local gaols. In 1800 James Hadfield tried to shoot the King at the Drury Lane theatre. He was found to be insane. The result of the case was

that, only four days after the trial, a bill was passed with a long title: 'A bill for regulating trials for High Treason and Misprision of High Treason in certain cases, and for the safe custody of Insane Persons charged with Offences.' The main part of this became the Criminal Lunatics Act of 1800. This established the idea of the lunatic being kept at His Majesty's Pleasure, and although it anticipated in some ways the McNaghten Rules, formulated in 1843 after Daniel McNaghten's attempt to assassinate Robert Peel, it was not accurate or learned on the matter of what constituted insanity. But it did require the detention of an insane person, the disposition being done without any work on the part of the judge. It was an automatic destination for men like Hadfield. Before this Act, any person acquitted because of insanity simply walked free unless the judge wanted the person detained. In that case there had to be a civil hearing. The only option open to the court was to use the 1744 Vagrancy Act which enabled criminals to be detained in a house of correction. But as a defence, a claim of insanity was very difficult to establish. It was a matter of the expertise of the lawyer, and even then, proving insanity before a felony such as murder or treason was very hard. Luckily for Hadfield, he had plenty of people to speak for him, and it was only because the charge was treason, not murder, that there was full opportunity for a sound defence to be arranged. He had arguably the best legal mind in the land on his side too. Lord Birkenhead, writing in 1910, pointed out the significance of the case: 'This brief, real-life tragedy is unique… it brought a royal Duke into the witness-box and a former royal orderly into the dock.'[9]

Before this and the notion of 'His Majesty's Pleasure' and criminal lunatics, the annals of the insane in court and in gaol make painful reading. For centuries the courts, without any real medical knowledge as advice, nor any understanding of insanity and its treatment, filled the gaols with the mentally ill as well as with the real criminals. But to take a positive spin on this, it has to be said that those found insane were sent to Bridewells rather than to the gallows or to the transportation ships. Asylums were used as well, of course, as is shown in the case of Susannah Millicent, who stole a petticoat in 1794. She was deranged when finally fit to stand in court, but the lawyers and jury saw that she should be acquitted and confined as insane.

Between the seventeenth century and the early nineteenth century, asylums were small and privately run, but the criminally insane would generally be sent to prison. We know from John Howard that in France, Austria, Bavaria, Spain, Greece, Norway and Prussia between Howard's visits around 1780 and the 1850s, codification of criminal law took place, and so there was always a consideration of the issue of insanity. However, with so little understanding of mental illness in these years, their destiny was either the 'bedlam' part of a prison hospital or within the main prison population and they were simply held with more restraint and observation.

Howard visited several European gaols and gave a detailed account of French penal policy, just before the new criminal legislation was presented to *Parlement* in 1791. The focus for the insane in France was in places such as the 'Force' system, which was a prison-within-a-prison for special care or restraint, or in the massive places such as the infamous Salpetriere for women in Paris, matching the male equivalent of the Bicetre; clearly, Howard saw the problems and the lack of sensible planning and administration:

> 'The majority are the poor, who wear a coarse brown uniform, and seem as miserable as the poor in some of our country workhouses; the insane; and those that have the venereal disease. Each sort is in a court and apartments usually separate from the others, and from criminals... such a number confined together in idleness, must produce a great corruption of manners.'[10]

In France, there was no theoretical and practical study of the varieties of insanity which would encroach on criminal classification until the work of Jean-Etienne Esquirol, whose *Mental Maladies* (1838) included writing on affective disorders such as paranoia, pyromania and kleptomania.[11] But enlightened individuals were aware of the follies described by Howard. Philippe Pinel (1745-1826) is reckoned to have struck off the chains of the insane in the Salpetriere and the Bicetre. Basically, if the doctors did not understand or agree on the proper treatment of the insane, how could the courts hope to make any decisions other than the simple ones of incarceration of some kind? That was the thinking at the time.

With hindsight, it is a dreadful thought that the criminality in the insane is still partly an element of penology which has no solution, as there is no all-embracing definition of the condition that satisfies everyone. All that can be said is that a comparison of Bedlam (the Bethlem Hospital) with Broadmoor explains the limits of our ability in this respect, and the same applies across the world. Bedlam was a place where, say c. 1800, the mad were restrained and beaten and were sights for the fascinated wealthy to visit and wonder at, whereas Broadmoor, first built as an asylum, not a prison, of course became the home of those criminals who are considered to be in need of totally supervised incarceration. Not until 1948 were the terms 'criminal lunatic' and 'criminal lunatic asylum' abolished. These terms had been used since the 1860 Criminal Lunatic Asylums Act. The new term was 'Broadmoor institutions.' The 1948 Criminal Justice Act noted: 'The expression 'criminal lunatic' shall cease to be used and there shall be substituted for it... the expression 'Broadmoor patient.'[12]

ENLIGHTENMENT THEORISING

To understand the beginnings of reform and the later effects of the Enlightenment, some consideration of Cesare Beccaria's thought needs to be given. He wrote in an age in which harsh corporal punishment was in general practice. Integral to his thought on prisons and punishment was the contemporary perspective on liberty and the individual. He raised issues such as the right to punish and the consequences of punishment. He refers to 'tangible motives' taken by men to ensure that the law is preserved. These motives lead to an acknowledgement that there is a right to punish transgressors. This is all very well, but he sees in the application of punishment a number of failings, chiefly that the language and process of the law is hermetically sealed from the ordinary citizen, and that punishment is often thoughtlessly done. He argued for the promptness of punishment, and reasoned, as many had done (as in China notably) for the punishment to fit the crime. What Beccaria opposed to the set functioning of the criminal law was gleaned from historical example and some universal reflections on transgression:

'It is impossible to prevent all disorders in the universal conflict of human passions. They increase according to a ratio compounded population and the crossings of particular interests, which cannot be directed with geometric precision to public utility... A glance at the histories will show that disorders increase with theconfines of empires...'[13]

The Enlightenment meant many things, but one notable aspect of that switch in perception about the nature of the individual was that he or she had 'inalienable rights.' More and more writers and thinkers saw the gap between social function and individual freedom. Across Europe as individuals were increasingly squandered in wars, through disease, and through man's inhumanity to man, liberty became the hot topic of debate and reflection. Prison and slavery were the obvious primary targets of reform, and a generation of reformers such as Howard and thinkers such as Beccaria put ideas into the melting-pot of debate and hoped for change to happen in the hands of the practical men of politics and affairs.

The changes happened, but slowly. We can see this in two clear examples, from England and France. In England, Samuel Romilly set about abolishing some of the worst excesses of the punishment doled out in the justice system. One outstanding example is the law of petty treason. The homicide of a husband by a wife was defined as murder and he would usually hang; the killing of a husband or master by a wife or servant was petty treason, and the culprit would be burned at the stake. This state of affairs existed until 1790, and Romilly, with others, acted for the abolition of the offence in terms of wives.

In France, Louis-Michel le Peletier (1760-1793) began his career as a lawyer working in the Chatelet prison. After being elected to the *Parlement* of Paris he was honoured as deputy in the States-General, and in the Constituent Assembly, he laboured for the abolition of the death penalty, the use of the galleys in prison sentences, and branding. Beheading he saw as barbarous, and in France the ritual and suffering involved in execution during the *Ancien Regime* was horrendously inhuman, seen as a debt of honour to the sovereign, with a slow death being the ideal.

Michel Foucault, in his seminal work, *Discipline and Punish* (1973) saw this period before the arrival of the great penitentiaries – at least in its expression in France – as 'the gentle way in punishment' and le Peletier was a key campaigner in that crusade for reform. Foucault gets to the heart of the subject when he says: 'The penalty transforms, modifies, establishes, arranges obstacles. What use would it be if it had to be permanent? A penalty that had no end would be contradictory…If incorrigibles there be, one must be determined to eliminate them. But for all the others punishment can only function if it comes to an end.'[14]

A significant case study in enlightened penology is found in the Netherlands. Not only were they early in the chronology of establishing a house of correction (1596) but at Ghent – then Austrian Flanders – started with a prison attached to an abbey. Then, just a few years before Howard visited, a house of correction was built. The place was designed as an octagon, and had separate sections for men and women. Its regime put other nations to shame, in terms of care and cleanliness. Howard saw that it was conceived as a 'house of industry' but unlike the English workhouse, it was a model of advanced thought in penology. Howard described the process:

'In order to the admission of a prisoner, previous notice must be given by the city or province that sends him. When he comes he is shaved and washed; a surgeon examines him; and if healthy, he is clothed with the uniform of the house, viz: a clean linen coat and breeches, and cloth waistcoat, which are marked with the number of his room; to it he is conducted by one of the most orderly of the prisoners…'[15]

This may seem closer to a clinic for care and supervision than a prison, but sentences reached up to 20 years and there were the equivalent of refractory cells there – simply rooms without beds.

The end of the story is disappointing. A few years later, on a second visit, Howard found it had failed and that standards had slipped markedly. But Foucault commented on the previous place at Ghent and saw the Flanders approach as being entirely representative of the new thinking, seeing it as, '… a house that would in a sense provide a universal pedagogy of work for those who had proved resistant to it.'[16]

THE ORGANIZATION MEN

The first ideas about work as the foundation of correctional measures was there in the sixteenth century, but by c.1790-1800, as Foucault's main thesis describes fully, the 'gentle way in punishment' had come very close to the idea of the workhouse, with the hardened criminals and the insane still offering an insoluble problem for the law and its administrators.

By the mid nineteenth century prison had become something worthy of attention to the new social sciences, inspired by the credo of Positivism, scientific method, and a belief that crime could be understood and classified. As biological and genetic knowledge grew, thinkers came along who were convinced that there were categories of offenders who could be placed in textbooks in the same way as one might write a study of butterflies and place them in cabinets. Central to this was Cesare Lombroso (1836-1909) who wrote with the assumption that there is no factor of free will involved in transgression, so criminals are born with the capacity to offend, and so consequently, the social context should be open to control and preventive measures put in place. To demonstrate this, he produced his masterpiece *L'Uomo Delinquente* (Criminal Man) in 1876. The germ of this was an examination of the brain of a notorious robber called Vilella. Lombroso noted that there was a specific location in the man's cerebellum which tallied with the same feature in rats. This led to an assemblage of 'types' with photos and profiles covering the types of offenders related to each category of crime. But he did concede that there were two overall versions of criminality – born and made. Some of the ideas appear to be hare-brained today, such as comparing acute vision with that of eagles and hawks and then drawing conclusions about criminality.

All this was just as academically suspect as the popular 'science' of phrenology in the mid-Victorian years, in which bumps on the head were supposed to relate to personality types. But society at this time was desperate to have a set of rules and a reference base for what was so hard to understand – crime as a possibly incurable disease. By 1846 the professionalisation of penology began with the first international prison conference at Frankfurt. This was followed by more and more large-scale ones, peaking perhaps in 1872 with the International Prison Congress held in London, and attended by representatives from the USA, South American states, France, Italy, Switzerland, Belgium and Holland. At the meeting, Russia, Greece and Sweden agreed to attend the next one.

This group took on the role of help-mate and inspector for any member who had troubles in its application of prison establishment, and in 1872 France was seen to be in need of help. *The Times* reported that the group was to 'appoint a commission of fifteen members to make enquiry into the actual state of the prisons and reformatory institutions in France, and to study the whole subject of penitentiary discipline and reform.'[17]

It was the age of the penitentiary and of a will to streamline and accelerate the process of mass handling of deviants, in line with the mechanical and systematic methods of the Industrial Revolution. Michel Foucault asks the question: 'How did the coercive, corporal, solitary, secret model of the power to punish replace the representative, scenic, signifying, public, collective model? Why did the physical exercise of punishment... replace... the social play of the signs of punishment and the prolix festival that circulated them?'[18] He was trying to ask why the chaos of the human mess that was the house of correction and the local gaol gave way to what he calls 'discipline and regulation.' On the surface, this is seeing prison as something much more acceptable than the random hold-all dens of darkness and deprivation that Howard and others saw in the Georgian years.

One answer seems to be that prison was beginning to be seen as a concept needing time, management and a trajectory of using time as the alternative of the hellish limbo that it had always been. Time and prison are close brothers. In a cell, the construction and maintenance of life by hours and the calendar fade away; a long sentence had always been a seemingly infinite road to the nowhere that could be defined. The new age brought in what today is called 'sentence planning' and phases of a sentence were described and planned in order to maximise the chances of reform and rehabilitation. The long process of making a prison far more than a space for holding deviants, beginning in several European locations in the sixteen century, had led to a situation in which our modern management culture had stepped in.[19]

Notes and references

1 John Howard, *The State of the Prisons* (London, 1929), p. 166.

2 Donald Thomas (Ed.) *State Trials*, (London, 1972)), p. 103.

3 Ibid. p. 107.

4 See Elizabeth Melling (Ed.) *Crime and Punishment: Kentish Sources* (Maidstone, 1969), p. 274.

5 C J Davison Ingledew, *The History and Antiquities of Northallerton* (London, 1858), p. 22.

6 *Gentleman's Magazine* 1802 p. 220.

7 Stephen Wade, *House of Care* (Welshpool, 2009), p. 31.

8 Melling op.cit. note 4 p.

9 The Earl of Birkenhead, *More Famous Trials* (London, 1930), p. 479.

10 John Howard, *The State of the Prisons* op.cit note 1 p. 132.

11 See Roy Porter *Madness: A Brief History* (Oxford, 2002), pp. 134-135.

12 See *The Criminal Justice Act 1948* (London, 1948), section 61 p. 93.

13 Cesare Beccaria, On Crimes and Punishments in McLaughlin, Euegene, et alia *Criminological Perspectives* (London, 2003), p. 22.

14 Michel Foucault, *Discipline and Punish* (London, 1991), p. 107.

15 John Howard op.cit note 1 p. 114.

16 Foucault op.cit. note 12 p. 121.

17 *The Times* June 28, 1872 p. 4.

18 Foucault op.cit note 1 p. 131.

19 For an interesting account of the sixteenth century measures, see Philippa Hardman, 'The Origins of Imprisonment' in *Prison Service Journal* no. 177 pp. 16-22.

Chapter 5

Work and Pain: From Penal Colonies to Gulags

The concept of a penal colony appears to be very simple: prisons in the metropolis where the criminal knows and has social contacts means expense and no end of emotional problems in the long-term care. Therefore, send the convict to the other side of the world and forget him. Set him to work making buildings and bridges and use chain-gangs. As to control, well, use the military. They have nothing to do when there is no warfare.

The Russians had shown the way with the use of Siberia but from the seventeenth century onwards, as the European empires of Spain, Netherlands, Britain and France expanded, there were then some suitably isolated and God-forsaken places to send the mass of urban deviants who otherwise would have had to be fed, clothed and set to work with the eyes of the prying world upon them. Inspections, visits, reporters, Christians and the rest, so the thinking went, would add such a burden of care. But in Australasia or South America, or even in the myriad islands of the China Sea and Indonesia, the process of anonymity and oblivion could carry on regardless.

This cynical tone is applied on purpose to give the reader a sense of just how little the criminal justice systems of the great empires exploited criminals, as they had done slaves. The arrival of the penal colony was something akin to planting a flower in a desert and then being perplexed when it failed to grow.

The first instance of a distant place being used by a European state as a penal colony is Madeira, discovered by the Portuguese in 1420 and used to hold some prisoners from home; later, Jewish minorities were taken there. Following this, Britain used the method of indentured servitude from the early seventeenth century. America, as far as Britain was concerned, began its life as version of gaol. France arrived on the scene much later in this respect, using Les Iles du Salut off Surinam, and notoriously, Devil's Island, from c.1850 when a massive number of prisoners were sent there and French New Guinea.

Even the phrase itself conveys misery and isolation. Franz Kafka wrote an imaginative piece called simply, *In the Penal Colony* which begins with an imminent execution and describes the place as 'a small, deep, sandy valley closed in on all sides by barren slopes' and adds that the condemned man is linked to others by connecting chains. In the opening, Kafka immediately defines the worst result of such penal servitude in isolation: 'The condemned man had such a dog-like expression of resignation that it looked as if one could set him free to roam around the slopes and would only have to whistle at the start of the execution for him to return.'[1]

In the mid and later nineteenth century, colonies expanded and there was an increasing number of prisoners sent there for political reasons. France led the field in emulating Russia in this respect, even sending 70 Socialist delegates from the Paris arondissements to Guiana in 1852. The topic of penal settlements had been gradually introduced from the 1830s. In 1837 there was a report on a debate in the *parlement* which clearly shows the 'spin' of the time in action:

'As to the proposed penal settlement on the isle of Bourbon, the "salubrity" and "delicious climate" cannot make us forget that transportation was the favourite means adopted in evil days for the maintenance of domestic oppression and when a loud laugh followed the fantastic description of the island by M. Rosamel Depui was right in calling the Deputies to order...'[2]

FRANCE AND ITS COLONIES

France and Russia had shown the way to succeed – if that is the right word – in the penal settlement enterprise. Distance and deprivation worked well as a solution to deal with political and religious dissidents as well, so the imperialists soon saw the advantages. Napoleon I had created the monumental *Code D'Instruction*

Criminelle in 1808. In the debates leading up to this, there had been criticism of previous penal policy, and the outcome was a public process, structured around two juries, and the second would confirm the sentence and conviction of the offender. Areas were to have holding centres, and prisons commanded by a *prefet*. Prisons were termed *maisons de force* – basically incarceration with hard work. All this was impressive, but did not change the penal colonies.

Napoleon III, almost fifty years later, was very fond of penal colonies, and after his country was officially defined as an empire again in 1852, he started a programme of establishment and expansion, notably in Guiana and New Caledonia. In 1853 the Montaigne d'Argent in Guiana opened, taking 300 convicts from a total of 3,000 destined for that place. The settlement was built by the convicts, so they lived in tents while building their own prison. Half of them died in the first year. The death toll in the whole enterprise was horrendously high: just three years later, of 8,600 transported there, only 3,600 were still alive.

The first fleet arrived in New Caledonia in early 1864 at Port de France, and soon there were 25,000 convicts there. The idea behind the enterprise, as explained famously in Henri Charriere's best-seller *Papillon* (1969) was that convicts with sentences of over eight years had to stay and settle there permanently. There was even a special home for the elderly attached to the settlement. By 1880, there was a massive area of 180,000 hectares there allotted to penal settlement which was run by a special administrator and a justice of the peace.

French Guiana, including the notorious Devil's Island, had been a place of exile since the Napoleonic era, but by the 1850s it was a large penal colony comprising the Salvation islands, Cayenne, and other smaller locations. On the islands of St Joseph and Royale the less dangerous prisoners were held. Many died of disease of course, and it was on Devil's Island itself that the political prisoners were kept, perhaps most famously Alfred Dreyfus, who had been 'fitted up' by a conspiracy of officers and sent there for a period from April, 1895 to June, 1899, transported, as the Governor said, 'like a low wretch.' He bore the whole horrible sentence with fortitude and he was released thanks to work done by friends back home in France.

Dreyfus's ordeal tells us a lot about the fate of political prisoners. At times he was restrained by the barbarous method of being shackled to his bed by a double buckle. He had been labelled as a traitor, and so his ordeal was the worst imaginable, described by some as a regime of sheer terror.

There were solitary confinement units there. Guiana as a penal colony survived into the 1950's. Henri Charriere, who escaped by making a raft of coconuts in a number of sacks and floating to freedom on the mainland, explained the system, as explained to him before arrival:

> 'The preventive detentions go straight to a prison called Saint-Jean... The right convicts are separated into three groups. First the ones labelled very dangerous: As soon as they are out of the punishment block they are transferred to the Iles De Salut... The convicts don't go to Devil's Island, that's for *politicals*... Then comes dangerous, second category, they stay at the Saint Laurent camp.... when there's a need for men they're sent to the very tough camps – Camp Forestier, Charvan, Cascade, Crique Rouge and Kilometre 42, the one they call the death camp.'[3]

TRANSPORTATION: VAN DIEMAN'S LAND

The use of transportation by the British government for dealing with criminals stretches back to 1607, and the notion of establishing this punishment within the criminal justice system begins officially with the Transportation Act of 1718. This started the use of America as the main location of convict settlement, but after the War of Independence and the loss of the American colonies, Britain looked elsewhere for distant colonies, and in 1787 the first fleet sailed from Portsmouth for Botany Bay.

The settlement of the mainland of Australia had begun, but in 1803 a young lieutenant called John Bowen was sent to create a British foothold in the south of Tasmania. A year later, Hobart was established, and Van Dieman's Land was named. Abel Tasman had been to Tasmania in 1642 and he named it Anthoonij van Diemanslandt after the Governor-General of the Dutch East Indies.

The name was to resonate through popular culture and the press through to our own day, with oral history, folk music and film maintaining the image of the place as one of the worst, most brutal penal colonies in history. There is some exaggeration in that, as many of the most horrendous destinations for convicts were in the secondary prison locations around Australia, but Van Dieman's Land is a name that has dominated the criminal history of the antipodes.

In the Regency years, when there were over 200 capital crimes on the statute books. Transportation was seen as a viable and desirable alternative to long prison sentences, but unfortunately, the hulks (prison ships in estuaries) were used as gaols before the prisoners were transported, and it is estimated that between 1776 and 1795 over a third of the 5,722 prisoners died. One writer of the time wrote: 'There were confined in these floating dungeons nearly 600 men, most of them double ironed... with horrible effects rising from rattling chains and the filth and vermin naturally produced by such a crowd of miserable inhabitants.'[4]

Who were these people – 75,000 in total – sent to Van Dieman's Land? They certainly had a reputation, becoming known as 'Vandemonians' so that the play on words would suggest something devilish and evil. The fact is that many were criminals who robbed or assaulted through desperation and suffering were sent there; poachers and pickpockets, sellers of stolen goods, and of course nasty characters who would have hanged for serious crimes were also destined for one of the Tasmanian colonies. Typical examples are these cases from 1833:

William Stephenson (21) charged with stealing a black cart mare: *transported for life.*
James Bedford (41) shoe maker, charged with feloniously killing a yearling sheep: *transported for life*
Isaac Johnson (46) charged with feloniously stealing one pair of boots: *14 years trans.*[5]

But there were also political prisoners, such as the Welsh Chartists who conducted a rising in Newport in 1839. They were convicted of treason and the sentences commuted to life at Port Arthur for their radical beliefs, such as the right to vote and the abolition of child labour. There was also William Smith O'Brien, who led an insurrection at Ballingarry, Tipperary, and who was condemned to death but then sent to Port Arthur and was there from 1848 to his release in 1854. As his status was political, he had a separate house, prominent on the slope above the penitentiary.

There were some transportees who were famous of course. George Loveless, one of the Tolpuddle Martyrs of 1834, was sent to Port Arthur (the others were sent to Sydney). The 'Martyrs' had been involved in attempting to form a trade union, and so Loveless was a special case for the authorities in Hobart. He was constantly under supervision, as his biographer wrote: 'Loveless reported three interrogations – one on board ship and two ashore – of which two were conducted by the police magistrate and one by the Governor himself...'[6]

Among the Hobart Town convicts there were 'hard cases' – known as 'incorrigibles' – and when the assignment system started, in which convicts were assigned to settlers to work, there was friction, resentment, and all kinds of problems related to work and integration. Before the penitentiary at Port Arthur, there were convict bases at Macquarie and Maria Island. Macquarie was established in 1821 mainly to take Huon pine trees for boat-building, but by 1830 there were severe problems, the main one being that the harbour there was very dangerous. Maria Island also did not really work and escapes were common. A surveyors's report then described the suitability of a bay within an isthmus. Thomas Scott wrote that the place was 'a deep and safe harbour, with stands of timber on all sides coming down to the water's edge.'[7] The first period of the convict settlement there was one in which security and a tough regime were a priority. The geography was the main factor: the Tasman Peninsula is joined to Forestier's Peninsula by a narrow strip of land known as Eaglehawk Neck, and so that was the only possible escape route by land for escapees. Otherwise they would have had to cope with the ocean or with the vast Norfolk Bay.

On Eaglehawk Neck a line of huge, vicious dogs was in place. There were also dogs and armed troops on the shore across from the isthmus so that any convict who tried to swim, and who survived the sharks, came ashore in front of the mastiffs. One report described the arrangement: 'The land is only seventy-eight yards across, and double sentinels are posted day and night... a line of eighteen dogs extends across... and being kept separate, are most ferocious...'[8]

Wearing his Hessian jacket and trousers, the convict would rise with the bell at dawn, have a drink of hot water and flour called *skilly*, and start the day's hard labour. He would have Sunday free and on Saturday afternoons he could have a bath and some recreation. As today, there were areas for exercise and, of course, the chapel for worship. This was built on the principle of the 'silent system' so that each convict sat in a cubicle from which he could see no others so that his silent prayer was aided by isolation.

Discipline, particularly under George Arthur, was hard. Flogging was used, as it was in the army and at times in British gaols at home for the most recalcitrant offenders. The man being punished would be fastened to a three-legged frame, then placed in a bath of salt after the cat o' nine tails had been applied. There was always a doctor present in case things went too far and life was threatened.

There was a system in place that used convicts as constables, and as with prisons through history, there was 'prisoner power' in which punishments were applied for unacceptable behaviour. Men who had 'grassed' and who were sent to another settlement or to court for witness duty, had to return, and there they would face retribution. There were cases in which such men begged the Governor to be sent elsewhere, to escape death at the hands of fellow prisoners.

Convicts worked in gangs on building projects. A typical example of this is the work done at Richmond, north of Hobart, which was named in 1824 and which developed quickly, becoming a military centre and needing convict labour and a gaol to hold them. This form of slave labour (which in effect is what it was) enabled roads and bridges to be made. The bridge at Richmond was built by convicts in 1825 and was originally called Bigge's bridge. It is the oldest bridge still in use in the whole of Australia. Further up the coast towards Bicheno, travellers may see a classic example of this work done by labour gangs, at Spiky Bridge, completed in 1843.

The gaol at Richmond is typical of the type of small local establishment needed to house the convicts. It is a grim place, with solitary confinement cells and a flogging yard. It must have been hell for the prisoners. In the 1830s the gaoler complained that he had an overcrowding problem with forty prisoners held in a space of only nineteen square metres. The gaol had twelve sleeping rooms, a small airing yard and eleven day rooms. There were separate solitary cells for women and a cookhouse. The remains of the foundation used for the flogging frame are still visible, and it must have been a harrowing experience to suffer punishment there. When not out on local building projects, convicts in the gaol would fill their time by painting, cleaning, doing all the housework chores, and sometimes having a little recreation such as draughts, as we know from a draught board which was cut into a floor.

Convicts mostly started their penal time as assigned labour. Some of this was on public works, but also many prisoners were assigned to settlers. Governor Arthur was strict in his rules concerning this system, insisting on firm discipline and religious worship and bible study within the working week. Alcohol was strictly forbidden and the masters taking on convicts were directed to force their convict-workers to pray and to observe the Sabbath; they even had to buy bibles for the convicts.

As Robert Hughes makes clear in his massive account of transportation *The Fatal Shore*, without assignment there would have been no colony in Van Dieman's Land. He points out that there was no labour but convict labour and that 'The mere fact of living as a free settler in a penal colony meant that a man must accept the paramount values of penal discipline.'[9]

There were all kinds of difficulties in the system of course. Peter Brannon, for instance, who was just twelve when sentenced to life transportation for stealing a sock, was assigned to a Mrs Green in Launceston where he was constantly rebellious and disobedient. He was always answering charges and appearing at trials; his punishment was to be put on public works, but he absconded and was then given a period of hard labour. Patrick Murphy, from Liverpool, ran off from his assignment with Thomas Reibey at Entally House, Launceston, and his punishment was work in a chain gang, constantly in irons.

For many of the convicts, their destination was an unmarked grave on the Isle of the Dead, out in the bay beyond the penitentiary and used from 1833. A minister of the time described it in his journal: 'This it appeared to me, would be a secure, undisturbed resting place where the departed prisoners might lie together until the morning of the resurrection. No stone marks where he slumbers, as no tombstones or other mark is allowed to be placed at the head of the graves.'[10] The religious life was crucially important of course, as the

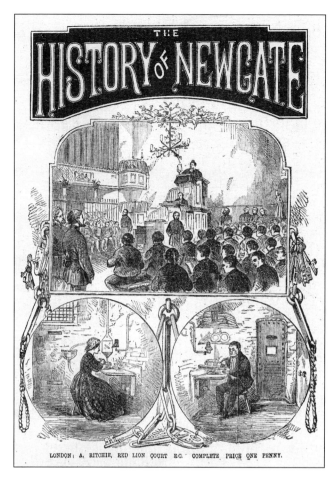

Newgate. One of the very oldest London prisons, and the place of execution when Tyburn was closed down. Anonymous booklet, published 1880s

A typical image of a dungeon: the Bradford gaol where all varieties of offender were held in the 18th century. William Scruton's *Pen and Pencil Sketches of Old Bradford* (1890)

JOHN NELSON IN THE BRADFORD DUNGEON.

'A hole' – an image of oblivion from the Middle Ages. This one is from Scarborough Castle.

A typical prison wing of a Victorian radial prison design. Courtesy of HMP Northallerton

Cobb Hall, a corner of
Lincoln Castle, a medieval
stronghold with a
dungeon. Author's collection

Dublin Castle: a symbol of imperial
strength and a place of detention.
Author's collection

A list of convicts: 1760
publication. Number 0020

A SELECT and IMPARTIAL

ACCOUNT

OF THE

Lives, Behaviour, and Dying
Words, of the moſt remarkable

CONVICTS,

From the Year 1725, down to the preſent Time.

CONTAINING

Amongſt many Others, the following, *viz.*

Catherine Hayes, for the barbarous Murder of her Husband.

Edward Bunworth, Wm. Blewit, and five more, for the Murder of Mr. Ball, in St. George's-Fields.

James Cluff, for the Murder of his Fellow Servant, Mary Green.

John Gow, alias Smith, Captain of the Pyrates, for Pyracy and Murder.

Mr. Maynee, one of the Clerks of the Bank of England, for cheating the Bank of 4420 l.

Mr. Woodmarſh, for the Murder of Mr. Robert Ormes.

John Sheppard, who made his Eſcape out of the Condemn'd-Hole, and likewiſe out of the Stone-Room in Newgate.

Robert Hallam, for the barbarous Murder of his Wife, by throwing her out of Window.

Mr. Skelton, the Apothecary, a Highwayman.

Sarah Malcomb, for the barbarous Murder of Ann Price, Eliz. Harriſon, and Lydia Duncomb, in the Temple.

John Field, Joſeph Roſe, Wm. Buſh, and Humphry Walker, for entering the Houſe of Mr. Lawrence, and Mr. Francis.

Fælix quem faciunt aliena Pericula cautum.

VOL. II.

LONDON:

Printed by J. Applebee, for J. Hodges, at the Looking-Glaſs, on London-Bridge ; and ſold alſo by C. Corbett, at Addiſon's-Head, oppoſite St. Dunſtan's-Church, in Fleet-ſtreet. M,DCC,LX.

The Hulk *Discovery* at Deptford in 1829. Old print. Author's collection

An iconic image of a convict prison: Dartmoor post card, c.1920.

A gaol plan c. 1800 showing the mix of offender categories. Author's collection

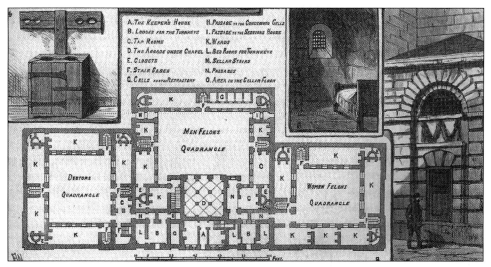

A wing entrance at Port Arthur, Tasmania. Author's collection

Port Arthur: the penitentiary. Author's collection

Solitary cell at Richmond gaol,
Tasmania. Author's collection

A typical treadmill or
treadwheel, invented
by William Cubitt
c.1820. Vicki Schofield

The Bastille from *La Prise de la Bastille*, 1965.

Frontispiece from the memoirs of Mr Linguet, a former prisoner, 1884.

A sketch of Devil's Island with the special enclosure made for Alfred Dreyfus. From The Dreyfus Case, 1937

A comrade's court at Sokolinki Camp. From *Soviet Russia Fights Crime*, 1934

The main entrance at Alcatraz island. Author's collection

A lower cell block at Alcatraz. Author's collection

San Francisco from Alcatraz. Author's collection

Interior of a cell at Alcatraz. Author's collection

The pentitentiary ruin, Alcatraz. Author's collection

Lubianka, Moscow. Les Baynton

What a convict would have looked like in the colonies. Author's collection

A Plan of Bermuda, one of a string of penal colonies, from a 17th century print.

The prison at Salerno. *Graphic, 1858*

The Chinese cage. An Englishwoman was put in this, in 1838, after a shipwreck. *Graphic, 1838*

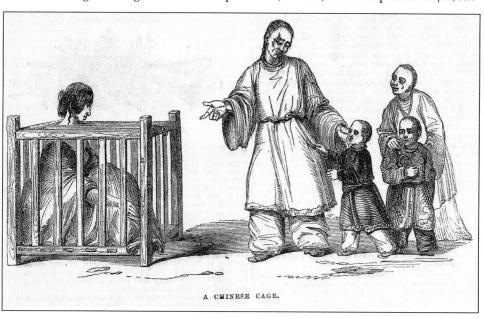

A CHINESE CAGE.

The execution 'suite' A feature of many prisons in the nineteenth century. From Arthur Griffith's *Secrets of the Prison House* (1894)

'Escapes from Siberian Prisons.' A feature in Hamsworth Magazine, 1895.

concept of the prison in the Victorian period was that it should include an effort towards salvation and redemption and a long period for reflection on past ill deeds done to others. The separate prison chapel was conceived along the lines of the first chapels in the new convict prisons back home in London, such as Pentonville. Henry Mayhew's description of the typical chapel is exactly what Port Arthur's place of worship would have been like:

'The seats are divided off in the same manner as the pit-stalls at a theatre, but in appearance they resemble a small box or pew…the reader has to imagine the ordinary pews of a church to be arranged on an inclined plane, one above the other.. and each divided into a series of compartments just large enough to hold one person…'[11]

The Sunday routine included opportunity for that introspection which the Victorians believed to be an essential part of the work towards reform. When the new penitentiaries were built, the chapel and time with chaplains was considered to be integral to the prison establishment.

Clearly, with hard physical work at the heart of the penal regime, and the frequency of infectious disease in the prison community, the medical men were of paramount importance. In fact, for the journey from Britain over the oceans to Van Dieman's Land, the surgeons' logs and journals provide some of the best information for researchers on the convicts and the illnesses they suffered. At Port Arthur, one considerable achievement in terms of health and care was the building of an asylum and a hospital. The latter was made of brick and sandstone and opened for business in 1842, though there had originally been a small wooden hospital. The place had four wards, with facilities for around 80 patients. As with military provision in these matters, the system included convict orderlies. Although there were limitations in medical provision, one interesting point is that the food available was recorded as being of good quality. Reports often noted that the convicts' food was better than that provided back home in Britain.

The asylum was not made until the end of transportation, but it illustrates an important development: the convicts who had stayed in

Tasmania and who were free after their ticket of leave (a kind of release on licence) and eventual freedom. The fact that there were many people with mental illness problems indicates some of the emotional and mental turmoil and suffering of those who had been in fact banished from their families and from their homeland. The various shades of depressive illness we now recognise were at that time only understood in very limited ways. But again, this reflected the same developments back home, as new large-scale local asylums were built from the mid-century.

The last two ships to arrive in Van Dieman's Land came in 1851. There had been a steady increase in numbers sent there as fewer were sent to New South Wales, and just before the final ships. There had been around 5,000 arriving each year. All transportation to the place was abolished in 1853 and two years later the island was renamed Tasmania. Finally, in 1868 all transportation to Australia generally ceased. The number of convicts who had made the journey there over the previous eighty years was approximately 162,000.

An 'old colonist' writing to *The Times* in 1853 took issue with some statistics and his comments give an insight into the state of affairs at the time the ships stopped arriving in Hobart: 'The noble earl says that of the convicts sent out, 99 out of a hundred were so far reformed that after their liberation they maintained themselves by honest industry instead of crime… If the proportion of criminals permanently reformed had been give as 1 out of 100, it would have been much nearer the truth.'[12] But on the credit side, the case of Abraham Hood shows that people changed. He had been sentenced to transportation for stealing a horse, but by 1829 he was working as a constable in Hobart, then became a watchman at Port Arthur, and finally entered settlement life as a baker, which is what his trade had been at home in Dalkeith.

RUSSIA: FROM KATORGA TO GULAGS

In his story *Punin and Baburin* (1874) Ivan Turgenev describes a scene at which a young man, Yumil, from a huge peasant-run estate, is sent to Siberia:

> 'The unfortunate boy was being transported to a settlement; on the other side of the fence was a little cart loaded with his poor

belongings. Such were the times then. Yumil stood without his cap, with downcast head, barefoot, with his boots tied up with a string behind his back and his face turned up to the seigneurial mansion.... A stupid smile was frozen on his colourless lips...'[13]

In the penal system of the Russian empire known as *katorga*, Siberian work camps provided the ideal destination for the underclass who could be used on public works to develop those regions which were several time-zones away from Moscow. These camps were first established back in the seventeenth centuries when it was realised that no-one could escape, as they were in one of the most inhospitable regions on earth. Supervision was therefore no real problem and if a few prisoners did take a chance against nature, then they were expendable. When the penal laws were overhauled in 1847, with the rise of nationalism and a growing number of dissidents who had to be removed to the extremities of the empire, these exiles mixed with peasant and criminal classes. Other minorities were sent there also, notably the Poles, who were known as Sybiraks.

In the 1870s, there was a renewed interest by intellectuals and students from Moscow and St Petersburg in the peasant, as an idealised type with special virtues. This movement made people generally more aware of the vulnerability of the peasants, as in Turgenev's account of the boy, Yumil. In other words, people could be sent to the camps by the Russian equivalent of manorial lords, as well as by judicial professionals. The *narodniki*, the intellectuals who were fervent for the cause of the land-workers, helped to make the nature of *katorga* more visible and understood. One of the most forthright accounts of the system comes from the writer Anton Chekhov who went to Sakhalin island, known formally as Sakhalin Oblast, a remote island north of Japan over 400 miles long.

For a *katorga*, this was as far east as anyone could go in Russia. Chekhov went there in 1891 to investigate conditions, mainly in a medical role (he was a doctor) and the result was his book *The Island of Sakhalin*. In his letters home, he wrote about the long journey there by carriage and river boat. After the time there, he was savage and indignant on the whole *katorga*system. This passage from a letter to his friend Alexei Suvorin encapsulates his criticism:

> 'Sakhalin is a place of unbearable suffering, on a scale of which no creature but man is capable, whether he be free or in chains. People who have worked thereor in that region have faced terrifying problems and responsibilities which they continue to work towards resolving. I am not a sentimental person, otherwise I should say that we should make pilgrimages to places like Sakhalin as the Turks go to Mecca, and sailors and penal experts should study Sakhalin in the same way that soldiers study Sevastopol.'[14]

In terms of the political exiles, as opposed to the criminals, there were marked differences. What was called the 'Administrative Process' was applied, meaning a secret tribunal – a trial with no press reports. The English traveller, Harry de Windt, travelled to Siberia at the same time that Chekhov was on Sakhalin, and de Windt explains: 'A man may be seated quietly at home with his family, in his office.. when the fatal touch on the shoulder summons him away, perhaps for ever. The sentence once passed, there is no appeal to a higher court...'[15]

Exiles usually spent up to two years in a prison in the west before Siberian exile, and then they went on their very long journey. They lived at various stages in their sentence in string of towns across the far east of Russia. As de Windt noted, there were concessions: 'On arrival at Irkutsk prison-dress is discarded, although he remains under lock and key and in close charge of the Cossack who is responsible for his safe delivery.'[16] The most detailed picture we have of life in the *katorga* in the nineteenth century is from Dostoievky's *Memoirs from the House of the Dead*, in which we have the place from the viewpoint of a political exile. He was sometimes in irons, wore regulation clothes according to his category, and worked as the common criminals did. But there was clearly a split between the criminals as such and what Dostoievsky calls the 'gentlemen prisoners'. As in every community, though, there were ever lower echelons in which prisoners resided, and in this case, it was the category of Polish prisoners. The 'gentlemen' were at first reviled and had to win respect: 'They watched our sufferings, which we tried not to show them, with delight. We were particularly severely cursed at work at first, because we were not as strong as they were...'[17]

The camp projects were mainly road-making and timber work and the Amur Cart Road, an incredible achievement which involved constructing a road 2,000km long through massive area of swamps and desolate taiga wasteland. It took eleven years to build, being completed in 1909, and was on a scale almost as large as some of the later Gulag projects. The conditions of life and work in Siberia were extremely severe, as Harry de Windt describes: 'Let the reader imagine, if possible, the blank despair of existence under such conditions: day after day, year after year, nothing to do or look at of interest; tortured by heat and mosquitoes in summer, perished by cold and hunger in the dark, cruel winter...'[18]

Siberia extends for 4,830,000 square miles – eighty-three times the size of England and Wales. Organising penal colonies across that vast space and beyond meant having a system of area managers. There were magistrates and police officers, but the army was the real presence in terms of overseeing the exiles and prisoners. There were as many complaints from members of the administration as there were from writers and travellers who, like Chekhov, lamented the desperately hard conditions of life.

It is important to clarify the difference between *katorga* and the forced settlers. The latter were technically not in prison, but were in exile; this was different from criminal prison sentences. It has been established that the forced labour system goes back to the eighteenth century, when, in 1722, Peter the Great passed a law to force labour at the Dauriya silver mines in far Siberia. There had been some kind of eastern exile in Russian society since 1649, when it was thought to be less severe to send people to Siberia than to keep them detained while also mutilating and knouting them. In 1736 an act was passed which enabled estate owners such as the woman in Turgenev's story to dispose of undesirables in the locality. The unfortunate individual would find that his property had been acquired and split up across the community and then he or she was expected to find a home elsewhere. Failing that, exile to the east was the only possible next step. Anne Applebuam has pointed out that in the nineteenth century, the numbers of *katorga* workers declined, while forced settlers increased in numbers. She explains: '…in the nineteenth century, *katorga* remained a relatively rare form of punishment. In 1906 on the eve of the Revolution, there were only 28,600.'[19]

The fact is that the vast areas of Russia to the east of Moscow and the other cities of the old Rus region needed a population, and they had huge natural resources waiting to be tapped for massive profits. Just as Rome had done in her method of having slave colonies established for mining and quarrying, so Russia sent large numbers of expendable people to the Far East. The system did achieve the aim of having a certain level of permanent inhabitants, however, as many exiled forced labour groups did indeed stay. Anton Chekhov met some of these, and he noted that: 'The majority of them are financially poor, have little strength, little practical training, and possess nothing except their ability to write, which is frequently of absolutely no use to anybody.'[20]

AFTER THE REVOLUTION
Research has shown that, by 1920, when the Revolution and the ensuing civil war had raged across the continent, two prison systems were in place in the new Soviet Union. The usual, established criminal prison establishment was organised by the Commissariat of Justice, with an element of corrective labour. In contrast, the Cheka , later the OGPU and KGB, controlled what were at first known as special camps. The important fact about the latter is that they were outside the normal criminal justice system. Their administration was unknown and was closed to all but authorised persons such as the official visit to Solovetsky by the writer Maxim Gorky in 1929. This camp system, which became the Gulag from the words *Glavnoe upravlenie lagerei*, equated to one of the most terribly resonant acronyms in Russian history. It was to last until Stalin's death in 1953.

At first, there was confusion and great disparity in the treatment of prisoners across the land. The prisoners of the Cheka were the intelligentsia and other deviants, and there was a period of overlap before Lenin's penal philosophy was consolidated. Therefore, in some prisons there was what seems on the surface to be an enlightened regime, as at the Moscow Butirka prison, where inmates had clean linen, books and health care. In contrast, at Arkhangelsk, as Anne Applebaum relates, matters were extreme and brutal: 'Some guards took matters into their own hands. In April 1921, one group of prisoners in Petrominsk refused to work and demanded more food rations. Fed up with this insubordination, the Arkhangelsk regional authorities ordered all 540 of them sentenced to death. They were duly shot.'[21]

In the years up to 1929, when a pattern had settled in as to the best model of a labour camp, as Alexander Solzhenitsyn makes clear, the new regime created special names for various classes of enemies of the state, and the negative labels all reinforced the spectrum of so-called deviant behaviour that Lenin identified. Trials took place without proper defence of objective hearings, and people were simply taken to a quiet spot and shot if that was the simplest way to achieve the latest target. Solzhenitsyn explains: 'As we begin to understand our judicial practices, we realize now that the public trials were only the surface indications of the mole's tunnel… At these trials only a small number of those arrested were produced in court… The majority of the engineers, who had the courage and intelligence to reject and refute the interrogators' stupidities, were tried out of earshot.'[22]

The Solovetsky Islands lie off the north-west of the Russian federation, comprising mainly Solovetsky, Anzer, Zayatsky Ostrov, Bolshaya Muksalma and Malaya Muksalma. The Solovetsky archipelago was to form the template for the gulags with the 'first camp.' Life there in the 1920s, particularly under the direction of the influential commandant, Naphtali Frenkel, was to provide the blueprint for what was later defined as the SLON work camp. SLON was yet another acronym, referring to 'northern work camps of special significance' In effect, this meant that the inmates undertook massive operations of public works, and the one that set the standard for the norm was the digging of the White Sea Canal. Although this came a little later, in 1932-33, the achievements at Solovetsky had made it clear that with Frenkel's methods, massive undertakings such as this canal of 150 miles, from close to Medvedhegorsk to a point a little south of Kem on the White Sea, would be achievable.

Stalin commanded that this canal had to be built by prison labour and to an outsider, the whole project seems an impossibility. The materials to be used were limited to wood, sand and rocks. The tools used were pickaxes, saws and hammers. All along the route, the prisoners had to build their own wooden huts, and food supplies were distributed very poorly. The gargantuan task went on, with the system of rewards for the workers who excelled themselves in productivity quotas.

Considering the deadly isolation of the Siberian camps, the question of escapes seems on the surface to be a pointless one: surely, the escape into the hard *taiga* [forests] and the endless wastes would be a form of suicide? The fact is that people did run off into the wilderness. Back in the Tsarist days, there was clearly a massive social problem with violent and desperate escapees. In 1900 a feature on this in *The Harmsworth Magazine* gave accounts of this experience from prisoners who had made it back to the west. The anonymous writer made the point that the life of the Siberian prisoner had three phases: the pre-settlement holding, the time away, and the remainder of his life, usually as a permanent settler of the region. On that basis, the need for some to risk their lives in escaping into the vastness of Eastern Russia might be understood.

The result of this was a numerous population of vagrants on the road and in the forests; as the article makes clear, and the communities along the route were well aware of this shiftless and needy type of runaway:

> 'The vagrant, it may be, turns westward in the hope of regaining the land of birth, and retraces his steps along the great highway, from which he can easily slink into the forest should he wish to avoid his fellow men… The passportless wanderer finds no place where he can rest the sole of his foot; and when the first of the night frosts in September heralds the approaching death of the year, and it is no longer possible to lie out on a mossy couch, he sees before him one of two prospects – a tragic end in the woods or self-surrender at some penal station.'[23]

Many would be destined to return to a settlement, give an assumed name, and start again on a sentence.

As for the worst of the Tsarist prisons, there were plenty of accounts available in the early twentieth century, so comparisons were made with the labour camps. Tolstoy applied to visit a state prison to add to his research, and he was told that, as he wanted to see the dungeons: 'There were only three persons in the Empire who could leave them having once entered – the Tsar, the commandant of the fortress and the chief of the gendarmes.'[24]

The late Victorian and Edwardian popular magazines took a great interest in the camps, delighting in showing drawings and photographs of men chained to wheelbarrows or displaying letters branded on their faces. Escaped convicts were said to 'infest' Siberia and a stress was placed on the very worst punishments, such as the treatment of Mongolian prisoners who were sometimes fastened to a board with their heads through holes.

Returning to the gulags, by the 1930s there had been increases on a massive scale. Generally, the years 1937 and 1938 are regarded as the Great Terror, when the worst atrocities took place, and the nature of the human commodity in the camps fell to the level of a valueless, work animal who was also a non-citizen. At that time the secret police in charge of the system, the NKVD, issued quotas for each region, and the labels used were 'category' – meaning that a 'first category' people were to die and the 'second category' were to be placed in what was effectively a concentration camp. Consequently, such bold and harsh figures as those for Georgia in 1937 indicated that 2,000 were to die and 3,000 were for the camps. Even the tiny Kalmyk area had to have 100 for execution and 300 for the camps.

In this period, no-one was safe and even camp administrators could find themselves called 'enemies' of the people and taken away to die or to rot in the far east. One camp survivor, Yelena Sidorkina, described this fear and uncertainty: 'Nobody knew what tomorrow would bring. People were afraid to talk to one another or meet, especially families in which the father or mother had already been "isolated." The rare individuals foolhardy enough to stand up for those arrested would themselves be automatically nominated for "isolation."'[25]

Ten years later there was a period of rearrests. The war with Hitler had ended and Stalin was arguably even more paranoid, relying on his usual line of thought with regard to supposed enemies – hit them hard and fast, and of course, do the unexpected. That way, all citizens would have a tinge of fear in their lives. Reading Solzhenitsyn's epic account of the gulags, published in 1973, the tone of sarcasm and dark humour, even in translation, gives a lucid perspective on the sheer scale of chaotic and uncertain administration, as in his account of being at Presnya prison at the end of the war: '…not only the prisoners who arrived there but even the most high-ranking officials and even the heads of Gulag itself were unable to predict who would proceed where.'[26]

The gulags were in one sense an extension of what Russia had always known, yet in another sense they were the absurd and barbaric creation of a deranged mind given absolute power. History will always view the gulag system as an instance of the worst that dictatorship can achieve in negating humanity, on a par with the Nazi concentration camps. Indeed, that comparison has to be made, but there were very marked differences between gulag camps and Auschwitz or Dachau. The Nazi creation was a genocidal programme and although the victims were in a sense 'criminal' and 'political' as the Russian prisoners were, the groups concerned were chiefly racial victims and the objectives, though horrific, were clear. What Stalin's motives were may perhaps remain an inexplicable subject. Yet in spite of contrasts, there is no doubt that hard labour was at the heart of both systems, as was the creation of a prisoner at the level of a slave with no identity. The dark paradox which was the focus of the impetus of revolution in Russia is surely akin to those movements for freedom in France in 1789 and in other locations of popular insurrection, yet the gulags, as consequences of the Communist imperative, bear no comparison with the aftermath of other evolutions, The French Terror was short and violent, but a new penal and legal code emerged, and citizens had rights. Soviet Russia erased the list of human rights as formed in the Enlightenment and most powerfully in the American state after its break from Britain. The penal system was the centre of the mindset of security, placing it in comprehensive control, above codification of law with rights integrated.

In a state with persons and 'non-persons' prison comes to occupy a primary place, becoming the potent arm of repression, the employer of a vast staff of administrators and guards, and the provider of the most destructive of all its effects – a metaphor for that fearsome limbo created by man for man. It is possible to gauge the scale of the atrocities by noting some regional examples. At a place called Levasho Moor, for instance, near St Petersburg, there are almost 20,000 victims of Stalin's Terror buried in mass graves. The museum there has an exhibit which hints at the extent of the human suffering involved because it is a collection of poems by the children of those who died. Catriona Kelly has commented on this: 'Between 1917 and 1953, millions of Russian families were torn apart as spouses of the arrested followed the supposed criminals into the camps of exile. The luckier children went to live with relatives; the less fortunate were placed in special children's homes run by the NKVD, with foster parents, or left to fend for themselves.'[27]

From around 1960 onwards, there has been a gradual gathering of material of course. This has provided masses of future sources for historians and given us a much more detailed account of the human testimonies from the camps. One influential collection in this respect came from Alexander Berkman in his collection of *Letters from Russian Prisons* (1999) and there we have hundreds of first-hand accounts from camp inmates, such as the definitions of oblivion, typified by this from 'G.A.N.': 'Yurko had been banished to Ust-Kulom, 27 versts [about 18 miles]from Ust-Syssolsk, on the river Vytshegda. In the Zyrian language Ust-Kulom means"The Gates of Death."This is what he writes: "The village deserves that name. A hole, a gap in human culture. The village is not marked on any map…"'[28]

The rapid displacement and transfer of the inmates is well documented, and the contrast between the early times at the Butirka in Moscow, and the shipping out of those inmates to distant camps is a large area of testimony, as one prisoner wrote: 'On June 4, when I was preparing to put Marusia to bed after giving her a bath I was called out of the room by the investigator of the Cheka, who arrived with some other persons and told us that we were to be transferred immediately to another place. I explained that a sudden transfer like this would have very bad consequences for her. To my declaration the following answer was made:"I must carry out my orders."'[29]

The history of the gulags has been written in phases and after the archives were recently opened to historians, the volume of material has grown considerably. What the whole miserable enterprise does show the historian of penology is that at any given time and in any autocratic society, a prison system may emerge that will begin as an *ad hoc* facility and end in genocide.

Notes and references

1 Franz Kafka *In the Penal Colony:* Franz Kafka Online Translated by Ian Johnston, 2010.

2 *The Times* 27 Jan. 1837 p. 4.

3 Henri Charriere, *Papillon* (London, 2005) p. 65.

4 Alex Graeme-Evans, *A Short History Guide to Port Arthur 1830-1877* (Hobart, 2001) p. 6.

5 Sentences of the prisoners at the Lincolnshire lent Assizes 1836 *Convicts of Lincolnshire* (Lincolnshire County Council, 2001) p. 6.

6 Joyce Marlow, *The Tolpuddle Martyrs* (London, 1974), p. 106.

7 Op.cit note 3 p. 8.

8 See Robert Hughes, *The Fatal Shore* (London, 2003), pp. 406-407.

9 Ibid. p. 388.

10 Op.cit. note 3 p. 13.

11 Henry Mayhew and John Binny, *The Criminal Prisons of London* (London, 1862) p. 512.

12 *The Times*, 2 July 1853 p. 5

13 Ivan Turgenev, *Punin and Baburin* Literature Network 2010.

14 Anton Chekhov, *A Life in Letters* (London, 2004), p. 204.

15 Harry de Windt, *From Paris to New York by Land* (London, 1903) p. 112.

16 Ibid. p. 113.

17 Fyodor Dostoievsky, *Memoirs from the House of the Dead* (Oxford, 2001) p. 32.

18 Op.cit note 15 p. 110.

19 Anne Applebaum, *Gulag* (London, 2003) p. 17.

20 Ibid. p. 17.

21 Ibid. p. 38.

22 Alexander Solzhenitsyn, *The Gulag Archipelago* (London, 1974) p. 47.

23 'Escapes from Siberian Prisons' *Harmsworth Magazine* (London, 1900) p. 309.

24 Ibid, p. 311.

25 Applebaum op.cit note 19 p. 109.

26 Solzhenitsyn op.cit note 22 p. 558.

27 Catriona Kelly, review of *Children of the Gulag Times Literary Supplement* 4.3. 2011 p. 13.

28 Alexander Birkman, *Letters from Russian Prisons* (Westport, 1999) p. 63.

29 Ibid. p. 77.

Chapter 6

Reform and the Penitentiary: The American Experience

Attention now turns to the origins and development of two systems: one based on silence and close confinement, and the other on collective assembly for work and for learning. In the USA these became the axis of debate and eventually opened up the nature of the penitentiary for further refinement as time went on. But first, before telling the story of the American system, we need a case study of failure to show the weaknesses.

The first penitentiary in England was built at Millbank and stood where the Tate gallery now stands. It had three miles of corridors, a thousand cells, and was a convict prison where the inmates were forbidden to talk to each other for the period of the first half of their sentence.

The concept of the giant penitentiary we owe to the philosopher Jeremy Bentham, who conceived of what he called the 'Panopticon.' This literally means 'seeing everything' and the plan was to have a prison with radial wings emanating from a central viewing-place. The Victorian prisons still in our current system all have this radial design, but the penitentiary was on a much grander scale.

Bentham proposed this in opposition to the expanding operation of transportation to the new Australian colonies after the loss of the American colonies after the War of Independence of 1777. He saw the use of transportation as a wrong move, and that large-scale prisons at home would solve the problem of prison over-population, much as Titan prisons were proposed in 2008 to remedy the same problem. Bentham battled long and hard for his panopticon to be created and he finally abandoned it by 1820. But Millbank was created as an experiment. The first forty prisoners arrived on 26 June 1816, after being carried in vans and chained together, from Newgate to Blackfriars Bridge, where they were put on board a barge and taken under police guard to the new prison.

Penitentiaries were not new: there had been a Penitentiary Act in 1779, as explained earlier, thanks to the work of John Howard and others. That Act merely made state prisons a possibility, though the plan was long term. Much of the Enlightenment thinking, as expressed by Howard and Romilly, was put into practice. The work was tough but there was pay; religion was integrated into the regime and reforming the individual was the priority. The Governor was also the chaplain in 1837. This was Daniel Nihil, appointed by the inspector, a Reverend Whitworth Russell.

Nihil was severe and unflinching. He believed in harsh discipline and a firm belief in demanding physical work. Although this new national prison was supervised by a committee, Nihil was the master. Even his name suggests an irony, being Latin for 'nothing.' It was certainly hard to get anything out of him. At one time he was challenged with evidence that the strong insistence on separation at all times was having a detrimental effect on the sanity of prisoners, and his response was: 'What I object to is a nominal separation accompanied with secret fraudulent communication. Health is certainly a consideration, but are morals less?'

Nihil's regime included the scandal of three little girl prisoners who had been in solitary confinement for a year, but 1822-23 was surely the *annus horribilis* of the penitentiary. The Governor then was John Couch. In September 1822 two convicts, Edward Chubb and Elizabeth Collis, died in the prison. The coroner's inquest decided that Chubb, who had had a 'scrofulous infection of the neck', and Collis, who had suffered from tuberculosis, died of natural causes. But just one month later there was a similar inquest on the death of teenager Jane Downes and the surgeon, Dr Hutchinson, gave a long and garbled account of his treatment of her, including the admission that she had 'fallen down' at one point. He was not convincing and questions were asked as to whether the girl was assaulted. Eventually a verdict of 'visitation by God' was decided on as the doctor could give no explanation.

Then, six months later, the doctor was dismissed from his post. It seems that he was not culpable as the too frequent deaths and illnesses were due to a lack of proper food. The doctor had tried to fight the committee on the matter and had failed. His friend, Morton Pitt, wrote on the subject: 'I have often lamented the jealousies and cabals amongst the officers which from an early period have been so prevalent at the penitentiary.' He claimed that: 'Too much detail has been undertaken by the committee and in point of fact they have been *governing* …'

Soon after, the worst happened with a truly dreadful inquest into the death of a girl prisoner. *The Times* reported: 'The jury, being sworn, adjourned to view the body, which was reduced to a mere skeleton, but bore the relics of a once very pretty woman. 'The surgeon and governor were questioned and at one point, this interchange took place:

Juror: 'What quantum of meat is allowed per day? Six ounces'.
Coroner: 'Gentlemen, I don't know if you are aware that several acts of parliament are made for the better regulation of the penitentiary…'
Juror: 'All we want to know is whether the meat be good and I should like the Governor to produce a sample.'[1]

No sample was produced.

The whole sorry saga of Millbank led to the scurvy scandal of 1823 (the press reported that '400 unhappy wretches are now in the infirmary') when the prison was cleared, the women pardoned and others sent to the hulks. The first penitentiary had failed. There had been endless tales of violence coming from the place, typified by this story from a writer later on who had been deputy governor:

'The Governor told the prisoners that the new brown bread would have to be continued until the next meeting of the committee, whereupon many resisted when their cell doors were closed and others hammered loudly on the woodwork with their three-legged stools and this was accompanied by the most hideous yells... Four prisoners were especially refractory and entirely demolished the inner door and every item of furniture. One of them, Greenslade, assaulted the Governor with part of the door frame and I was compelled to knock down one of them Michael Sheen...'[2]

THE WALNUT STREET EXPERIMENT v THE AUBURN SYSTEM

Well-meaning ideas from the Enlightenment had led to the penitentiary experiment. Jeremy Bentham's panopticon was just one of many theoretical notions to enter the arena of penology as the nineteenth century began. In Britain the situation was the dual one of the silent system and the separate system for most of the century, but in America, the first phase of prison reform began with the Philadelphia Quakers, and a slightly different dual development was to happen as time went on.

William Penn, as early as 1682, had considered confinement as a location for corrective measures to be applied. A century later the Philadelphia Society for Alleviating the Miseries of Public prisons advocated the creation of a humanitarian penitentiary. The Penal Code of 1786 had been somewhat draconian, closer to medieval prisons than to the British Bridewell regime, with manacles being used and chain gangs for public works. The new Quaker thinking was based on withdrawal of alcohol and solitary confinement. The prototype for this was the Walnut Street Jail, opened in1790, which was based on a more far-reaching categorisation method than the one in Britain. There were four classes comprising confinement offenders, select class, probationary class and repeat felons.

There were separate quarters for women prisoners and debtors, and dangerous offenders were placed in solitary. In these measures, the Walnut Street custodians were ahead of the British house of correction development, and in fact had applied most of John Howard's recommendations. Although there was social time for most, with a large room in use (with supervision) segregation was the organising principle, and the experiment impressed other states so much that the regime was also established in six other states by 1812, including New York in 1797 and Maryland in 1811.

In New York, the new prison was named Newgate after the prison which had become almost a synonym for a prison in general (Dublin, for instance, had its Newgate, in Green Street). This was the brainchild of Thomas Eddy who had been deeply influenced by the Philadelphia approach. But this Newgate was only for felons. Eddy had ideas about 'contamination' which were not fully recognised elsewhere. But there was a worm in the bud of the Walnut Street Jail – this was the facility for night-room congregation. Eddy saw that this was a weakness as the ideal was, he saw, to have *single* cells for the night.

Both Walnut Street and the New York Newgate were based on a strong belief in reformation of the offender with religious practice and hard work as the cornerstones of the regime. Unfortunately, events transpired which would, as they did in Britain, cause a re-think about the potential for rehabilitation and change in the individual – this was mainly evinced in a riot of 1802. The tendency for the more lenient approach to work, but with reservations, led to the alternative model known as the Auburn system, after the creation of Auburn prison in Cayuga County. In Auburn the regime was originally an extreme version of the Pennsylvania system, in that prisoners were isolated all day, even when working. The result was a disaster as the number of individuals with mental illness increased alarmingly. The result was the silent system in which prisoners could congregate, but in silence.

At Auburn most of our modern stereotype images of an American prisoner were conceived, as Tamsin Spargo has described:

'Auburn created many of the features of prison life that swiftly became visual clichés, such as striped prison uniform and close-cropped hair to symbolize the convict's changed status. The prison also introduced a special walk, called "lockstep" in which each prisoner shuffled along holding the man in front, as they moved between cells and workshops or the dining hall.'[3]

Arguably, the years up to the last few decades of the nineteenth century, in terms of prison reform, were dominated by different moral ideologies. The Walnut Street ethos was one in which an innovative penology worked towards more explanations of the causes of criminality, whereas the Auburn system was based more on ideas linked to the thinking of discipline with punishment. Michel Foucault's influential ideas on the growth of the penitentiary at this time are relevant here. Foucault saw that the multiple strands of impersonalisation of state-designed factory-like existence spread across all social institutions for the containment of deviance, whether that might be a workhouse, a hospital or a prison. He argued that the panopticon, which gave rise to the British radial design of local prison, was also expressed in many other ways, ultimately to achieve total supervision and observation on the institutionalised individual. The two American systems may be referenced to see this emerging: the Pennsylvania approach tried to take a meliorist view of man (satirised in Voltaire's fiction *Candide*) while at the same time acknowledging that dangerous and extreme behaviour had to be contained. In contrast, the Auburn model created the 'cog in the machine' design, something Marxists would call reification, making a person into a 'thing.'

The Auburn model, similar to the British nationalised model from 1877, made the prisoner a number, a statistic, a unit – an item to be managed and to be made to fulfil the needs of a regime with pointless physical labour such as the treadmill and the crank (the latter being a mechanical device fixed to a cell door having a handle to be turned by the inmate so many times per day.) Indicative of the American approach in the years after the New York Newgate was the attitude of Louis Dwight. He founded the Prison Discipline Society in 1826 to inculcate religious worship and hard work. Dwight described his admiration for Auburn with a tone similar to that of the masters and managers of Foucault's new age of discipline and production: 'It is not possible to describe the pleasure which we feel in contemplating this noble institution, after wading through the fraud, and the material and moral filth of many prisons. We regard it as a model worthy of the world's imitation... upon the whole, the institution is immensely elevated above the old penitentiaries.'[4]

The Auburn model's physical establishment was important also, as Larry Sullivan explains:

'The Auburn/Sing Sing type consisted of a central office building that also housed mess halls and chapel, connected to multi-tiered cell blocks. The tiny cells were built inside, in five layers, back to back … on the prison grounds were shops or factories, hospital facilities and a power plant…'[5]

Between the Civil War and the end of the century, the emergence of social science and new viewpoints on how prisons should be defined and run gradually created a stress on managerial ability together with detailed study and documentation of institutions. This was to be a lasting influence in America and the germ of this kind of thought may be seen in Enoch Wines's massive *Report on the Prisons and Reformatories of the United States and Canada* published in 1867. This work advocated state control and argued for a philosophy of sentence progression, similar to that instituted in Britain by Edmund Du Cane a decade later. There was a belief that a social scientist could effect change in terms of rehabilitation and that knowledge was the key, very much in the mould of the earlier Positivism of Auguste Comte. The thinking here included demographic patterns, classifications of criminal, and a belief in predictive criminal behaviour. In the thinking of Zebulon Brockway the new attitudes may be seen, with his stress on having indeterminate life sentences, professional staff and openness to reformation. For Brockway, the right term to use was that of 'adult reformatory.' These ideas were applied with plenty of social education and hard physical work at the Elmira Reformatory in New York. Although the concept of the social contract, famously expressed by jean-Jacques Rousseau, has been largely taken as a fundamental statement of human rights, it is worth noting that Rousseau writes about the criminal in these terms: 'Every wrongdoer, in attacking the rights of society by his crimes, becomes a rebel and a traitor to his country. By violating its laws, he ceases to belong to it, and is even making war on it.'[6] The problem is, when a society accepts that and therefore sees the criminal an a 'non-person' then either he must be kept, fed and preserved, either he is a non-person in penal limbo, or he is a commodity which may or may not one day be a citizen again who accepts the social contract. In America, by the end of the nineteenth century, there was no prison 'system'– that is, each state could decide on how its prisoners related to Rousseau's notion of wrongdoers. Each state in the union had its own general and local prisons and made its own laws, as it does today.

By c.1900 a federal prison was explained by Charles Richmond Henderson, a sociology professor, as being there for 'the confinement of persons convicted in the United States courts of crimes against the United States and sentenced to imprisonment in a penitentiary, or convicted by courts-martial of offences…'[7] In the early twentieth century, as Henderson noted, there was no master plan: 'Most of our states, without much order or system… develop regular, constant and adequate agents of administration.'[8]

However, efforts towards progressive reform developed up to the 1950s with a succession of academics and administrators, but the work ethic at the centre of all prison regimes was a bone of contention. The work regimes were done differently at various times in American prison history and two systems were used: the contract and the leasing versions of prison work. In the contract system, inmates worked for outside firms, and in the leasing system the firms outside actually maintained the prison, so it worked as a profit-based concern, an extension of the company itself. Naturally, the progressive thinkers disapproved as in their view work had to be a part of a broader plan for rehabilitation. Hence, for decades, there was always going to be a split and a cause of dissension and debate in this context. At the heart of all regimes, though, was the warden, and much depended on his attitudes when any innovation was considered. Surely Alcatraz is the outstanding example of an initiative away from the norm.

WARDEN JOHNSTON AND ALCATRAZ

Alcatraz Island, just a mile or so into the bay from San Francisco, was a fortified military camp and lighthouse until 1934 when the federal penitentiary opened there. It lasted until 1963. Alcatraz was to be a 'super prison' to house the most dangerous criminals from across the United States. In a massive logistical operation, the inmates of the new prison were moved by train from state penitentiaries to the Bay harbour and then across to the island. Ensuring there were no escape attempts, or gang members on the 'outside' did not stage a breakout, was an affair of military precision.

We need to have some understanding about the man appointed to be the first warden, James A. Johnston, who believed in ensuring inmates had certain rights and building mutual trust. Johnston's background was in regional government and in business rather than in penology or in any form of social science. As early as 1912 he had made it known that he was for the new Progressive Republican ideas. This state governmental context meant that he was noticed, and after his thoughts on management and reform were known, he was appointed as warden of Folsom prison, but he had a vision, and he expressed it in this way:

'When I assumed the wardenship of Folsom, I knew a good deal about men but very little about prisons. However, I was not dismayed. I realized that the prison revolved around the prisoners, and they were men first and prisoners incidentally. I had a theory about treatment of men. I had faith in my ideas. Of course there was a possibility that they might not pan out practically. Judged by the way prisoners behaved and the way they worked, the absence of serious disturbance and freedom from outbreaks, the new penology obtained better results than the old.'[9]

Johnston followed this experience by taking over at San Quentin from 1913 to 1925. As with any attempt to balance order and discipline with any form of enlightened regime, he was the subject of much criticism. Reports circulated that his prison administration was 'lax' and eventually the prison board wanted to remove him. But after the election of Franklin D. Roosevelt in 1932, and the New Deal, there was a new attempt to handle penal administration by more sensible separation of classes of offender so that hardened criminals would have a very different sentence pattern to that of those who offended through the desperation of poverty. Hence the concept of Alcatraz was born.

At sixty years old, Johnston must have thought of retirement, but he received the call, the new island prison was explained to him, and he was asked if would he take control of it. He relished the challenge from the start, and he knew that he was to be looking after the most high profile gangsters of the land. Al Capone was there following a ten-year sentence imposed in 1931 for violating income tax laws, Robert Stroud, notorious murderer, and George 'Machine Gun' Kelly, the kidnapper. Johnston was determined to experiment with his more enlightened policies there, being in charge of an average of 260 inmates per year, with a total of 378 cells and ninety officers. The chronicles of the 'Rock' include thirty-six inmates involved in escape attempts; seven shot and killed, two drowned and two escapees who were recaptured. There was a total of twenty-eight deaths of inmates on the island, and five suicides.

Johnston's regime included the concept of work as a privilege, and men at first did the lowest maintenance jobs before being put to work in a glove or clothing factory or making furniture. There was a sliding scale of days taken from the full sentence, related to years worked in the factories, so that after the fifth year and succeeding years of work, five days each month were deducted from the sentence. The produced was contracted to the armed forces.

Johnston's method was to make a close study of his inmates and thoroughly research their lives and characters. He explained: 'After getting the broad picture of escapers, detainers and forfeited credits, I began to read the records and the reasons given for each man's transfer to Alcatraz. Every day I talked to a number of them, gave them instructions and advice, and as I sized each man up, I tried to penetrate his inner thoughts and feelings, and find a spot I could reach that would help me to help him and to handle him with the least trouble.'[10] Without being consciously aware of the fact, Alcatraz was very much a test case for the progressive approach. Johnston wrote about the people who came to visit and to interview him on his methods and he noted at one point that he was often asked about the possibility of reforming these desperate men. He said that his reply was that he believed 'every human has some good spot, that I always tried to find that spot, and that I never closed the door of hope on any man.'[11]

Just before Alcatraz opened, there had been the publication of a huge report called Penal Institutions, Probation and Parole by the National Commission on Law Observance and Enforcement, headed by George Wickersham. This report extended to almost 700 pages and amounted to a detailed critique of the prison establishment across the land, but also had a progressive slant, suggesting measures to improve the situation. The age-old topics of segregation and classification were important in its recommendations, and the progressive attitudes generally included attempts to return to the ever-present issue of parole. Parole had been the focus of heated debate in both approaches – the repressive silent system and the more enlightened penitentiary estate. The 1930 Probation Act had made parole administration centrally controlled. In some ways, the Alcatraz adventure was an acceptance that the most extreme offenders were a totally separate group, outside the normal classification, and yet many thought that its creation must not be seen generally as admission of defeat.

From the inmates' point of view, Alcatraz may be seen as the quintessential example of ultimate supervision and control, but with a paternal streak of apparent concern for the individual. Darwin Coon, for instance, who was a prisoner there from 1959 to 1963, recorded this, in terms which reinforce the theory of Foucault that the implications of the word 'discipline' extend to constant inspection and examination: 'The next day we got processed. The doctor gave us a physical, we met the warden and we were read a list of do's and don'ts … We weren't allowed to go to the yard for the first two weeks… That first weekend on Alcatraz was the two longest days of my life…'[12] He makes it clear that there were rules for every movement, every step taken and every request submitted. As is familiar from films of American prisons, the essential quality of the material nature of incarceration is the transparency of the cell. In rows in each cell block, the cells are like cages, open to inspection at any time, unlike the British and most European approach in which there is a level of privacy and slots for looking in on the inmate to check. In Alcatraz the cells were low and small so that although the inmate looks out on the passing people and movements, he feels the claustrophobic 'weight' of the low ceiling and the small space for movement.

If attempts have to be made to define this unique establishment in the American system, they have to explain such topographical and physical elements as narrow gangways in the blocks, the sense of isolation even when working outside, the apparent but deceptive closeness of San Francisco across the Bay, and most of all, the enclosed communal spaces which were hard to supervise (mainly the exercise yard and the canteen hall) so clearly where any man in a vulnerable situation was most open to attacks in the eternal prison threats of vendetta and spontaneous violence. Darwin Coon describes one such occurrence when a man fought back on a bully: 'On the advice of other inmates who were being harassed by the same man, the little guy looked around for something to knock the bully's brains out and came up with a big brass pipe... We learned later that the little guy had done a good job... he had completely knocked out one of the big man's eyes and given him a nineteen-inch skull fracture.'[13]

Yet it has to be stressed that, as with all prisons packed with lifers, the resources for education were well used and respected. The prison library and education facilities were extremely impressive and individuals who wanted to change or at least develop themselves creatively and educationally could do so. Visitors to the island today can still see the drawings and paintings done by inmates on display in the cells and the library, with its substantial stock. Somehow, two places within the prison seem to typify its massive contradictions: the cell where a guard was killed and the cell of a man who clearly had a talent for art. They are virtually next-door. The first still has a bullet-hole and the second has a sketch on display inside.

FROM RIOTS TO THE SUPERMAX

In any given society, prison riots and mutinies tend to be quite rare and they provide memorable dates to anyone following contemporary history. In England within the last thirty years there have been only a few, mainly at Hull in 1976, Manchester, 1990, and Lincoln, 2002. If such terrible events happen within a limited period, as happened with those in military prisons in 1946, they usually open up debate on significant penal subjects related to current practice. That was certainly the case in the USA between 1951 and 1953 when riot followed riot; the scale gradually escalating. Before 1950 there had been an optimistic feeling that the progressive attitudes and the regimes of paid labour had worked. But then, in February 1951, ten prisoners in Angda, Los Angeles, cut their heel tendons in protest at barbaric treatment there. Following that were more heel slashings and then a hunger strike in Mobile, Alabama, and no less than thirty-seven men slashing heels as a protest about whipping punishments at Louisiana State Pentitentiary in the summer of 1951.

Riot followed riot over the next eighteen months, with one of the most serious being at the State prison of Southern Michigan, which was a huge institution, overcrowded in spite of its accommodation for 6,000 inmates. There had been experiments with inmate councils up to this date, as that was a step towards the realization of progressive ideals, but inevitably, power conflicts began to emerge between inmates and the prison establishment. The scale of the problem is illustrated in the case of the trouble at Jackson, Michigan, where state troopers were called out and there was a hostage situation. As Larry Sullivan explains, the resolution came after prolonged meetings: '... the convicts accepted emendations and deletions to their demands and settled with the administration and the state's governor, but the warden, Fox, took a false step. Fox made a speech that in effect congratulated the inmates as honourable men. This naïve mistake cost Fox his job...'[14]

What had gone wrong? Answers to the question were expected, and in 1953 the American Prison Association provided a report which mainly attributed the trouble to administrative shortcomings, particularly in inadequate financial support, inadequate staff and too many idles in the prison population. Then what happened was a long debate amongst sociologists and criminologists, aided by experienced prison staff, about the real nature of power as exercised in a prison establishment. The realization gradually dawned that prisoners are an extremely varied group of people, and within areas of care and concern such as ageing and vulnerable inmates, educational attainment and levels of sociopathic behaviour, there had been very little knowledge or applied policy. The workings of prison politics, the shufflings and readjustments as the composition of the population changes, the ratio of guards to prisoners, and much more, became matters worthy of attention.

What had previously been seen as a universal concept which could be embodied in applied elements of theory was now seen as naïve by many. This was compounded by the diversity of categories of prison, from prison farms to massive penitentiaries. There was also the element of racial mix too – one of the strongest forces at work inside prison walls in the USA. Within such sub-cultures there were also gang activities and that issue still persists. But the bedrock of much of the trouble had been such common practices as chain gangs, corporal punishment and lack of close supervision. There were no easy solutions.

By the 1980s there were other problems, notably AIDS. Of all causes of deaths in prison in the late 1980s, AIDS was the most frequent. When Larry Sullivan wrote in 1990, he could say: 'In New York, for instance, AIDS has been responsible for over 50 per cent of all convict fatalities since 1984.'[15] This problem, together with overcrowding and a high proportion of prisoners aged over fifty, led to a sense of the progressive optimism being seen as a general failure. In 1990 there was a widespread feeling of despair at the end of such optimism. With hindsight, we may now see how dreamy some of the expressions of the wonders of 'the new penology' were. There is a huge rift between the actual routine of prison life and the millions of words of theory in the well-meaning textbooks of criminology. Looking at some essays by penologists of the time, it is easy to see how far reality has stepped in to ruin a good piece of academic system-building.

What then came along was the 'supermax'. This is a return to the first American penitentiary model – the solitary confinement version – and as Stephen Eisenman has written, it has not been popular:' ... it was resurrected in the late 1970s and 80s during the greatest period of growth of the penal state, and at a time of government anxiety about the rise of radical political movements.'[16] The current situation (2011) regarding prison population is a major cause of concern and does not indicate any measure of success for the supermax. The total prison population in the USA now is 2.3 million. In 2008 the number of the prison population was 762 per 100,000 compared with 221 per 100,000 in 1980.

One case study will illustrate this failure: that of Marion, Illinois, supermax. In 1973 a long-term control unit was created there (comparing loosely to the British one established at HMP Wakefield around the same time) and this meant that political radicals could be in solitary for up to thirty days. This was no less than a behaviour modification method; it was a return to the common practice in Europe c.1840. The result was sadly predictable: work and hunger strikes and a level of solidarity which created major problems. This might have been an impasse with a compromise, but then two guards were killed by Aryan Brotherhood prisoners and the result was repression. The 'lockdown' followed and a 'no tolerance' ideology grew. As Eisenman explains:

'The Marion lockdown, in turn, spawned a new generation of control unit, or supermax prisons, among the first of which was Pelican Bay in 1989, whose harsh regime, according to federal district court judge Thelton Henderson in 1995, "may well hover on the edge of what is humanly tolerable for those with normal resilience, particularly when endured for extended periods of time." Judge Henderson's ruling, in a large class action alleging multiple forms of cruel and unusual punishment placed the prison under the oversight of a special master and forbade the imprisonment of mentally ill prisoners in the Security Housing Unit at Pelican Bay, but did not end the use of long-term isolation for other men.'[17]

There is little doubt that, as this shows, the history of imprisonment in the USA developed in a rhythmic trajectory of care and repression, each phase following a new impulse towards trying to relate penal measures to current trends and influences, but that in the end, perhaps due to sheer high levels of population, reform has been doomed to failure. In contrast to the first steps towards a more humane regime at Walnut Street, the modern situation is enough to depress anyone who still holds Enlightenment opinions. But there is still hope in that other element of prison life – the humanity within the staff. Individuals will give, understand, work for compromise and find a workable system in spite of the hard and fast regulations. A survey of all prison history reveals this, as evidenced in autobiographies and documentaries. But of course, this is not a naïve view: it is based on an alternative literature which forms a secondary penal story, and this will be the focus of chapter 10.

In contrast, the discipline of criminology goes on, adapting and offering yet more answers to problems. There may also be some kind of solution from sheer necessity – that of economics – and Stephen

Eisenman suggests this: 'But even an ideology as powerful as the one that underlies the supermax may fall to the hammer blows of economic recession... decline in corrections budgets, combined with lawsuits in multiple states alleging abuse... have stopped cold the growth of the supermax regime...'[18]

The American experience provides a clear template for a pattern familiar to historians of penology: new beginnings influenced by theoretical models tend to attempt reformative systems; this then fails and control and repression take centre stage. Finally, the two approaches sit uneasily together, and change only happens when some extreme event occurs. Riots, mutinies and attacks on staff may be the obvious examples of failure, but in truth the more important factors indicative of a failure in a prison regime is detectable in the diurnal process of communication and phatic liaison. The latter is a useful phrase describing the often transient unions, agreements and pacts between staff and influential prisoners. Often in the American system, the powerful prisoners may exercise influence (through fear and coercion, threats and punishments) even from an isolation cell.

In America, the last forty years have seen the intensification of both repressive and enlightened applications of penology. This is a massive paradox: on the one hand, it is in the USA that we have one of the highest incarceration rate in world history, comparable to that of China and Russia. The International Centre for Prison Studies at King's College, London, asserts that the USA has the largest documented prison population in the world. In 2011 the figure of people in jail per 100,000 was 701. Yet on the other hand, some states have applied innovative strategies for the cultivation of the individual as an effort towards rehabilitation. In Texas, for instance, a programme called Changing Lives Through Literature is now in place as an alternative to prison *per se*. In a feature on this recently, Anna Barker explained how it works:

'CLTL is the brainchild of Robert Waxler, a professor of English at University of Massachusetts, Dartmouth. As an experiment, he convinced his friend, Judge Kane, to take eight criminals who repeatedly came before him and place them on a reading programme instead of sending them to prison. It now runs in eight States, including Texas, Arizona and New York...Repeat offenders... discuss literary classics such as *To Kill a Mocking Bird* , *The Bell Jar* and *Of Mice and Men* .'[19]

Because prison is so large scale and widely documented in America, the extremes have a profound impact in the mind of the general reader. The stress is often on the massive economic investment in penal establishment, or on the 'true crime' elements of death row and gang violence. In the first months of 2011 for instance, on various cable television channels running in Britain, there were features on escapes from American prisons, reoffending in California, jail powerbases and gang segregation and drug busts inside. Features on such topics as chain gangs and prison culture (tattoos, art, ethnic identity etc) have been common in recent years.

In America today we may see the verification of Foucault's reasoning with regard to the dominance of discipline in its widest and deepest senses as described by him in his chapter on the panoptikon in his book *Discipline and Punish*. There is expatiates on the proliferation of supervision, cellular observance, uniform movement and on the world of jail as one extreme instance of a universal application of populations at labour and in penance existing like drones in the hive. The first aim of prison is to extract individual identityand ever since the first professional jails in Europe after the demise of the house of correction, this has been so. The new prisoner arrives, is stripped, and a health inspection takes place. Prison garb is given and the person with a name is given a number and allocated to a cell. He or she is then slotted into the organic life of a community existing outside citizenship and indeed in a peculiar position. They begin to regard their former identity as something reified, a 'thing' separate from what they are now. The new identity is defined by their landing, wing and cell, and also in their categorization.

The US system has made a science of this, and as the criminal offences on the statute books continue to replicate, more and more people have some experience of imprisonment. Looking back to the early Philadelphia system, it is easy to conclude that philosophical bases of the Enlightenment have given way to a second or possibly a third managerial revolution.

Notes and references

1 *The Times* Oct.23 1823 p. 2.

2 Arthur Griffiths, *Millbank Penitentiary: An Experiment in Reformation* (London, 1890) p. 33.

3 Tamsin Spargo, *Wanted Man* (London, 2004) p. 84.

4 Quoted in Larry Sullivan, *The Prison Reform Movement* (Boston, 1990) p. 10.

5 Ibid. p. 12.

6 Jean-Jacques Rousseau, *The Social Contract* (London, 2001) p. 71.

7 Charles Richmond Henderson, *Modern Prison Systems* (Washington, 1903) p. 143.

8 Ibid p. 231.

9 Warden Johnston, *Alcatraz Island Prison* (San Francisco, 2001) p. xx.

10 Ibid. p. 44.

11 Ibid. pp. 281-282.

12 Darwin E Coon, Alcatraz: *The End of the Line* (Sacramento, 2002).

13 Ibid. p. 86.

14 Op cit. note 4 p. 47.

15 Ibid. p. 135.

16 Stephen F Eisenman, 'The Resistable Rise and Predictable fall of the US Supermax' *Monthly Review* November, 2009 p. 2.

17 Ibid. p. 5.

18 Ibid. p. 11.

19 Anna Barker, 'Novel Sentences' *The Guardian* 21.07.2010 Society supplement. There is a vast literature on the experiments with regard to applying philosophy, humanities subjects and open discussion of values and such topics as acculturation in several penal systems. This is dicssed further in my final chapter.

Chapter 7

Punishment as Commodity and Masterplan

Turning to the darkest, most sub-human conception of a prison, my focus is now on the 'concentration camp' – a term I have placed in inverted commas because the term is not limited to the Nazi death camps, but indeed has a history stretching back to the Spanish and British empires in the late 1890s. In some ways, the history of these establishments is inextricably linked to imperial power until the appropriation of the concept by Hitler and his panel of top-brass genocidal megalomaniacs converted the notion into a death factory. In the global history of prisons, the term was used first in its Spanish form of *reconcentracion*, but in some ways this was no different from Russian penal colonies in the sense that people were imprisoned not for any crime but for who they were.

The Anglo-Boer War in its last phase, and the actions of Lord Kitchener and others, is a formative period in the emergence of the concentration camp, and Trotsky knew of this, commandeering the idea in its Russian form with the word *Kontslager*; also, paradoxically, the German empire expanding into Africa adopted such camps after the British establishments in South Africa. The one element all the concentration camps have in common is that they were holding areas for non-combatants and so encompassed various mixes of racial, ethnic and ideologically 'unsound' minorities or oppositional communities.

ORIGINS: *RECONCENTRACION* IN CUBA

In a speech given by Senator RedfieldProctor fromVermont in 1898 we have a concise description of the first concentration camp on record:

'Outside Havana all is changed. It is not peace, nor is it war. It is desolation and distress, misery and starvation. Every town and village is surrounded by a *trocha* (trench) a sort of rifle pit, but constructed on a plan new to me, the dirt being thrown up on the inside and a barbed wire fence on the outer side of the trench. These *trochas* have at every corner, and at frequent intervals along the sides, what are there called forts, but which are really small block houses, many of them more like a large sentry-box, loop-holed for musketry, and with a guard of from two to ten soldiers in each. The purpose of these trochas is to keep *reconcentrados* in as well as to keep insurgents out…'[1]

There we have perhaps the Ur-image of the death camp, a racial concept, a holding operation by an oppressor which is conceived and maintained with minimal topographical complexity; it is essentially what became barbed wire compound and corner posts. Redfield saw this on behalf of the Red Cross and there is a profound irony in that what became later the death camps were in their first formation (holding camps) beyond any application of care and rescue such as the Red Cross might wish to apply. They were created to hold civilians who had been driven into compounds. As the senator added, they were prison yards 'where every point is within range of a soldier's rifle.'[2]

The Spanish-American War of 1898 began with a rising in Cuba, emerging from the collapse of the sugar market. The Spanish response was extreme and reports of atrocities reached America and elsewhere. The Cuban guerrillas would have been far more dangerous had they had support from ordinary people, and so Marshal Weyler created the first *concentrados*. But it is argued that the very first military leader to use tactics involving camps of non-combatants was General Sherman, and that Weyler had known of this while serving as an attache in Washington D C.[3] The United States entered the fray after the US battleship *Maine* was blown up in Havana harbour in February 1898 and Congress acknowledged the independence of Cuba. War with Spain began. But before all this, Weyler had imposed repression. He had previously been Captain-General in the Philippines where he became known as 'the butcher,' and was sent as Governor to Cuba where he had full powers. Faced with a guerrilla war, his strategy was to remove civilian support for insurgents and so the camps were made. By 1897 Weyler had 'relocated' more than 300,000 people.

Documentary reports of the time state that in the western Cuban provinces, 400,000 people died of starvation and disease. The now familiar concomitants of euphemisms and double-talk came with the regime. The peasants were referred to as being 'pacified', four western provinces of Cuba were essentially 'stationary', and transport of provisions was banned. The people who were thus 'concentrated' in cabins called 'Bohios' which were made of wood and palm. In the midst of all this organisation, there is the key word 'concentrate' as Senator Redfield noted in his report when he quoted Weyler's order: 'First of all the inhabitants of the country now outside of the line of fortifications of the towns shall within the period of eight days *concentrate...*'[4] Naturally, this was also backed up by savage repression and hangings were common after 'trials' which were far from being any such thing.

The toll on human life was extreme and the report adds this note on the results of life in enforced block houses: 'Deaths in the streets have not been uncommon. I was told by one of our consuls that people have been found dead about the markets in the morning where they had crawled, hoping to get some stray bits of food from the early hucksters, and that there had been cases where they had dropped dead inside the market, surrounded by food...'[5]

The course of the war through 1898 led to anarchy and revolution. The policy of *reconcentracion* created a mass of desperate people after the Americans entered the war and the island was packed with a mix of combatants of all kinds, from Spanish soldiers to gangs of insurgents and separate groups of what came to be known as *Reconcentrados*. By January 1898 *The Times* reported a telegram received from Havana in which the situation is clear: 'Yesterday morning about 100 army officers, incensed at the newspaper attacks on the Spanish army in Cuba, began smashing the windows and destroying the printing presses at the offices of the journals *La Discusion* and *El Reconcentrado* ... a mob of about 1,000 persons accompanied the officers, shouting "Viva Espana!"'[6] The then dispersed prisoners had their won representative newspaper. Strangely, a prison population had become a social minority with a sense of identity, albeit based on repression and a desire for liberty and social revolution.

Throughout the Cuban actions on the theatre of war between the USA and Spain, reporters and writer monitored change and some located the further activities of the *reconcentrados* and their involvement in the anarchy succeeding the escalation of the war. In September 1898 for instance, one correspondent went out into the wilds of the island to see for himself the repercussions of the concentration camp system when disintegration began and anarchy took over: 'I left to visit the rebel camp and headquarters of Major-general Jose Rodriguez who is in command of all the insurgent forces in Western Cuba which are distributed among the provinces of Havana, Pinar del Rio and Matancas, numbering 10,000 men armed with rifles and 5,000 with cutlasses...' Then, out on a visit, he saw the aftermath of the concentration camps, in one place: 'At San Francisco da Paula we found the place almost in ruins, many of the houses having been burnt by the insurgents in one of their raids. Here we found stationed a considerable number of Spanish troops, but we saw few inhabitants and these were mostly *reconcentrados* in a most miserable condition: white people, nearly naked, of horrible condition, some nearly naked and horrible to look at with their terribly shrunken limbs and hugely distended stomachs, a little remnant of some thousands who have here perished of famine and fever during the blockade.'[7]

By early 1899 reporters attempted to express conclusions and reflections on the Cuban situation, and impressions were given of the sheer scale of suffering and deprivation, much of it being the result of what the Marshal had started with his internment plan: 'In the town of Sagua the needs of the absolutely destitute, some 4,000 in all, have been attended to by the establishment of central kitchens erected under the direction of the *Alcalde*; a substantial ration is supplied each day to each deserving person.'[8] Central Committees were formed at Cardenas, Sagua, Santa Clara, Santo Domingo and Jovellance; rations and relief were finally distributed as violence gradually receded.

Senator Redfield pulled no punches in his summing up of the worst he had seen:

'I could not believe that out of a population of one million six hundred thousand 200,000 had died within these Spanish forts, practically prison walls, within a few months past, from actual starvation and disease caused by insufficient and improper food…. the Los Posos hospital in Havana, has been recently described by one of my colleagues… he visited it after Dr Lesser had renovated it and put in cots. I saw it when 400 women and children were lying on the stone floors in an indescribable state of emaciation and disease, many with the scantiest of rags, and sick children, naked as they came into the world. And conditions in other cities are even worse…'[9]

Reconcentracion had been imposed at the beginning of the conflict so Weyser's methods had generated repercussions he probably could never have imagined. It may have succeeded in isolating guerrilla forces but it also set a level of degradation and brutality we have come to know in more recent history as the most repulsive euphemism of them all – ethnic cleansing. He would not have intended such a measure but creating the camps undoubtedly established a major element in the anarchy in the island as the war, lasting less than a year, brought the deprivations it always does, and the already confined peasantry were there to be exploited. In some cases factories and work camps naturally emerged from the original concentration camps. Weyser had unleashed a quasi-military strategy which was to provide a useful gambit against non-combatant populations and the dark side of the military thinking was perhaps not fully realised in the contemporary press reports.

A precedent had been set; a ploy registered in the military history manual. With hindsight, we can see how valuable the notion of blockhouses and camp compounds would be to regular armies faced with the moves made in war by a civilian group working by unorthodox means or simply offering support to the fighting force of their own society. As the contemporary reports of the horrendous results of the policy show, it was a strategy commanders used when their line of thought considered the end as being more valuable than the means.

BRITISH CONCENTRATION CAMPS

Herbert Kitchener, surely best known as the stern face on the Great War poster proclaiming 'Your Country Needs You', was a great military leader who seemed to attract controversy as well as hagiography and myth. One early biographer, writing in 1910, expressed the complexity: 'That he wields some strange and subtle power over the crowd is indisputable. The secret of it may lie in the awe inspired by those marvellous successes he never fails to produce by the magic of his patient persistence...' Notice here the words 'awe' and 'magic' placed alongside words that are not directly heroic.

Kitchener's legendary steely eyes and dignified bearing could instil fear and he was seen by some as ruthless. But at the field of Omdurman, it was Kitchener who commanded the people of the town to go out and bring in the wounded from the field. Estimates of him vary greatly, but perhaps Richard Holmes's words in the *Oxford Companion to Military History* form the best appraisal: 'Kitchener was an indefatigable organizer who understood the absolute necessity of consolidating resources before striking a decisive blow.' On the other hand, Erskine Childers's opinion was that 'Kitchener was inclined to think too much of propelling and too little of educating his army – to look rather to the quantity rather than the quality of the work done...'

Kitchener was a strategist and a man with a presence in a battlefield. When events were developing in the process of a confrontation, he would appear at just the right time. He was expert in what we might call today the logistics of managing men, supplies and communications. More than anything else, it could be argued, he inspired men and glowed with confidence with the assurance that comes from good planning and research. From Wolseley he learned that the time given to finding the right man for the job is the secret of success. When journalist G. W. Steevens went with the Sudan expedition in 1898 to work on what would become the best-selling *With Kitchener to Khartoum* (1898) he wrote that the great general should be a national treasure, or in the words of the time, something that should be exhibited at a national exhibition:

'But it so happens that he has turned himself to the management of war... and he is the complete and only master of that art. Beginning life in the Royal Engineers he early turned to the study of the Levant. He was one of Beaconsfield's military vice-consuls in Asia Minor; he was subsequently director of the Palestine Exploration Fund... the ripe harvest of fifteen years is that he know everything that is to be learned of his subject. He came at the right hour. He was the right man.'[10]

Part of that art of war was the use of the internment camp.

South Africa had been the scene of a long-standing conflict; in 1880-1 there had been a small war in which the Dutch Boers had won at Majuba Hill. Britain had no real worries about giving independence to the insignificant states of Transvaal and the Orange Free State as they then were, but after the gold rush, things were different. By 1898 it was clear that the Boers' power could be a genuine threat to British supremacy in that part of the Empire. Of course, there was support from Germany for the Boers, and Germany made sure that it openly congratulated the Boers after they crushed the strange and wrong-headed Jameson Raid in which the Rhodes-backed Dr Jameson (2 January 1895) led a small army into the Transvaal ostensibly to stage a coup. The result was that by 1899 the Boers were becoming a formidable military force.

The turning point was around May and June 1900 after Mafeking was relieved, Roberts went into Johannesburg, and the Orange Free State was annexed. In October that year the Transvaal was annexed. It was from that point that the British intelligence involvement was to be particularly important. It was a lesson to be learned, as was the case with all major aspects of that war. As the Boer 'commandos' started their sabotage and skirmishing campaigns, they were fated to be up against Kitchener and his ruthlessly efficient tactics of defensive positions, internment camps and liaison with Colonel Henderson and with Lord Roberts in intelligence work. The scouting and reconnaissance work that went on was destined to be chaotic and dangerous. As has often been pointed out, mounted scouts combed the countryside and quasi-military intelligence officers ran spy-rings to track down resisters. There were atrocities, such as the episode in which Harry Morant of an irregular band of volunteers called the Bushveldt Carabineers was involved in killings of unarmed men. But that is simply something which has attracted popular historians as a spin-off narrative. The real atrocity was in Kitchener's use of the camps, following Weyser.

He took over command in the war in early 1900. The Boer's strategy of guerrilla warfare was winning as they were expert marksmen, were fighting on home terrain, andhad strong and clever leaders. Kitchener moved quickly, first streamlining the transport provision and then pressing on and taking the initiative. But the Boers would not accept any peace terms and the war resumed. Kitchener's plan to overcome the guerrilla fighting difficulties was to use a grid system over the country, making block houses and putting up barbed-wire fences. This was then further solidified by gathering the people – civilians – into forty-six concentration camps, following the practice of the Spanish in Cuba. These camps proved to be insanitary and harmful. The figures are debated, but possibly 26,000 interned Boers died of disease in the terrible open jails. Enquiries were made and the conclusion was that poor administration had caused the failure and lamentable death-rate there. In early 1901 the camps were transferred to be under the control of the Colonial Office.

The subject has been controversial. Historians have argued very differently about the nature of the camps, but from the Boer point of view this conflict was a war of independence. The first gambits from the British had been to destroy settlements and this was followed by the camps. The term used by the British for these places was 'volunteer refugee camps' and we have testimony from writers such as Emily Hobhouse and W. T. Stead that Britain was guilty of war crimes in creating these prison camps. Hobhouse gave lectures across Britain, for instance, in which she made the situation clear, as in this report from a lecture given at Leeds:

'The police attended....Miss Hobhouse, who secured an attentive hearing, denied at the outset having carried out a political propaganda in South Africa....Miss Hobhouse then drew a picture of affairs in South Africa, stating that telegrams did not agree with the facts as seen by herself. She reiterated her stories of horrors in connexion with the war and with the concentration camps, speaking of the country as devastated and denuded... the majority of the women and children in the camps had been exposed all night to the weather. Hundreds of children became skeletons for the want of vegetables. The rations were not good in quality and a famine loomed... the statement made by the press that Boer women did not attend to their children was a cruel libel...'[11]

Boer historiography points to sources such as the local and national press at the time which reported the fact that the camps were placed in the most unsuitable locations: Merebank, which was in a swamp, and Springfontein camp where twenty people were forced into one tent and had to sleep on the bare, damp ground. Part of the problem here in sorting evidence and sources is that extreme statements were made, such as Sara Raal's account in her book *Met die Boere in die Veld (With the Boers in the Field)* in which she states that ground glass and razor blades were put in the camp food.[12]

THE FINAL SOLUTION
A history of prisons has to cope with the extension of the concentration camp in the Nazi era and it is a challenge to explain how such places as Belsen and Auschwitz may be defined. They bear no relation to the Spanish and British notions of 'reconcentrating' non-combatants except in the tenuous link of dealing with 'problems' of an extra-military character. Prison within a state of total war was something totally new in 1940. The worst excesses of imperial penology and camps in settlements, however brutal their regimes, have nothing in common with the Nazi death camps. Results of the regimes may at times have caused deprivation, starvation and disease, but they were never factories of extermination.

There is one historical factor which is important however: the first German camps in their empire, well before the Nazi creations. In the German colonies of South West Africa, the word *Konzentrationslager* first appeared in the German language referring to establishments parallel to those of Britain a little earlier. But as Anne Applebaum has pointed out, these German camps were in some respects proto-Nazi:

'There are a number of strange and eerie links between these first German-African labour camps and those built in Nazi Germany three decades later.... The first imperial commissioner of German South-West Africa was one Dr

Heinrich Goering, the father of Hermann, who set up the first Nazi camps in 1933. It was in these African camps that the first German medical experiments were conducted on humans: two of Joseph Mengele's teachers, Theodor Mollison and Eugen Fischer, carried out research then on the Herero, the latter in an attempt to prove the superiority of the white race.'[13]

There is little doubt, however, that this treatment of the Herero and Namaqua people (from modern Namibia) was genocidal. The prisons began after a rebellion led by Samuel Maharero. The German commander, Lieutenant General Lothar von Trotha, adopted the concentration camp policies of Kitchener and Weyser, and various places were used, including Shark Island. By 1908 the mortality rates in the camps reached 45 per cent. The camps were encircled by thornbush or barbed wire, food rations were limited, and disease was rampant with dysentery and typhoid claiming many lives. The Windhoek camp held 5,000 people and there was hard physical labour, in addition to the deprivations and illness.

The is plenty of documentation on the Shark Island camp at Luderitz, Southern Namibia, an island linked by a causeway, so that the desert lies on the land side, and ocean beyond of course, at the other. Work was primarily on railway-building on the line from Luderitz to Kubub. We know from the writings of one witness that in 1906 almost 2,000 prisoners arrived there, and the commander in the following year reported that 1,700 people had died by the April of that year.

A plain conclusion from all this is that in a sense, this terrible situation was indeed a small-scale foreboding of what was to come in the 1930s, yet there have been counter arguments. Some historians have disagreed about the scale of all this and one argument is that von Trotha was more guilty of neglect than of purposeful genocide. But there is ample evidence to confirm that the atrocious nature of the camps led to alarmingly high death rates and much suffering. Arguments regarding neglect lead more convincingly to planned actions of allowing nature to take lives rather than actually imposing death sentences.

Whatever the truth of all this, the fact is that prison camps used to deal with concentrated populations had given a template by c.1930 which opened the way to the systematic mass murder of the Nazi death camps. In legal terms, one debate with regard to proto-concentration camps relates to military necessity, and the elasticity of the concept has left minority peoples open to exploitation as we look with the wisdom of hindsight at past abuses and exploitation. The central assertion in opposition to military actions embracing very nasty extensions of this guideline is put by A. P. V. Rogers: 'The principle of military necessity is encapsulated in the preamble to the St Petersburg Declaration: that the only legitimate object which states should endeavour to accomplish in war is to weaken the military forces of the enemy and that for this purpose it is sufficient to disable the greatest possible number of men.'[14] By 'men' the implication is that the interpretation of the words should be 'combatants.' The St Petersburg declaration of 1868 was one of the first attempts to codify legal elements of warfare. Clearly, this statement and some later ones, up to Hague Conference of 1907, had not the slightest notion of exactly what species of evil Hitler and his Final Solution were capable of. The conception of war in the Nazi ideology was one in which annihilation was designed and planned, regardless of protocols or declarations by civilised states.

One place to begin with the subject of the Nazi Holocaust or *Shoah* (Hebrew term) is arguably from the inside. The literature of internal testimony is immense, but perhaps the first insight to begin with is that of an observer who was 'neutral' in the sense of being a British serviceman, neither Jewish nor German. The experience of Denis Avery is exactly that. He smuggled himself into Auschwitz in order to describe the system, published eventually in his book *The Man Who Broke Into Auschwitz* (2011). There was a dual penal regime in operation: Jews for the death camp and other categories for the labour camps. Often, the labour led to death anyway, but Avery desperately wanted to see the worst – and as a Jew within the system. He describes how he achieved this transient documentary perspective: 'Evening was approaching and the British POWs would soon assemble for the march back to E715. The Jewish work Kommandos were getting ready to return. I made my move, striding towards a shed. Inside, I pulled off my heavy boots and put on the clogs. Hans followed on my heels [Hans had agreed to the temporary exchange, and of course Avery had to trust him!] I gave him my tunic.

The smell of filth and decay rose from the weave: I was conscious of creatures emerging from the folds.'[15]

Avery's account of the experience is one of the best introductions to the penal system which represents to nadir of the concept of incarceration as the negation of identity and the reification of the human:

> 'Auschwitz III was like nothing else on earth; it was hell on earth. This is what I had come to witness, but it was a ghastly, terrifying experience. I was hunkered down amongst those fading people but unlike them I had plotted angled and bribed to get myself in here. I awoke to a feeling of utter desolation. The *kapo* was storming through the hut, kicking the bunks and barking orders. The lights came on... a man was beaten for moving too slowly. Those who had deteriorated in the night were pushed to one side.... I was preparing for my next ordeal – how to get out.'[16]

The Holocaust prison was the ultimate expression of the state's power to annihilate the individual, to abolish the physical existence of a person and indeed, in aspiration, the rubbing out of a race. In one sense it was an extension of the penitentiary in terms of supervision and eradication of identity combined with all the aims of a radical ideology, but it also provides a counter-concept to all previous versions of a prison. In the latter sense, this is rooted in narcissism extended to the level of a national ethos, and that intensity of menace and destruction, applied to a prison, is a recipe for utter evil. Penal policies across the world until the Nazi era had, however extreme their punishments, preserved at least a semblance of the fact that prison has to relate organically with a criminal justice system, and that system – from imperial China to the dungeons of the manor courts across Europe – had linked to moral as much as political strictures. The Nazi Holocaust negated all that previous penal practice.

In fact, this 'scientific' process of genocidal intent, with its reduction of a human being to no more than a selection of residues, from metal tooth fillings to ash, and spectacles to hair, directed responses from survivors and commentators which help in the understanding of the depths of iniquity this prison system generated.

In Primo Levi's *The Periodic Table* for instance, we have a narrative of what may be described as an examination ofman by means of considering his disintegration. Philip Roth, in an interview with Levi, expressed something of this:

'The description and analysis of your atrocious memories of the German's gigantic biological and social experiment are governed... by a quantitative concern for the ways in which a man may be transformed or broken down and, like a substance decomposing in a chemical reaction, lose his characteristic properties. *If This is a Man* reads like the memoir of a theoretician of moral biochemistry who has himself been forcibly enlisted as the specimen organism to undergo laboratory experimentation...'[17]

The concept of the Nazi concentration camp also had the dimension of work, of course, with the now infamous motto of 'Arbeit Macht Frei' ('work makes one free') over the gateway. Again, as with the negation of identity, this twisted appropriation of the old 'work ethic' of Victorian jails creates such a dark irony that it cancels out all previous notions of work as a redemptive element in incarceration.

The vast literature created by those who saw and described the camps, together with the writings of those who experienced them as prisoners, is a discrete and unique body of work, giving future readers and historians a documentary profile of prison life which has no points of reference elsewhere. The writers involved in this struggled to explain the topography, but visual narratives ever since have effectively textualized the physical, material nature of the concentration camp. In Nazi ideology and military practice, the concept was separated from other strands of the establishment of incarceration in the Third Reich. Such groups as slave labour, prisoners of war, spies, and various fringe minorities, were held in prison in very different locations and the mix of manufacture, waste appropriation and extermination of life in the concentration camp *per se* offers something that calls out for explanation in terms other than the one central to Nazi ideology. Writers and thinkers have responded to this in phases. First, in mere description in attempts to delineate a landscape more akin to a dark dystopia of human imagination than to reality, then in more philosophical forms, and finally, in genres and categories which experiment with the ways in which we seek to comprehend enormity. In the latter, part of the material concerned has been in the source material of the Nuremburg trials and partly in the resources of poetry and film in which it is more receptive to expressing horror and revulsion where normal linguistic resources fail.

Auschwitz was a massive area surrounded by an electric wire fence and concrete posts. Supervision posts with armed guards looked across the open space and inside were the huts, ovens and factories. Workdays were generally timetabled for the hours of 1730-1200 and from 1230-1700, and classification was at first conceived in four categories related to levels of discipline and the nature of the ethnic/racial definition of the prisoner.

In order to define the prisoner experience in terms which relate at least tenuously to the norm of incarceration, reference should be made to a document of 1942 which was intended for circulation to Gestapo officers. It was written by Heinrich Himmler. He says:

'Imprisonment in a concentration camp, involving as it does separation from one's family, isolation from the outside world, and the hard labour assigned to the prisoner, is the most severe of punishments. Its use is reserved exclusively for the secret police, in accordance with precise regulations which specify the form of imprisonment and its term. In this matter I have reserved for myself a large measure of authority...'[18] In other words, nothing is clearly stated here, no reference to shootings of people in lines, followed by their collapse into mass graves, nothing about gas chambers, and nothing about medical experiment. Himmler's exclusive powers meant a *carte blanche* permission to commit any variety of amoral brutality in his imagination.

Understanding this horrendous history through the primary sources makes it clear that the conception and the execution of the 'Final Solution' was something understood in terms of that strand of German history in which anti-Semitism is traceable. Yet that is not the whole story. Hitler and his panel of top brass advisers approached the project as if they were entrepreneurs; businessmen with a brief to find the most economically viable way to achieve both the extermination of a race and the production of commodities. The creation of prisons has always been a challenge to the creativity of those who plan, and in Bentham's panopticon there is arguably a very high level of the absence of human consideration. Though he was concerned with economy, security, reform and self-reflection, and the Nazis aimed at annihilation, there is still a link between the logistics involved. At the base of earlier conceptions of prisons there was utility and economy, with the individual conceived as a commodity held within a system.

Of course, prisoners usually have committed a crime, but in Auschwitz the victims were innocent of any act or illegality. They were punished for being what they were. Hence, prison for identity was created, and in terms of war crimes, precedents were set for future judicial procedure. Naturally, prison within a war situation was always going to be re-examined and regulated in future, whenever and wherever possible. In simplistic terms, the concentration camps of Hitler's Reich illustrate what happens when absolute power exists on its own legal platform, and that law is devoid of human rights. In taking a prison system to the extreme of business logistics, the Nazis offered an anti-humanitarian establishment, shifting prison from the world of human community and the state to a netherworld devoid of morality. Prisons have always functioned on fragmented and distorted versions of the contemporary moral structures of society, but now, with Auschwitz, every country on earth was shown the counter-world, the absence of morality and humanity, as it exists in the mesh of obligation, respect and mutual reliance. The Enlightenment was negated also in the Nazi mindset.

The precursors of the Holocaust camps, as summarised above, seem horrific enough but they had parameters, boundaries. Beside the conveyor belt and locomotives of the process of death, they seem part of a previous, lost milieu of imperialism gone wrong, an extension of a method rather than being a chamber in hell. One factor of great importance in the earlier models of the camps is that they were absorbed as acceptable military strategy, and that implies that the state control mechanisms knew of the decisions to use the extreme methods of punishment and imprisonment of non-combatants. Prison was, in the European empires, used as simply one more resource of consolidation and of course, victory at any cost against irregular forces of resistance.

Cultural history and mass media have generated such a massive level of narrative and imagery relating to the Nazi camps that the eclipse of the atrocities in the first concentration camps is virtually complete in terms of popular knowledge and education, consigned to minority and specialist history. Consequently, the general notion of a concentration camp will, for most people, have no other connotations than the horrors of genocidal extermination, and revisionist history will surely have to continue the struggle to show how the idea of a prison was extended systematically into military affairs. Previously, civilians caught up in wars against empires had been destroyed, but in more openly direct methods of siege, starvation and execution – though only when caught up in risings and rebellions. Before the concept of a war crime, the restraints were religious and ideological. In the modern age of empire, morality was overlooked when necessity called.

Notes and references

1 Larry Daley, 'Documenting the Reconcentration, Cuba (1895-1898) 'www.ami gospais-guaracabuya.org p. 2.

2 ibid. p. 2.

3 Sherman removed all the inhabitants of Atlanta in 1864. He said, 'If the people raise a howl against my barbarity, I will answer that war is war, and not popularity seeking...'See Dr Nassir Ghaemi, 'General Sherman Would Not Have Invaded Iraq.' www. psychologytoday.com 7 Oct, 2008.

4 Op.cit note 1 p. 3.

5 Ibid. p. 4.

6 *The Times* 14 Jan, 1989 p.4.

7 'The Situation at Havana' *The Times* Sept. 20 1898 p. 6.

8 'The Condition of Cuba' *The Times* 6 Jan. 1899 p. 8.

9 Op.cit note 1 p. 5.

10 G W Steevens, *With Kitchener to Khartoum* (London, 1898) pp. 46-47.

11 'The Concentration Camps' *The Times* 26 June, 1901 p. 14.

12 See Elliott Lake: 'British Concentration Camps' in http://elliottlake.wordpress.com

13 Anne Applebaum, *Gulag* (London, 2004) pp. 19-20.

14 A P V Rogers, *Law on the Battlefield* (Manchester, 2004) p. 4.

15 Denis Avery, *The Man Who Broke Into Auschwitz* (London, 2011) p. 90.

16 Ibid. p. 90.

17 Philip Roth, introduction to Primo Levi, *The Periodic Table* (London, 2000) p. xiii.

18 See the web site: www.wintersonnenwende.com/scriptorum/english/archives or the full text of the letter from Himmler.

Chapter 8

Politicals, Enemies and Doing Time

In the winter of 1940, Joseph Czapski was sent to the prison camp at Griazowietz, in the Soviet Union. After a boring day of peeling vegetables, he joined a group of other Polish officers in an education and self-help group in which each person would talk on his own special interest. In Czapski's case his subject was Marcel Proust and his great novel *A La Recherche du Temps Perdu*. He had no books or other resources, but simply spoke from memory and enthusiasm. He did have the help of another prisoner, though, whose script became the basis of a short book called *Proust Contre La Decheance*.

Czapski then went on to extend his interest, as Adrian Tahourdin explains: 'Czapski was released when the Germans attacked the Soviet Union and spent the next two years organizing cultural life in the Polish army… after the war he lived mostly in France where he practised as an artist…'[1]

This is entirely in keeping with the spirit of the time before the gulags proliferated. Intellectuals in the Moscow Butyrka prison had the same kind of privileges. An important part of prison history is the occupations of prisoners when not engaged in labour. Sometimes this was the case because the people were locked up for political or state security reasons and relates to the long history of art, creativity and intellectual pursuits behind bars, as exemplified in the case of Czapski. This area of prison life also comprises the subject of categorization. A classic explanation of this is the case of the Chartists, as discussed in my introduction, when they argued that they should not be subject to the treadmill because they were 'political' prisoners, not criminals as ordinarily defined.

DARTMOOR AND OFFICERS' CLUBS: TWO CASE STUDIES

Prison for prisoners of war has never been all about scrimshaw art and chats about Proust. The more common experience is of utter depression, a constant concern for escape and liberation, and a sense of being superfluous – something leading to extreme apathy. Worse, the experience may be combined with brutality.

A useful place to start is by looking at prisoners of war. During the war with Napoleon, 100,000 French prisoners were held captive in Britain. For many officers, there was a parole arrangement, and although the French did not reciprocate, the British authorities maintained that. There was formerly a prisoner exchange system but that stopped in 1803 and so prison space had to be found for these vast numbers of men. After the battle of Trafalgar in 1805, almost 5,000 men were transferred to Britain.

The responsibility for accommodating the prisoners was given to the Transport Board, an organization working closely with the Admiralty. There were some war prisons, at Millbay, Stapleton, Forton and Portchester, but in 1797 a huge prison camp was created at Norman Cross near Peterborough, and then others were built: Dartmoor, Valleyfield and Perth. By 1814 there were nine such prisons, and Dartmoor, arguably the most notorious, had almost 8,000 prisoners of war by 1814.

More space was needed, however, and so the hulks were used. Of the various types of ships, the three-deckers were the largest, and they held 1,200 men. Incredibly, by 1814, there were 51 hulks in use. There was to be a massive problem with ill-health, perhaps more outstandingly so compared with harsh conditions and punishments in general. The Enlightenment thinking, with its humanitarian basis, was not always a matter of theory turning into applied reformed actions, but in this case, a lawyer called Emerich de Vattel had published *Le Droigt des Gens* (The rights of People) in 1758 and this was influential. Linked to this there had been the exchange system, which meant that there would simply be a short time of internment, and there had been the *parole d'honneur* – officers released on their word of honour that they would not re-enlist and fight in the current conflict.

The Transport Board had to cope with the frustrating paradox that French prisoners could be released by parole, by exchanges, or as invalids, but the French did not act in the same way. By 1803, 500 French officers had been released on *parole d'honneur*. But the fact remains that traditional prisoner-of-war procedure broke down. History is always biased and partisan, and the French writing on the lives of French prisoners in Britain insist on the treatment being brutal and heartless. But at times this contradicts the British records. For instance, one French writer wrote about prisoners on HMS *Prothee*: 'These dead people come out for a moment from their graves, hollow-eyed, earthy complexioned, round-backed, unshaven, their frames barely covered with yellow rags, their bodies frightfully thin.'[2]

Worst of all, allegedly, was the terrifying Dartmoor. Reports and letters to the press constantly argued that the regime there was barbarous. One opinion was that 'Men fit for service are killed, and then sent home to France to finish dying there.' But there were other bad reputations. General Pillet wrote that Norman Cross, for instance, was a place where he had seen 4,000 French prisoners buried. In 2010 the television archaeology programme *Time Team* set out to test the truth of this by conducting a 'dig' there. The prison at Norman Cross was constructed between 1796 and 1797 to accommodate 7,000 prisoners. It was known at the time as Yaxley barracks, was only 78 miles north of London and close to the sea, so communications and supply were not difficult. Great Yarmouth was to become a receiving port for prisoners, and they were taken to Lynn by sea and then by canal to Peterborough. But some had to walk, as this record shows: 'At Lynn the prisoners were packed into barges and lighters and were sent up river through the Forty Foot and the Paupers' Cut and the Nene to Peterborough, whence they marched to Norman Cross.'[3]

The French were allowed victualling each day to the value of seven pence and the total cost per man per day was one shilling and ten pence. They lived on bread, biscuits and some beef, but it is recorded that much of this was inedible. George Borrow, the Norfolk writer, noted that: 'The men's rations was of carrion meat and bread from which I have seen the very hounds turn away.' The local newspaper, *The Stamford Mercury*, gives us an insight into the place as over three thousand prisoners arrived in 1797: 'Exclusive of seven dead and three who escaped they passed under the care of seven turnkeys and the eighty men of the Caithness legion who guarded the Norman Cross.' These guards were 'fencibles' (regiments raised under the threat of invasion) who had served in Ireland, and were under the command of Sir Benjamin Dunbar.[4]

For such large numbers of prisoners, more military presence was needed; the Dragoon Guards and Oxford Militia were also present, the latter men escorting prisoners from Yarmouth.Later, there were Dutch prisoner also brought to Norman Cross. The numbers were certainly high, but was there a burial ground there for 4,000 dead, as claimed by the French? The academics from the *Time Team* venture found no absolutely hard evidence but the possibility is still not ruled out.

The Transport Board also had to cope with corruption: the problems lay not with the prison staff themselves, but with the contractors. The stipulated diet rarely in reality met the demands of the orders placed, so that often meat orders would be replaced by herring or cod, or even by vegetables. The Board did try hard to regulate matters and had regular inspections, often visiting prisons unannounced, as happens today. The Board had a doctor in their ranks, Dr John Weir, who also investigated and reported on prisons. He sacked surgeons who were clearly incompetent, such as Jeffcott at Stapleton and Kirkwood on the *Europa* hulk at Portsmouth.

There is no doubt that in the hulks there was a terrible death toll. In the Portsmouth hulks between 1817 and 1827 there were 222 deaths and 188 of these were due to illness. Of these, 115 died from one of these killers: pneumonia, consumption, dysentery and typhus. The inquest records, held at the Sign of the Packet Boat Inn, show the extent of the illnesses and deaths. The mortality rates in all the prisons were high but Dartmoor was the worst in that respect.

Sir Thomas Tyrwhitt, Lord Warden of the Stanneries, thought that a farming community could be made on Dartmoor, with Princetown at the centre but that did not work out, and so when the notion of a convict prison was broached, costs were done, and the fact was that running a prison was much cheaper than maintaining several convict ships. Work went ahead, and builders were still there when the first French prisoners arrived in 1809. The result was a powerful fortress, with barracks for the militia. The prison had two high circular walls, five blocks, a hospital and staff quarters. There was no heating in the cells and things started badly as 1,500 men were packed into cells meant for just one thousand.

In the hospital there was work for several nurses and washer men. The latter were paid six pence a day but their bonus was that they could share the clothing of the dead. Next to the hospital was a place feared by all. This was known as the 'cachot' – a sort of 'black hole' of massive stone blocks with a metal door which was a punishment cell for the escapees who were caught and for serious breaches of discipline such as assaults on warders.

The Governor was in the service of the Transport Office but was also a captain in the navy. From the very beginning, as the motto over the gate says – *'spare the vanquished* – the ideology behind it was as much ruled by caring as by punishment. But things could easily go wrong, as they do in all gaols. There were frequent deaths, many due to smallpox, but the total of deaths between 1908 and 1815 was the staggering number of 1,500. As Trevor James, historian of the prison, has said: 'More than fifty years later their bones littered the area, having been exposed by Dartmoor weather and wild animals.'[5]

The rations at Dartmoor were 'navy rations' – mostly soup, fish and bread – but there were wages for work so prisoners could buy and sell food at certain times as well. The daily ration was a 1lb of bread, 2lb of fish, 1lb of potatoes, and vegetables. Unlike civilian prisons, though, the discipline was organized by the prisoners themselves; rules were established and infringements were punished by flogging with hammock cords. Conditions and supplies were affected by corruption of course, and one of the worst cases was that of a contractor called Josh Rowe, whose malpractice was reported by the Governor, Captain Cotgrave. The Transport Office did an admirable job of dealing with contractors as a rule. Their advertisements for tenders stressed that: 'Each tender must be accompanied by a letter from two respectable persons, engaging to become bound with the person tendering, in the sum of £2,000 for the due performance of the contract.' Josh Rowe continued to exploit the system and Cotgrave had endless problems with him. After all, diet is a crucially important part of a prison regime for adequate food is essential to well being and reduces the chance of trouble and rebellion.

To illustrate the effects of adulterated food on the morale of prisoners, the tale one former inmate told shows how bad things could be: 'One day a man pulled out of the soup bucket of his mess a dead rat which he held up by the tail, whereupon heads and tails and feet were dredged up from every bucket...'[6]

In Dartmoor's history as a place for prisoners of war, though, the story that darkens the whole story, with horrendous and barbaric repression, is the occasion in April 1815 when, after American sailors who had been drafted into service with the British navy but who resented that and preferred to be prisoners of war, were taken to Dartmoor. They repeatedly made attempts to escape. Americans were taken to Dartmoor from 1813 until 1815. Britain had the task of deciding what should be done withAmerican prisoners from the beginning of this. At Dartmoor the Americans were segregated with the blacks being placed in barrack number 4. The long room would have a central area slung with hammocks. There was a high incidence of illness as the temperature was very high at times. The blacks were from privateers, and they were at first mixed across the prison population, but when segregated, communication was of course, easier. Therefore concerted action and revolt could be planned.

Such was the status of blacks at that time that at Dartmoor the blacks' barrack was used for punishment. In April 1815 records show that three Frenchmen found in the act of buggery were flogged and then put with the blacks'–'turned in amongst the negroes'. But as the prisoners controlled punishment most of the time, they were responsible for some of the most severe sentences within the walls, as in the case of one man whole stole ten pounds. He was to be flogged with 500 lashes and was cut down after the first seventy-five so there could be some healing before the next lashing.

Barrack 4 became a strong community which at one time, was led by a huge man called King Dick. He was very tall and strong and the records show that he had 'two comely lads' with him as an escort.

By March 1815 there was a plan to return the American prisoners, but before that could happen, the horrible events of April took place: Captain Thomas Shortland suffered the complaints of prisoners that the bread issue was poor. There was a feeling of unease about the prison, and when a hole was found in a wall – one leading to another yard rather than the open moor – Shortland treated it as an escape attempt and as some of the black Americans were by the gates of their yard, he ordered troops to open fire. Seven prisoners died and thirty-one were wounded. One prisoner who died was only fourteen years old. The irony was that just three months earlier, the peace treaty between Britain and the United States had been signed.

There is no argument that can possibly condone what the officer did that day, but it is certain that escapes of prisoners was a frequent occurrence and there was plenty of local confrontation between French paroled officers and British civilians, None of this, however, applied to American prisoners, so it is unlikely that there was a grudge darkening the heart of Shortland.[7]

Little more than a century later, during the course of the Second World War, it is possible to find plenty of evidence in memoirs and documentaries about the cultural and ideological basis of the treatment of POWs. There had been a distinction between the treatment of officers as opposed to regular servicemen stretching back to the mid eighteenth century, and a glance at one example from a book of 1943, in which the author visited a group of German POWs will show a sharp contrast. The assumption was that officers (as famously documented at Colditz for instance) acted honourably, though with a duty to escape. The deal was that prison for them could be a version of an officers' club, as long as they played by the rules. Travel writer H.V. Morton went to visit some German prisoners 'in the north' and he noted that officers and men were sent to different camps. He then recalled his meeting with the Germans in a country house 'camp.'

Morton was guided around the place by the Colonel in charge:

'The huge panelled dining room on the ground floor, in which the ship-owner once entertained his guests, is the German common room. It is furnished simply with a few chairs and a ping-pong table. The only decoration is a photograph of Hitler shooting out his arm in salute." Every prisoner is a hundred per cent Nazi" said the Colonel. "At first, when addressed by an officer they would come to attention and salute, with *Heil Hitler*. But we have stopped that…"'[8]

When Morton asked what they did all day, he was told that they played cards and ping-pong, but that the local Bishop had ordered some German books for them. The account he gives conveys a sense of a relaxed atmosphere, strangely outside time – 'for them the war was over' as the cliché goes. One young officer wept while Morton was there, and his reason was that he was no longer any use to his Fuhrer.

DISSENT BEHIND BARS

Prison as a punishment for unacceptable opinions, political dissent and perceived deviance, has always led to a number of categorizations and material conditions in the history of penal thought. In most cases the punishment has been extreme, and in earlier times the stress was on corporal punishment. A classic case is that of the Fenian prisoners in the late Victorian years. The journals reported on the harsh treatment meted out to the Irish republicans and Karl Marx wrote a scathing condemnation of this for the working class journal *L'Internationale* in 1870, in which he itemised such cases as these:

'*O'Donovan Rossa*, owner of The Irish people, was shut up for 35 days in a pitch-black dungeon with his hands tied behind his back day and night. They were not even untied to allow him to eat the miserable slops which were left for him on the earthen floor'

O'Leary, an old man of sixty or seventy who was sent to prison, was put on bread and water for three weeks because he would not renounce *paganism* (this is what a jailer called free thinking) and become either a papist, Protestant, Presbyterian or even Quaker, or take up one of the many religions which the prison governor offered to the heathen Irish.'[9]

In other words, attention turns to the history of prison for dissent, deviant thought and counter-cultural activity. Before open debate and legislation on human rights, repression was the response, as in the frequent, pragmatic suspension ofhabeas corpus by various governments. Legal codes across the world have always sought, at least on the surface, to integrate human rights to some degree, but everyday practice in criminal justice systems will always vary in the extent to which the dictates are applied. In Imperial Russia, for instance, the priesthood of the orthodox church were expected to act as an element in the apparatus of repression, even conveying information about individuals gained in the confessional to the police.[10] Of all aspects of prison history, the chronicle of prison for dissent or unorthodoxy has most enlightened the society in the immediate context.

As the history of classical Greece and Rome makes clear, changes in political ideology may happen rapidly with such massive causal factors as war, poverty, civil disorder and factional rivalry being ever-present. The casualties of defined deviance may be yesterday's party men, the bedrock of what used to be orthodoxy. In numerous cases studies across the stage of world history, examples may be found of political deviants being thrown into dungeons and even if we separate the gulags and camps from such matters as house arrest and political exile, the subject is fraught with contradictions and contrasts. For instance, in his exile in Van Dieman's Land, William Smith O'Brien could read, talk, reflect and exchange or express ideas, but only within the walls of his villa on the slopes above Port Arthur.

Totalitarianism in the twentieth century has brought with it the use of imprisonment as part of the machinery of the suppression of identity; if one takes away liberty and freedom of thought, with the exchange of humanitarian thought and interplay, then George Orwell's world of Big Brother has arrived. The modern classic template in this sense is in China. As I write this in 2011, Bob Dylan has given a concert in China, and his songbook was vetted by the authorities. They allowed him to sing everything on his programme except 'Blowin' in the Wind' and 'The Times They Are a Changing.' This is just one in a myriad examples from past time in which authoritarian ideology has interfered with art, intellectual endeavour and social commentary, of course, but in China the process has been patently open for the world to see. In December 2010 this was most blatantly transparent when the Nobel peace prize recipient Liu Xiaobo was due to attend the prize-giving ceremony in Norway; at that point, Liu was two years into an eleven-year sentence for anti-state activity.

The list of prisoners in China, held for alleged charges such as 'espionage' is very long indeed. In many cases, the 'crime' is that of simply writing history or any humanitarian discipline which may tread on the sensibilities of the state. Dolma Kyab, who writes as Lobsang Kelsang Gyatso, was sentenced to ten years in prison for 'stealing state secrets' when in fact the focus of his transgression was his book *The Restless Himalayas*, in which the Lhasa history teacher merely wrote about the history and culture of Tibet. He was tried secretly by the Lhasa Intermediate people's Court, and in fact there still has been no statement about what offences he has committed. English PEN, fighting for the rights and freedom of writers across the globe, has explained the situation: 'This book alone would not justify such a sentence under Chinese law, but according to Dolma Kyab, the Chinese government has accused him of espionage and stealing state secrets, one of the most serious political offences in China.... this may be because another of Dolma Kyab's manuscripts includes information on the location of military camps...'[11]

At the core of imprisonment for action or thought against the state is treason. The majority of criminal codes have some use of, or relation to, the key Treason Act in English law, of 1351. The wording of that act covers all aspects of harm done or considered against a sovereign. The important phrasing is 'Compassing or imagining the King's death' and 'levying war against the king in the realm' / 'adhering to the King's enemies in his realm; giving aid and comfort here and elsewhere.' Distinctions between 'treason' and 'high treason' were defined in states across the world, as in, for instance, the criminal codes of Canada, Germany and New Zealand; in other states, treason has multiple related offences, as in Switzerland and France. However, punishment is extreme in all cases, and in imprisonment for treason, there has always been the element of what we would call today 'indeterminate sentences.'

The huge body of material in the State Trials gives a series of variations in this respect. Thomas More was in the Tower for just one week before he was executed, whereas Sir Walter Raleigh's execution was postponed, and as Lord Denning explains: 'The King spared his life. He was committed to the Tower, there to remain during pleasure. He was well treated. He had apartments in the upper storey of the Bloody Tower where he had his wife and son with him, and their personal attendants. He had the use of a garden. The young Prince

Henry was most friendly and visited him there. He wrote *The History of the World* and did experiments in chemistry.'[12]

The records of the Tower provide ample support for the view that imprisonment for treason led to all varieties of suffering, from long periods such as the term served by Lord Grey who had been in the Tower for eleven years after being reprieved at the last moment as he stood on the scaffold, to the suicides, as in the case of Arthur, Earl of Sussex who cut his throat in July 1683. Although many aristocratic prisoners lived inside that fortress for long periods, enjoying a life of comfort and all amenities, the word 'Tower' conveyed a sense of oblivion, and prison histories from all countries and regimes with regard to punishment for treason provide chronicles of misery, harsh treatment and usually, a long and painful death. But modern times have brought changes. In the Second World War Churchill wanted all captured German soldiers who had been tried for treason to hang, and the prison periods of waiting for the scaffold were mercifully short.

The treatment of prisoners for the crime of treason and of sedition, or related offences such as espionage or even, in some societies, blasphemy, has origins or parallel ideologies in ancient notions of taboo, and an interesting feature of modern history when compared to tribal moralities in anthropological studies, is that imprisonment replaced such punishments as banishment or of course, death. In Shakespeare's plays, banishment is seen as something worse than death or imprisonment. Coriolanus banishes victims with these words:

> You common cry of curs! Whose breath I hate
> As reek o' the rotten fens, whose loves I prize
> As the dead carcasses of buried men
> That do corrupt my air, I banish you.
> *Coriolanus* (III iii. 118)

Prison has been combined with corporal punishment and torture for crimes against the state, and the common law in Europe, with Roman Law have both had this element. Incarceration in this respect has often been subject to the whims and moods of tyrants or to the long legal process and ritual involved when authority punishes its political transgressors. Yet prisons across the world and in history have ample examples of the other side of the coin – the toleration of creativity in imprisonment – and the vast literature of political detainees is evidence of this. Therefore, in a paradoxical sense, the history of prison has contained for many the history and literature of counter-thinking, revolution and free thought. On the one hand we have the slaughter of the French Revolution and the unacceptable thinkers and aristocrats led to the guillotine in the tumbrels, and the other we have the canon of classic works written or conceived in jails.

Prison and torture for treason was conceived in terms of the great metaphor of the body of state and the 'body' of the state in its hierarchies and the status of individuals; hence the notion of petty treason when the body of the victim was of a higher social order than the transgressor. But this same metaphor led to the extremes of torture and the imposition of a slow, languishing death, notably in the punishments of a 'debt of honour' to the sovereign and in England of the victim being hanged, drawn and quartered. On the credit side, we have the long tradition of the prisoner left to live the life of the mind, while the body was confined. Not only the categorization of inmates, but also the material nature of the prison was affected by the fact that places had to be found for crimes of dissent and opposition to the state. This also played its part in the long search for alternative ways to punish people. As a result of all this, it would be no exaggeration to say that there has always been an unseen, alternative curriculum inside prison walls: a culture of the autodidact. After all, 'doing time' is the simplest expression to convey the double meaning of (a) simply watching time pass and (b) actively making time valuable.

One of the most fascinating examples of this is in those cultures in which education and self-development, philosophy and critical debate are valued and also exist in the religious or educational foundations of the society. This has always been found in Jewish societies, for instance, where there is a foundation establishment of discussion and debate emanating from study of the Talmud. Ingrained in Jewish learning is the minute discussion of the annotations to the books of law, achieved by rabbis through the centuries. Consequently, in the literature of the Holocaust, we have Jewish writers of various nationalities, articulating what is in some ways beyond articulation. There is a sense in which the experience of imprisonment is incommunicable an all contexts, but arguably, the experience of the concentration camps is more so. In fact, one of the key statements from that literature is Theodor Adorno's statement: '…to write a poem after Auschwitz is barbaric, and that corrodes also the knowledge which expresses why it has become impossible to write poetry today.'[13] Yet, the writing from the camps and ghettos was immensely important, as Milton Teichman has written: 'The truth-telling of writers…did not hurt the Germans while genocide was taking place; nor did the efforts of writers lessen the destruction of the Jewish people. But as a result of their eye-witness accounts, the mountain of evidence of German crimes against Jews… is larger…'[14]

Moreover, there is no need to refer to the great traumas of prison life. In the everyday experience of jail across America there has been a massive literature spawned. H. Bruce Franklin summarized this: 'The tidal wave of great literature … that poured out of America's prisons from the mid 1960s to the mid 1970s did not emerge by chance. Tens of millions of Americans were being drawn into the global struggle against colonialism and imperialism, a struggle that swept into America in the urban rebellions that began in 1964 and culminated in April 1968 with revolts in 125 U.S. cities the week after the murder of Martin Luther King…'[15]

In some ways, the alternative history of prison is most clearly perceived through the intellectual ways of 'doing time' as evidenced in such classics as prison notebooks, memoirs or essays of several celebrated prisoners such as Antonio Gramsci, Oscar Wilde, Nelson Mandela, Eldridge Cleaver, Florence Maybrick or the Suffragettes. When there is a large-scale issue concerning human rights, these writings are even more valuable as examples of alternative perspectives on prison.

South America provides a useful modern example of this history of political detention, with a number of case studies of what abuses and cruelties may yet persist centuries after the Tower of London or the first concentration camps. In a 2008 study by the Geneva Academy of International Humanitarian Law and Human Rights, Democracy, Human Rights and Prison Conditions in South America, the context of abuses in jails in Chile, Brazil and Argentina was described. The aim of the research was to account for serious infringements of human rights. One overall comment was: 'Serious violations of human rights are found in the continuous practice of torture of prisoners, abuse, and disparaging conditions of maintenance of people placed in prisons in those three countries.'[16]

The prison experience in these states was arguably one of the worst anywhere at any time and the report notes: 'The police and legal structure were used mainly to fight political crimes performed by those in opposition to the military regime and in addition several other actions performed by the State happened aside from the law increasing the violation to the rights of individuals.'[17] Mass imprisonment expanded in the 1990s across many continents, and the authors of the report make it clear that criminal policies adapted in the three South American states under scrutiny were influenced by 'new parameters established in developed countries'.[18] The repressive apparatus was consolidated and widely used, and the statistics of incarceration make alarming reading: the imprisoned population in Brazil, Argentina and Chile respectively in 2007 was: 422.590, 60,621 and 48,855. Between the years 1992 and 2007, the rate per 100,000 in Brazil averaged almost 200.

The report concluded that in these prison systems 'the maintenance of good order and discipline is constantly under threat. Practices of violence and corruption are frequent and render prison environments places of even broader human rights violation.'[19] There have been frequent riots and disorder and violence to staff. In terms of concepts of freedom, the report makes a case for the fact that notions of freedom in this context relate more to social behaviour and individual success than to social hierarchy and mobility, and hence the rigid definitions of the lower and criminal classes, together with the status of dissidents, have been confirmed in a repressive manner.

One case study which highlights this state of affairs relates to a modern classic of prison literature - *Tejas Verdes: Diario de un Campo de Concentracion de Chile* by Hernan Valdes. After suffering several hours of torture he wrote: 'All I knew about evil until now was only caricature, only literature. Now evil has lost all moral reference.'[20] Tejas Verdes existed between 1974 and 1974 and evidence given from former prisoners there was logged as part of the process of forming indictments in 1976 against a number of retired military officers. One typical example is of Rebecca Espinoza:

'have testified that they saw the three persons who are today 'disappeared' in a very bad physical condition. In the case of Rebecca Espinoza, 40 years of age at the time of her detention and mother of four, witnesses testified that she was enclosed in a small wooden shack, and not allowed to communicate with other prisoners. The fingers of her hands were broken, she was nearly unconscious and was frequently raped at night. The last time witnesses saw Rebecca, two military men were leading her towards the Maipo River.'[21]

The prosecution used a leading precedent – *Tibi v Ecuador* from 2004, and ultimately from the Nuremburg trials. The legal principle adopted there is the 'jus cogens' – a 'compelling law' with a status in international jurisprudence stating that no nations may break its ruling. The Tibi case exemplifies the situation *vis a vis* some South American prison practice and human rights. Daniel Tibi was arrested in 1995 in Quito while driving his car and was flown to Guayaquil where he was placed in a cell and held for 28 months without trial. He claimed that he had been tortured, being beaten, burned and almost suffocated, as police worked for a confession from him on drug trafficking charges. He alleged that when admitted to a penitentiary he had to pay 20,000 sucres to a prison guard, in order to have a cell. He claimed that such a deal was common practice, to get a 'safe' cell.

The evidence was deemed to be admissible. A long debate took place on habeas corpus and other writs, and the nature of the international legal position on such a plea. Tibi had tried all possible actions with regard to domestic law in Ecuador and had failed to find help. The nadir of his horrendous experience was surely when he was offered his freedom if he admitted involvement in another case; he claimed he had received death threats in order to persuade him to confess. Statements to the court included an account of his treatment: 'He was handcuffed and taken to a room where he received blows about the body and face. His lower limbs were burned, this time resulting in his ribs being broken. On other occasions, he was dealt blows with baseball bats…'[22]

The report by the Centre for the Study of Violence by the team at the University of Sao Paulo concludes that actions urgently needed to apply some regulation in this context include changes to the basic configuration of the criminal justice system, participation of civil society organizations in monitoring conditions (such as the British Independent Monitoring Board) and a description and analysis of violations of human rights, covering such topics as prisoner deaths, torture, abuse and material conditions.

CAT AND MOUSE

If an example had to be chosen from the history of prisons at any time or in any place in which prison was used in abnormal circumstances for dissidents and free thinkers, the experience of Suffragettes in the UK and Ireland would provide the outstanding illustration.

At the heart of this was the Cat and Mouse Act of 1913 - properly termed the Temporary Discharge for Ill Health Act – by which women prisoners could be released and then immediately arrested again. Force-feeding was used within the prisons – hence causing the 'ill health'.

In August, 1892 a woman prisoner at Walton gaol was brought to appear before the committee of prison visitors. She had tried to wreck what she could in her cell and assaulted the matron. Her punishment for this misdemeanour was to be shackled for four days with her hands tied behind her back. The governor had directed the irons to be put on for a period without a limit, and that was his mistake. He was in the wrong. The case highlights the long history of brutal repression of women prisoners there.

Sidelights on history such as this make us wonder who committed the crimes in days long gone. Another seventeen years after this incident, and again in Walton, there were events which make us ask the question again. This was what the Women's Social and Political Union was to call 'Atrocities in an English Prison' in their newsletter. The writers claimed: 'Two English women have been assaulted, knocked down, gagged, fed by force, kept for consecutive days and nights in irons.' The article was about Selina Martin and Leslie Hall who had been remanded in Walton for a week, bail having been refused.

But the Suffragettes were to provide an even more sensational story in Liverpool, as a member of the top English aristocracy, Lady

Constance Lytton, came up with a plan to be arrested and taken to Walton to experience and write about the kind of treatment that was being given to her fellow protesters for women's rights. Her father had been Viceroy of India and her mother was at one time lady-in-waiting to Queen Victoria. Now here was Constance, a militant for the feminist cause, who had taken on the identity of 'Jane Warton' when arrested in Liverpool. It was, from one point of view, an undercover job, an investigation, with herself as the subject of the 'atrocities' claimed.

Liverpool had not experienced a great deal of militancy over the period of activist campaigns and there were only ten incidents in the city at one of the most energetic periods of unrest between 1913-14. But Edith Rigby, a secretary of a branch of the WSPU, did place a pipe bomb at the Liverpool Exchange Building in 1913. The bomb actually exploded. It didn't do the general debate any good at all that Rigby's husband approved of what she was doing. Such events helped to cause more division and mistrust, but on the positive side it made the men with more entrenched conservative view sit up and take notice.

Real militancy in the campaign started in October 1905 when Annie Kenney and Christabel Pankhurst heckled MP Sir Edward Grey. They went to prison for a week after refusing to pay a fine. From then onwards, the WSPU would have a militant 'wing.' Women in the regions were asked to participate more actively in local campaigns. Deputations to the House of Commons followed, and after 1909 the government began the 'force-feeding' of women who were being held in Holloway. Then hundreds of women in all areas were held and force-fed.

'Jane Warton' was born. There is a photograph of her which shows a tallish, thin women wearing a long black coat (with badges on the collar) and a large-brimmed hat to put a dark shade over her face. It would have been hard to see the famous Lady Lytton under all that. Lytton went to Walton gaol where there was a crowd, and with the intention of being arrested, she committed her 'crime', as described in her memoirs: 'I took to running and urging on the crowd... I began discharging my stones, not throwing them but limply dropping them over the hedge into the governor's garden. Two policemen then held me fast by the arms and marched me off to the police station.' Lytton explained the reason for going to Liverpool: 'I was sent to join in working an anti-government campaign during a general election in 1910. Just before I went, there came the news of the barbarous ill treatment of Miss Selina Martin and Miss Leslie Hall...I heard too of another prisoner in Liverpool, Miss Bertha Brewster who had been re-arrested after her release from prison, which she had done as a protest at being fed by force.'

The conditions in the gaol were harsh. Lytton upset the authorities in lots of small ways such as her attempt to combat the intense cold by wearing her skirt fastened around her neck. She wanted to speak to the governor when he made his first visit, but his windows had been broken in the protest outside, and he was in a bad mood. At least she had a gas-jet for some degree of light in that pokey, dark place, with its tiny high window.

Warton/Lytton refused food for four days when inside the prison which meant that she would have to be force-fed. Her memoirs provide an account of what that was like. A gag was placed between her teeth, then a tube was put down her throat 'which seemed to me much too wide and was about four feet in length' she writes. This is what happened next:

> 'Then the food was poured in quickly; it made me sick a few seconds after it was down and the action of the sickness made my body and legs double up, but the wardresses instantly pressed back my head and the doctor leant on my knees. The horror of it was more than I can describe. I was sick over the doctor and wardresses, and it seemed a long time before they took the tube out...'[23]

This was so horrendous that reports about attempts at resistance make painful reading. 'Force feeding was threatened so Mrs Martin barricaded her cell' is the kind of sentence often encountered in reading these records. As for Jane Warton, she was 'found out' and attitudes changed, and so there was a furore. The doctor, knowing who she really was, said: 'You are absolutely not fit for this kind of thing. How could your Union send a woman like you to do a thing of this kind?' What better evidence could the militants have than this? The implication was that it was quite acceptable to force feed and manacle working-class women, considered to be 'more robust'.

This issue and the general consequences of the Jane Warton case, led to energetic leaders and letters in *The Times*. On February 10 1910 Home Secretary Edward Troup was forced to make a statement to the press. He wrote: 'I am directed by the Secretary of State to say that the statement that Lady Constance Lytton was released from Liverpool prison only when her identity was discovered was untrue. The release of "Jane Warton" was recommended by the medical officer… upon purely medical grounds.'

The facts are that Lytton was force fed eight times. She had been entered in the prison books as having refused medical examination, so how could the medical officer's assessment have been made? The case highlighted more than the different treatment given to militants of different classes: it also brought to the public attention the inhuman treatment of female prisoners that had been going on for decades, and in Liverpool some of the worst examples of this are on record. It was not illegal; the prison authorities were within the law, but that is a matter for debate as to the justness of such punishments as shackling for many days at a time.

Constance Lytton died in 1923 after being handicapped by paralysis eleven years before. Her last days in Walton included an interview with the governor and the doctor, and she reported that they were 'courteous' on that occasion. Her courage was incredible and her time in Walton not only highlighted some of the inhumane treatment that had been part of the prison system for years, but also the sanctioned attitudes and treatment given out to women with startling callousness. Even the notorious death of Emily Davidson under the King's horse in the 1915 Derby had seemingly not changed some of these attitudes to female suffrage.

One of the most dramatic and controversial sagas from inside its walls is that of the women of the Irish Women's Franchise League. In 1912 the suffragist paper *The Irish Citizen* threatened a hunger strike in Mountjoy. The focus for this was Mrs Mary Leigh, who, with others, had been given long sentences for trying to burn the Theatre Royal on the night of Herbert Asquith's visit. The *Irish Citizen* made clear its position on that act and its significance:

'The savage sentences inflicted on the convicted prisoners, cannot, of course, be allowed to stand. The judge himself was sufficiently ashamed of them to express the hope that they would speedily be revised by the proper authority... The Irish public must not fall behind the disagreeing jurymen in the appreciation of the political motive of Mrs. Leigh and her comrades. They must be accorded the full rights of political prisoners.'[24]

And so a hunger strike was planned. There was fury that Mrs Leigh had a term of five years to serve. These were of penal servitude so there was no stretch of knitting and sewing to be considered. Force-feeding had begun by 3 September when it was reported that Mrs Leigh was 'in a state of collapse.' A supporter, Mrs Grace Roe of Dublin, went to speak to the Lord Lieutenant about the matter. She was told that it was policy from England that was the cause: Asquith and Lloyd George wanted it done, and even Lord Aberdeen could not persuade them otherwise. The two women in question, Leigh and Miss Evans, were reported in *The Times*. In the autumn of 1912 the news was not good, with the Dublin correspondent writing thathe had no reason to believe 'that Sir James Dougherty gave Miss Roe ... absolutely no hope of the early release of the prisoners...'

By October, though released on compassionate grounds, Leigh was facing trial for yet another offence. She had thrown a hatchet at John Redmond, a Home Rule supporter of Asquith, on that same occasion of Asquith's visit. Mr Justice Kenny announced that there would be a full investigation with regard to that second charge against her.

In December the Cat and Mouse Act began to take effect on Leigh and Evans. In lawyer speak, they had 'failed to comply with the terms of their licence on release from Mountjoy.' They had not reported to police by the time set and so were to be returned to gaol but were bailed pending an appeal to the King's Bench with the objection that they were not in fact obliged to report while on their licence.

These various case studies show the diverse range of issues and moral or political debates with regard to the treatment of political prisoners, and also highlight the paradoxical and complex consequences of categorization and the penal policy with regard to 'special' category of inmate. The history of this area of prison life is destined to be under a dark shadow of inhuman and brutal applications of repression. If we look for one instance in which this paradox is most clearly seen, surely this has to be the story of Oscar Wilde in Reading Gaol where he was given books, cups of tea and other small comforts, while all the while he was subject to hard labour and a diet that took its toll on his constitution. He may have accelerated his death in that regime, but it gave him time to pen one of the most incisive and philosophical reflections on prison existence – his great essay *De Profundis* in which he wrote of the most perceptive statements about the intellectual and sensitive person inside prison walls: 'But we who live in prison, and in whose lives there is no event but sorrow, have to measure time by throbs of pain, and the record of bitter moments. We have nothing else to think of. Suffering –curious as it may seem to you –is the means by which we exist, because it is the only means by which we become conscious of existing…'[25]

As a coda to the discussion on unacceptable opinions, we might note the contrast in treatment of the lower classes as opposed to writers and intellectuals such as Wilde and thousands of others. In 1805 *The Observer* carried this report:

'On Thursday a private received 400 lashes in the Horse Barracks-yard at Ipswich, for uttering seditious expressions in a public-house in that neighbourhood. Detachments from all the regiments in the garrison were present at the punishment.'[26]

Notes and references

1 Adrian Tahourdin, 'Memoirs' *Times Literary Supplement* 25 March, 2011 p. 27
2 Gavin Daly, 'Napoleon's Lost legions: French Prisoners of War in Britain 1803-1814 *History* Vol. 89 no. 295 2004 pp. 361-380 p. 374
3 See Friends of Norman Cross at www.friendsofnormancross/a-detailed-history/5-the-prisoners
4 Ibid.
5 Trevor James, *About Dartmoor Prison* (Crediton, 2001) p. 14
6 Ibid. p. 22
7 For a full account of this, see 'The paradox of Dartmoor Prison' at www.american heritage.com/articles/magazine/ah/1975
8 HV Morton, *I Saw Two Englands* (London, 1943 p. 259

9 Karl Marx Letter to *L'Internationale* 21 Feb. 1870, see www.marxists.org/archive/marx/works pp. 1–7 p. 2.

10 See Orlando Figes, *Natasha's Dance* (London, 2003) p. 292.

11 See PEN site www.englishpen.org/writersinprison: Location: P.R.China/Tibet section.

12 Lord Denning, *Landmarks in the Law* (London, 1984) p. 13.

13 Theodor Adorno, *Prisms* (London, 1967) p. 30.

14 See Milton Teichman, quoted in 'How Writers Fought Back: Literature from the Nazi Ghettoes and Camps' in http://findarticles.com.

15 H. Bruce Franklin, 'From Plantation to the Prison-Industrial Complex: Literature of the American prison' Paper delivered to the MLA Convention, Dec.2000 on Http://andromeda.rutgers.edu/~hbf/MLABLACK.htm.

16 'Democracy, Human Rights and Prison Conditions in South America' Centre for the Study of Violence, University of Sao Paolo: www.memoriayjusticia.cl/english/en_rights-tejas.htm p. 1.

17 Ibid. p. 3.

18 Ibid. p. 5.

19 Ibid. p. 7.

20 Quoted in 'First Indictments for Torture at Tejas Verdes' www.memoriayjusticia.cl/english/en_rights-tejas.htm p. 2.

21 Ibid. p. 1.

22 See University of Minnesota, Human Rights Library, for a full account of the trial. This is Report 90/00 Daniel David Tibi at http:// www1.umn.edu/humanrts/cases/90-00.html.

23 Constance Lytton, *Prisons and Prisoners* (London, 1988) p. 261.

24 See Roger Fulford, *Votes for Women* (London, 1958) p. 260.

25 Oscar Wilde, 'De Profundis' in *The Works of Oscar Wilde* (London, 1948) p. 884.

26 Collected and reprinted in Yvonne Ffrench, *News from the Past 1805-1887* (London, 1940) p. 18.

Chapter 9

A Short History of Modern Failures

It is not a difficult task to gather a vast amount of material to show conclusively that in the last fifty years across the world, prison has not worked. The disenchantment behind that statement lies in the nature of the failures, from Australia to Alaska. The worm in the apple has been the extension of foundation ideas which themselves related to fundamental philosophical lines of thought on liberty and humanitarian reform. In short, models from the Old World provided ready-made templates, and proliferation went forward with no impact from genuine thought on the amelioration of man as a convict, a transgressor, regardless of which moral or legal system was in existence in relation to the offence.

Documentation on the extent to which prison has not succeeded in terms of rehabilitation and a reduction in recidivism is ample and easy to obtain. But the practical and political explanations, concerning pragmatic decisions with reference to expanding prison populations resulting from the proliferation of offences, and a lack of viable alternative sentences, takes second place to a more philosophical explanation. Sociologists and philosophers have offered explanations and theories, yet basically the deepest explanation for failure is arguably to be found in the implications and resonances of the idea of liberty.

Erich Fromm has produced a lengthy exposition of the profound impact of social and religious change in this respect, finding the roots of social unrest and deviancy in the events of the Reformation and in the commercial revolution of the early modern period. He ties together both Luther's conception of Protestantism and the cash nexus enterprise behind the modern state, materialism, and the profit ethos, locating a fearful loneliness and moral vacuity in the condition of modernity. One implication of this is that because social cohesion and communication, along with shared beliefs in ontology and the religious imperative of togetherness, modern man, in spite of the Enlightenment, became subject to the disciplines of anonymous existence. Because he was reified – often being a 'hand' rather than a 'worker' or defined by statistics and production figures, he found himself in a milieu in which transgression took multiple forms. This was exacerbated by the consolidation of state power with religious establishment. Fromm expresses this well in this passage from his classic work *The Fear of Freedom*:

> 'The individual became more alone, isolated, became an instrument in the hands of overwhelmingly strong forces outside himself; he became an "individual" but a bewildered and insecure individual. There were factors to help him overcome the overt manifestations of this underlying insecurity. In the first place his self was backed up by property. "He" as a person and the property he owned could not be separated… the less he felt he was being somebody the more he needed to have possessions…'[1]

The broad argument from Erich From and others is that the growth of the commercial imperative and the cash nexus between people, creating master and servant, led to the series of industrial revolutions beginning c. 1770 as steam power was developed and applied to production, and that this uprooting of traditional social relations and integrated community made property and materialism central to life. If we apply this to criminality from the first industrial changes and the burgeoning of empires to the managerial revolutions of the 1950s, with their influence from Behaviourism, then we find that in the first hundred years or so, from c. 1700-1820s, crime against property was rife, leading to repressive laws and numerous capital offences. This was followed by an escalation in white collar crime, as individuals were caught up in faceless, bland large-scale organisations.

Underpinning all this was the religious element: the church courts across Europe and the new empires, for instance, for many years ran alongside the criminal courts and the sheer range of potential transgressions by an individual multiplied. A person could find prison his destiny through debt as well as through seditious activity, and through any number of crimes against property and against the person, as the rich increased in power and status, and the poor became labelled as the 'underclass.' It is not difficult to find strong links between Marxist thought and the proliferation of prisons; after all, if a person lives in a state with no social welfare and he only has his labour to sell, then loss of the one source of income will drive him to crime to avoid ruination.

The new concepts of prison came alongside all this, and the criminal statistics were further fuelled by the rise of gin shops and beer shops, pubs and clubs through the eighteenth and nineteenth centuries and those destined for prison became largely victims of some or all of these sicknesses and shortcomings of what we now call modernity. Modernity and its penitentiaries, as we have seen, struggled to offer more than a dark hole of oblivion. Yet by the mid twentieth century, the evidence points to the failure of prison, and within the last twenty years there has been a widespread effort to create alternative punishments. However, the signs for some kind of wholesale backing to redemptive penal trajectories and a confident swath of reformed offenders returning to society without criminal tendencies are rare and harder to find as each year passes. Prison populations rise and the same familiar failures reoccur.

There were concerns about this early in the twentieth century, long before the social sciences began to develop to such a level that they would play a part in prison establishment and policy. For instance, in 1935 when standard minimum rules for all sane persons imprisoned had been stated and promulgated by the International Penal and Penitentiary Commission, the Howard League for Penal Reform (formed in 1866) published an appeal in the national press for observation of the rules worldwide. Their statement included four basic demands, including a verification by all states that they accepted the rules; an insistence that all states must then publish the acceptance; that the League of Nations 'should address to the Commission a formal request for their views as to the best way of ensuring that the Governments they represent should in future observe all standard minimum rules, and that the existingrules should be extended to deal with 'such questions as imprisonment without trial.'[2]

The Howard League made it clear that there were some states which disregard the rules, but would not publish their names 'but all the instances given relate either to Europe, the United States of America or the British Empire.'[3] These minimum rules related to the subjects of food, work, accommodation, health, punishments, prison staff, religious services and assistance to liberated prisoners. The League had found terrible abuses worldwide, and noted that they research document included material on '…physical torture and ill treatment' and these were reported widely. 'In many countries corporal punishment is recklessly used and beating is common, as punishment by official order or at the whim of the prison officer' they added.[4]

Ten years previously, Margery Fry of the Howard League located the nature of the shifting logistics of prison philosophy and application of experimental ideas: 'The study of the best methods of preventing crime…is much wider than that of prison organisation; to subordinate it to the latter is like treating public health as a branch of hospital management. There is now little excuse for this. When the century opened our childish doggerel, 'Him as takes what isn't 'is'n/ when he's cotched shall go to prison' may almost have represented the sum total of penal resources. Today things stand differently.'[5] She understood that the visionary and innovative ideas in penology were going to struggle to have any real impact.

Here, I will look at three case studies of such failures: the Australian camp at Palm Island, the Mau Mau insurrection in Kenya and the condition of the prison system in the Irish Republic. They have little in common in terms of any broad generalisations but what they share is the kinds of failure which tend to be based in degrees of abuse, neglect and poor administration. One feature they have in common is a marginal place in the media and in universal dissemination of information. In fact, the Mau Mau camps of 1957 have only recently become widely known because files from the Foreign and Commonwealth Office were opened for scrutiny in 2011. These examples will illustrate failure at various levels: some prison systems have not advanced in step with their neighbours simply in minor matters such as cell facilities or education, whereas others show obvious infringements of human rights. My summaries of these three examples will present them as issues and debates, not as established negatively disseminated instances of abuse or neglect.

PALM ISLAND

There is now no doubt that the history of Australia had a hidden narrative for much of its existence. That story was a shadow behind the development of white Australia, and it concerns the treatment of the Aboriginal people. That history has been nothing less than genocide, beginning in the nineteenth century with horrendous massacres and reprisals by white settlers who had rifles against the fighters of the black Australians with their spears. After that, in the mid twentieth century, the genocide took the form of 'breeding out' the 'Blackfella' in the age of the stolen children – an attempt to use the nasty procedures of genetic annihilation as historian Phillip Knightley explains in his account of A. O.Neville, the man with the ironic title of Chief Protector of Aboriginals for Western Australia in 1937:

> 'Neville asked: "Are we going to have a population of one million blacks in the commonwealth or are we going to merge them into our white community and forget that there were ever any Aboriginals in Australia?" The key resolution at the conference, *The Destiny of the Race*, passed unanimously, called for the absorption into the white community of all non full-blood Aboriginals. Taking part-Aboriginal children from their mothers and families by force was part of this ambition.'[6]

This was nothing less than eugenics; the type of social engineering familiar from late Victorian notions of the decline of the quality of populations in industrialised nations, and indeed, parallel to the Nazi experimentations. Phillip Knightley has no qualms in comparing what happened in Australia to the Nazi era, writing that 'lawyers can argue about the definition of genocide but for power and simplicity it is hard to beat Hannah Arendt. Writing in *Eichmann in Jersusalem* she said that genocide was the desire to make a distinct people disappear from the earth. That was the shameful desire of the

Australian government for at least sixty years.'[7] Knightley was working as a journalist in various parts of Australia when this process was well known, but yet never had any knowledge of it.

The turning point came, and the testimonies of suffering finally reached print, notably in Lorna Cubillo and Peter Gunner's landmark case against the Australian government in 1999. They were both eight years old when they were forcibly taken away from their parents to be assimilated into institutions and then raised with a white family. What emerged then was that there had been 30,000 people in similar circumstances, and they were labelled the 'lost generation'. Cubillo and Gunner's case in a Darwin court eventually led to something not quite defined as an apology after their terrible testimonies of cruelty and abuse was ruled as admissible by Judge Maurice O'Loughlin who heard evidence which included accounts of people being beaten, sexually abused and treated as slaves.

It is in this context that we must understand what evolved at Palm Island. This was a former black penal colony, explained by Cameron Forbes: 'Palm Island was the prime example of the paternalism of the Queensland government. The superintendent was near supreme ruler, with an iron control over daily life, including habits of orderliness and cleanliness and "dancing or other native practices". Bells rang for curfews, housing was doled out, children and unmarried girls were segregated in dormitories.'[8] In 2010 Palm island was reported as still being a 'purgatory' for its inhabitants, but by that time documented testimony was widely available, such as this report by Keith McEwan:

> 'In explaining the harsh and arbitrary treatment inflicted on those sent to this penal settlement off the coast of Queensland, near Townsville, a woman confined there in 1956, stated, "Mail had to be smuggled out of the settlement otherwise if we post letters through the office on Palm Island they are opened up and destroyed and we are called up before the Superintendent and severely punished. We are put in gaol and only given two blankets and fed with bread and water for a week."'[9]

McEwan gathered other reports, including stories of the island (established in 1918 as a detention centre and penal settlement), such as accounts of girls who had tried to escape being shaven bald and were given a bag to wear as a dress after being locked up for six weeks.

In 1987 the Royal Commission into Aboriginal Deaths in Custody was established and one conclusion was that police officers were not responsible. But the statistics say a great deal about the penology. In 2009 an Aboriginal person was fourteen times more likely to be in prison than a non-indigenous Australian, and 18 per cent of deaths in custody in Australia between 1990 and 2007 were of Aboriginals.[10]

Then the case of Mulrunji Doomadgee reached the headlines. Doomadgee had been arrested for drunkenness in 2004 and taken to a police cell on Palm Island where he died. The inquest revealed that an officer, Sgt. Hurley, had hit Doomadgee so hard in the stomach that his liver was almost split into two. In 2007 the officer was acquitted of charges relating to cruelty and manslaughter. Yet the case does not end there, because in early 2011, the Queensland police announced that no action would be taken against six other officers who had earlier been detailed to investigate the officer's conduct and had not allegedly done their duty in that regard.

The case highlights much that is undesirable and abusive in Palm Island: there were riots after the death of Doomadgee and these were mercilessly quelled. Kathy Marks, writing in 2011, summarises the unbelievably unacceptable update on the case: 'Hurley is now an acting inspector on Queensland's Gold Coast. One of the officers involved in the investigation – which the coroner, Brian Hine, found riddled with lies – has also been promoted. Another has retired on medical grounds…'[11]

In the nineteenth century, unhampered by any talk of human rights except in the dusty philosophical works on the shelves, there was no need even to imprison Aboriginals. They were simply murdered, as in a typical case in 1834 from Western Australia, '…soldiers under the command of Captain James Stirling, the state's first governor, butchered a sleeping camp of eighty Aboriginal men, women and children from the Nyungar tribe near Pinjarra. Their leader, Yagan, had learned English and tried in vain to explain Aboriginal law and culture to the settlers.'[12] One would have thought that some progress would have been made by the late twentieth century, some kind of new understanding and attempts to live together, but the 'stolen children' years and the penal camps have done irreparable damage in that respect.

THE MAU MAU CAMPS

In April, 2011 the Foreign and Commonwealth Office released papers from the 1950s relating to the Mau Mau troubles in Kenya. *The Times* reported that this uncovered 'a vast cache of documents' which revealed 'efforts to cover up one of the darkest episodes in British colonial history.'[13] But this is all not that much of a surprise. A trawl through the newspaper archives revealed a great deal about the whole episode and its suppression.

As early as 1950, writers were explaining the rise of secret societies in Africa, and witnesses described seeing meetings held late at night in the Naivasha area. Some locals were beaten and forced to take oaths, as in this account: 'One said he was made to stand in the middle of a circle made of grass on the hut floor while one of the accused passed a banana leaf, containing the blood of a ritually sacrificed sheep, round his head.'[14] The phrase 'mau mau' means 'something that has to be done quickly' and the society's aim was to evict all Europeans from Kenya.

By 1952 matters had escalated, and oaths were being taken far more widely and by large numbers of Kenyans, as was the case with a man convicted of slaughtering stock on a European farm. He told the authorities that he had taken seven oaths before the attack, including: 'If I reveal any secrets of members who are Africans, this oath will kill me.'[15]

The attacks increased and the British army arrived in great numbers. Some of the main combatants were the Lancashire Fusiliers and the King's African Rifles. Insurgents were rounded up and kept in gaols, then later in camps. In November 1952 for instance, over 2,000 Mau Mau members were detained and put behind barbed wire. Emergency regulations were in place for magistrates and military forces. Gallows were erected. All this we know from press reports. Then, in 2011 the archives were opened, and a group of aged Kenyans arrived in London to plead their case of abuse and torture at that time.

Yet again, a scandal relating to the empire in Africa had opened up. David Anderson, Professor of African History at the University of Oxford, told the press: 'These documents were hidden away to protect the guilty... and it's not just in Kenya. What other colonial skeletons are rattling around in the FCO basement?'[16] Evidence points to the killing of around 12,000 rebels, and the estimate of numbers kept in the camps is 70,000. The Kenyans who came to London had lawyers of course, and the official statement from them was that there had been a system of torture and degrading treatment applied by police and other members of security forces with the knowledge of the Colonial Administration.

Ndiku Mutwiwa Mutua was a Mau Mau suspect detained in 1954 for supplying food to rebels hiding out in a forest. His story is that he was a prisoner in the Eastern province, then this happened:

> '... he was allegedly handcuffed and pinned to the ground, with his legs pulled apart, and tied or strapped down. Having been rendered completely powerless and vulnerable Mr Mutua claims that he was castrated by one or more of the officers present....for two days he was allegedly left without medical attention and then liberated from the camp by Mau Mau rebels...'[17]

The important element in all this is that essentially nothing had changed in this particular version of imprisonment since the Victorian era of empire. Once again, the rift between principles of human rights and actual penal practice was very wide indeed. The establishment attacked the Mau Mau phenomenon as, in Trevor Huddlestone's words: '...a movement which in its origins and in its deeds is entirely evil. It is the worst enemy of African progress. It has about it all the horror of the powers of darkness.'[18] There were certainly killings and a reign of terror, but once again, the question of judging a civilization by the way it treats its prisoners rears its head and demands the issue of justice to be asserted as historical change brings about revisionary perspectives.

ANOTHER IRISH QUESTION

In terms of more regular prison – the incarceration of criminals in European society – the case of modern Ireland is contentious and illustrative of the same rift. The Irish prison service found that it was the subject of an inspection by representatives of the European Committee for the Prevention of Torture and Inhuman or Degrading Treatment of Punishment. This body is directed by the Council of Europe whose delegates have unlimited access to places of detention and who interview'persons deprived of liberty'in private. The visits of inspection are every four years and there is co-operation with all relevant authorities. It was created in 1989 and builds on Article 3 of the European Convention on Human Rights which provides that:'No one shall be subjected to torture or to inhuman or degrading treatment or punishment.'[19]

Prisons across the liberal democracies are quite accustomed to endless dialogues concerning human rights and national legislation (which of course varies according to each legal code employed) and the prison newspapers, prison lawyers, and professional advisers such as Independent Monitoring Boards, having their say about conditions inside the walls. In 2010 it was Ireland's turn to cope with the kind of material that IMBs and inspectors of prisons write and publish online every month. In early 2011 the criticisms were summarised by Conor Lally, crime correspondent of *The Irish Times*: 'A European committee against torture has strongly criticised "degrading, inhumane and unsafe" conditions in the Republic's prisons and has questioned plans for a new super-prison to address chronic overcrowding.'[20] In that sentence it is possible to detect in miniature everything that has gone wrong with the prison ideals first fully formulated by John Howard in 1777. The criminal justice system is packed with offences having custodial sentences yet few alternatives to prison exist and the pragmatic way to deal with the situation is therefore to build bigger jails. That process has been replicated in dozens of prisons across the world. Statistics of sentencing back up the criticisms: the prison population had risen by 30 per cent in the three years since the last visit; the numbers being imprisoned for six months or less had risen from 3,000 in 2005 to 5,000 in 2008.

In spite of the costs involved, and of criticisms of super jails by many theorists, in July 2010 it was announced that the massive Thornton Hall prison was to go ahead. It is to be close to Dublin, have a capacity of 2,200, and is to be built in a series of phases on a site extending to 140 acres at Kilsallaghan. The first phase is planned to be complete by 2014. There is always a counter argument to that of criticising size and scale. The Minister for Justice at that time, Dermot Ahern, said that the jail was needed because most people were going to jail for serious crimes – something that contradicts the European report.

The report from the European Committee had criticisms to make on several jails, including Cork which was called 'unhealthy, with three sleeping in one-man cells and where the air was "rank and humid'. At Dublin's Mountjoy prison the criticisms were aimed at prison gangs, overcrowding, and unsafe conditions for all, and the note was recorded that stabbings and attacks were 'an almost daily occurrence'. In the Midlands prison, a case was quoted in which versions of an assault by a prisoner and by an officer 'did not tally with CCTV. No action was taken'.[21]

The Head of the Irish prison service, Brian Purcell, has done what all governors do – reject the criticisms as being distorted. He did not accept that any Irish prisons were unsafe and his records logged that out of 117 reported incidents in Mountjoy, only twenty-one involved knives. He added that prevention of torture complaints were given 'prior to the introduction of the new procedures.'[22]

Historian Tim Carey, in his book on Mountjoy prison, published in 2000 expressed uncertainty even as new developments and expansion were taking place. He refers to a new prison opened at Castlerea and another being built at Portlaoise, together with a new female prison at Mountjoy, but he adds: 'Such additions may give the system a certain amount of breathing space (one of the most talked-about changes is the proposed re-introduction of in-cell sanitation in the male prison at Mountjoy. But no-one is too sure about the end result.'[23]

This case study from Ireland relates very closely to a pattern established by all mechanisms for jail inspections. As long as there have been prisons there has been some kind of prison visit by either charity workers or official regulative or advisory bodies. From the beginnings of the prison systems in America and Europe, regulation was piecemeal and often ineffective. An objective observer may have hoped for the twenty-first century to have brought improvements in this balance between the prison regime and its watchdogs. The cycle goes on repeating itself: new prisons, new theory, a revised method of regulation, perceived failures of care, then new prisons.

There is no reason why Ireland should be singled out here as its shortcomings are almost universal, but it has to be said that some states have thought very differently from the norm. Vivien Stern, for instance, offers this account of innovation from Sweden: 'In some Swedish prisons…when you ask to see the visiting room, perhaps expecting a large area with tables and chairs and a refreshment corner, you are shown instead a corridor off which are a number of small rooms with beds and chairs. These are the individual visiting rooms and visits are in private.'[24]

A study of *Inside Time*, the national prison newspaper in the UK, will immediately make clear to anyone who has never been inside a prison what the important issues are regarding rights and the prison regime, and this would apply in prisons anywhere on earth. What matters is the attitude of the prison staff and the Governor's discipline with regard to every perceived punishment over and above the deprivation of freedom. In other words, topic such as visits, health care, association time, education, physical exercise and time with probation and legal advisors, are some of the principal areas of importance in this respect. Lifers, for instance, who have with little hope of ever being outside in society again, create a pattern of individual and communal culture and interchange which helps to make incarceration bearable. Any small detail which takes away an element of that culture may be very harmful to the individual.

This is why regulation, official visits and inspections matter, and why unannounced visits are particularly valuable. Yet, as history has repeatedly shown, mechanisms for regulation and objective reporting have always been inherently created as something separate from each prison; that is, if all kinds of checks and scrutinies were regularly made available, and with local personnel involved, researchers and politicians would not have to rely so often on formal reports by people who perhaps have no real knowledge of the immediate circumstances such as cultural factors and crime patterns impacting on the prison in question.

The last word has to be that governing a prison is an extremely tough task and always will be, and that governance still entails a great deal of power in the hands of one person at the top. The implications of that sentence need to be considered, as multiple case studies from the past make clear.

Notes and references

1 Erich Fromm, *The Fear of Freedom* (Oxford, 2010) p. 104.

2 See 'Treatment of Prisoners' *The Times* Sept. 16 1935 p. 9.

3 Ibid. p. 9.

4 Ibid. p. 9.

5 'Penal Reform' *The Times* 19 Jan. 1925 letter from Margery Fry p. 8.

6 Phillip Knightley, *Australia: A Biography of a Nation* (London, 2001) p. 112.

7 Ibid. p. 121.

8 Cameron Forbes, 'Palm Island Case Study' on www.qsa.qld.edu.au.

9 Keith McEwan, 'Bells Tolling for Palm Island' in www.cla.asn.au/0805/index.php/articles/2010.

10 See Australian Bureau of Statistics ABS. http://www.abs.gov.au.

11 Kathy Marks, 'Aborigine Race Row Deepens as More Officers are Exonerated' *The Independent* 18 March 2011 p. 29.

12 Op.cit. note 6 p. 110.

13 Ben Macintyre, leader, *The Times* 5 April 2011.

14 'Secret Societies in Africa' *The Times* 5 June 1950 p. 3.

15 'Mau Mau Youth's Seven Oaths' *The Times* 8 Oct. 1952 p. 5.

16 Op.cit note 12 leading article.

17 Ben Macintyre, 'Tales of brutality and Violence That Could Open the Claims Floodgate' *The Times* 5 April 2011 p. 6.

18 Letters page of *The Times* 13 April 2011.

19 See the Council of Europe web site at http://www.cpt.coe.int/en/about.htm.

20 Conor Lally 'Conditions in Republic's Jails 'Unsafe' *Irish Times* 8 Mar. 2011.

21 Ibid.

22 Conor Lally, 'Prison Chief Rejects EU Body's Criticism' *Irish Times* 9 March 2011.

23 Tim Carey, *Mountjoy, The Story of a Prison* (Dublin, 2000) p. 245.

24 Vivien Stern, *A Sin Against the Future* (London, 1999) p. 23.

Chapter 10

History from Inside

Every great metanarrative, either of a nation or of a region, of a theme or of a life, has an inner narrative too which is often inaccessible. The great overarching story has within it countless smaller tales, biographies inextricably mixed with the large, transparent series of events. Prison is no different. There is the story of the systems, the regimes and the influential people and ideas, but there is also the other history – from inside the cells and on the wings. This is a people's history, rather than any official or well established history. Usually it takes the form of out-of-print memoirs, books published by small presses or reports and enquiries with voluminous personal testimonies.

One of the most powerful and comprehensive of these sources is found in government reports. In the nineteen-century parliamentary papers, for instance, intertwined with the dutiful and plain prose of the inspectors we have thousands of voices coming across time to the modern reader, as if he hears the voice of a prisoner, an officer or a chaplain from a Victorian prison establishment. These are often related to scandals, as was the case with HMP Birmingham where the regime of Lieutenant Austin and Dr Blunt at the prison became the subject of a government enquiry in 1854. The commissioners reported in July that year. Mr Welsby, Captain Williams and Dr Baly wrote their report and a number of inhuman punishments at the prison came to light. They based their enquiry on the stipulation in the 1823 Gaol Act that although in common law a gaoler has no authority to punish (merely to restrain), some punishments were allowed: close confinement, and bread and water diet for no more than three days. Lieutenant Austin and Dr Blount had done far more than that, being fond of several cruelties in their regime. From the extensive report, the voices of prisoners and staff speak to us, as they rarely do in the history written from the overall nature of the establishment. How rare are the voices of prison staff, but here are the actual words from a warder at Birmingham, relating to one of the most disgusting cases of abuse at the prison – the horrendous treatment meted out to young Samuel Grey who was admitted in October 1852. Grey was paralysed down his right side, suffered from the onset of consumption, was deaf and had a speech impediment. It was also noted that he had a rupture. Yet this young man was made to run in the exercise yard. At the enquiry, warder Norton gave evidence:

> '...on the 18th November, when the prisoner was in the exercise ground, under the superintendence of the warder Jeffries, upon being ordered by him along with the rest of the prisoners, to exercise at the double, he tried to run, but had gone a little way when he fell down, and discharged a considerable quantity of blood from his mouth...'[1]

The point about murderer John Straffen's long prison life is that it was unknown. Like so many thousands of others, he left nothing on paper or on record; his experience was all internalised, until that day when prison officer Robert Douglas saw him, and so the general reader and citizen outside the world of prison had another perspective offered about what is essentially an hermetically sealed microcosm. In spite of true crime memories, television documentaries and film narratives, the actual first-hand feel of the cell door shutting on you and the forgotten prison world closing in, the history of *being in prison*, as opposed to prison as an institution, is still largely out of the radar of most people's knowledge of their world.

On the other hand, some prisoners make a resolution to write about their prison experience in great detail. There are instances in which a person's entire adult life has been in prison – unlike most serial killers in fact. The representative of this most familiar today is surely Charles Bronson, who has even written a guide to all English prisons, as seen from the cells, rather that on a visit or from an office in the administration block. There are several examples from history of similar prisoners: those spent so long under lock and key that their identity and achievement as writers and artists relates almost entirely to prison experience. One sensational example is the Austrian soldier of fortune and hero of the British Empire, Rudolph Slatin.

Slatin was born in Vienna in 1857 and his first education was commercial. This led to the first link with Africa in his life when he acquired a post as an assistant to a bookseller in Cairo who needed a clerk and tutor. He worked with an explorer for a while and then worked in Khartoum and in the Nuba mountains. He was gaining a great deal of local knowledge when General Gordon arrived on the scene. Gordon gave Slatin a government responsibility: first the work was in financial administration and later it involved inspections of outlying areas. This led to his most powerful position under the Khedive (the ultimate ruler of the Sudan): governor of Dara in Dar Fur. Gordon, operating under Khedive Ismail, needed Europeans in his management team and so Slatin was a valuable acquisition in that respect. But it was tough for Slatin, who soon found himself acting in a military capacity. He had experience in Austria as he had served as a sub-lieutenant in the forces of Archduke Rudolf (the 19th Hungarian Infantry). But his troops in Dara were unreliable. Though Slatin had fought several battles, eventually his men left and he had to surrender to the Mahdi. The Mahdi was Muhammad Ahmad, a man who had won power and influence leading a jihad against the 'infidels.' The word 'Mahdi' means 'guided by God' and Ahmad convinced his followers that he was that man. What could Slatin do to survive and still play a part in the war against this charismatic figure? He converted to Islam.

Slatin lived in captivity in a mud dwelling and was in chains up to the death of the Mahdi. A drawing exists in which 'Slatin Pasha' is shown staring at the displayed head of Gordon being carried by two Mahdists. In Slatin's memoirs we have a very rare document: an account of imprisonment not in any great state or empire, but in a tribal outpost of East Africa, under the power of a despot. For some considerable time he contrived to exist as an adviser, always under supervision, and playing dangerous games with what may be called diplomatic moves, but one day, he was taken to a dark tent and forced into chains, without knowing why:

'Accompanied by my gaoler and some eight others, I went to the tent, where I was now directed to sit on the ground, and chains were now brought out. Two large iron rings, bound together by a thick iron bar, were slipped over my feet, and then hammered close. An iron ring was placed a round my neck, and to this was attached a long iron chain with the links so arranged that I had the greatest difficulty in moving my head. I endured all this in perfect silence...'[2]

The remarkable aspect of this is that the reader is given an insight into marginal, unchecked, whimsical imprisonment – something outside any system or modality of a justice programme.

But this amazing character began a new role when Khalifa Abdullahi succeeded the Mahdi in 1885. Slatin was very poor but managed to fulfil a role at court, though many thought he was a British spy. By September 1900 he was Inspector General of the Sudan, but he did renew his links with family and native land, going to Austria every summer. However, he was still destined to move in high places: he could have worked for the Turks or the Germans, but would not work in any capacity against Britain. His last work was for the Red Cross and he refused the post of ambassador in London, for Austria. Rudolf Slatin died in 1932 after one last visit to the Sudan as a guest of the government.

For most testimonies to prison 'from the inside' however, the location is not as obscure and small-scale as this: for the most part, prison writing or oral witness deliveryhas always been focused on materiality. Interestingly, as well as the creative material produced, there has always been a tradition of thinkers, philosophers and social theorists behind bars. After all, a time spent in a cell is an opportunity for radical change, profound reflection and the formulation of political ideas. Antonio Gramsci, the great Italian Marxist, planned his great work *The Prison Notebooks* while in Ustica prison, Milan, and wrote themlater in prison in Rome, after being granted permission to write in his cell in 1929.

EXPLAINING THE INTERIOR LIFE

The alternative history of prison, written by prisoners, has predominantly been concerned with the privations, sufferings and mental anguish of being shut away from the world of business, family and citizenship. Documentation from the early civilizations gives much information, such as the drawings done by prisoners of the Assyrians which show people being blinded or the death penalty of being hoisted on poles.[3] In the medieval period, knowledge of prison life often comes from pleas and complaints, or legal and official records, as in this commission from 1285: 'The number of persons who have died in gaol is positively appalling, and no words can describe the horrors and iniquitous treatment meted out to poor helpless prisoners. Although they were sometimes allowed the stated sum to purchase food and other necessaries of life, these were only obtainable through the gaolers... if they complained, they were mercilessly placed in heavier irons and placed in dark dungeons.'[4]

Literature *per se*, as distinct from more prosaic documentary evidence, has often given valuable information on general features and often plays up the idea of prison as metaphor. But such seasoned prisoners as Francois Villon have left powerful accounts of the material state of being confined:

> 'Come see him here, in his pitiless plight,
> Noblemen, free of tax and tithe,
> Holding nothing, by king or emperor's right
> But by grace of God of paradise.
> Sundays and Tuesdays he fasts and sighs.
> His teeth are as sharp as the rats' below...'[5]

At times, in rare and impressive works on the nature of prison, writing comes along that goes more deeply into the nature of prison as seen from inside. With regard to the American correctional facility, John Cheever's 1977 novel *Falconer*, does exactly that. Its roots are in the 'prison' of alcoholism in Cheever's case, and he uses the metaphor of being on the surface the relaxed and quiet writer of provincial America, yet also a man with inner demons in order to access the nature of being incarcerated. The quintessential nature of prison experience is the need to relate to others. What does not figure in the general history of prisons is that muddled, fearful, yet essential being in a community – yet it is a community with its own norms, rules and safeguards. The intimate and ambivalent relationships – those of inmate to inmate and inmate to authority – have to be expressed either in sociological writing or through the imagination. In *Falconer*, Cheever manages to create authentic scenes from degradation and pain through to the legal and official issues, such as the lawyer's visit: 'He carried a clipboard with a thick file of papers. "Here are your facts," he said, " I think I've got everything here. Armed robbery zip to ten, Second offence, that's you isn't it?"' The lawyer has got the wrong papers. The prisoner, Farragut, has been attacked and is on crutches. The result is a quality something like Kafka's protagonists but placed within a convincing, detailed prison establishment.

That quality of isolation mixed with the slippage of identity is what writings from prisoners have added to the massive body of the historiography of prisons. The heart of this writing is in most cases given by those who for obvious reasons, are educated and who are able to find the words to express such complexity. One difficulty with the literature on record is that it has been written by people who have known prison so well that it becomes their 'material' and their knowledge is based on experience that is perhaps outdated. Yet there is no doubt that in certain places at certain times the radical counter-culture absorbed imprisonment as a determining and organizing principle in creative writing. The American Beats of the 1950s have this quality. Gregory Corso, for instance, born in New York in 1930, provides a template, being placed in a boys' home initially and then in New York City jail, followed by a three-year sentence at Clinton State Prison. The combination of rebellion, philosophy, and the experience of various versions of confinement gave his creativity an original element.

In contrast, surely historians would long for information on prison conditions in obscure corners of the world, referred to throughout recorded history. Typical of this is the memoir by Miles Phillips about his imprisonment by the Inquisition in Mexico in 1574-5. He makes an effort to explain what torture was imposed and how executions were carried out, but for actual reference to prison we have: 'Thus we remained closed imprisoned for the space of a year and a half, and others for some less time; for they came to prison ever as they were apprehended.'[6]

In the last thirty years much has changed in this respect: the prison memoir is now an established genre, and the reader expects a 'warts and all' approach. Organizations such as the Writers in Prison Network and the programmes carried out across American jails based on creative writing have confirmed everyday prison experience as a viable area of writing and expression in visual and dramaticarts. Charles Bronson typifies this development. Hehas produced a body of writing that is like nothing else in the prison literature: what his life presents is a story ofconsciousness caught up completely inside the prison life. There is a 'jail head' in the prison system. This is a man whose entire waking moment is devoted to small victories in the ongoing battle with the establishment. Everything thrown at him, every small regulation and order, will be an appeal to conceive a battle plan. He knows every inch of the material microcosm of the prison: the kitchen, each wing, the education block, segregation, laundry, health care, gym, exercise yard and workshops. The plan and layout of the place are imprinted in his mind. His identity ceases to be the person known by relations and friends outside. When they visit they see only that one-dimensional figure who talks about the weather or what is on television. The man who returns to his pad is already scheming.

This is Bronson. Because so many men inside have developed that mindset, they see in him the absolute extreme of that profile: he had fought in every arena open to him. The trajectory of dissent in a prison career goes from adjudications to escalated offences, then to a reputation for trouble that sticks like superglue to his prison name and number. Charles Bronson has done this and more: he has taken it to the level of a finely tuned performance. His imagination has formed his projected self into a warrior. His endless press-ups become combative against his own standards. His confrontations become more extreme. The result has been, as he put it himself: 'The world left me behind more than a quarter of a century ago. I'm a lost man –what more can be said?'[7]

The alternative history of prisons is accessible often merely in scraps, in tantalising snippets of experience. In addition to the testimony of inmates, there is the question of staff. There were no real professional prison staff, in the modern sense, until the mid nineteenth century. Of course before that, in cultures across the globe, the staff were military personnel. The warders and guards of earlier times, along with the executioners, are mostly in the shadows of history. For centuries, turnkeys were no more than minions who maintained security through fear and threat – that is, if prisoners escaped, their jobs or heads might go. Globalization has meant that the pattern for prison staff has been imposed across former empires so that penal colonies and local jails kept by magistrates across the continents ruled by the three or four great modern empires, had staff with similar status and qualifications for the job. In India, for instance, prison as punishment came with the British from the 1770s, and the Indian prison rules date back to 1894. As Vivien Stern pointed out, writing at the end of the twentieth century, referring to Tihar Central jail: 'Apparently the jail is still administered according to the rules of the 1894 Act.'[8]

The writings of prison staff have indeed been rare. In the late Victorian period, a handful of staff produced memoirs, such as the anonymous work on a female prison 'by a prison matron'[9] and very few such items have followed. A book such as Robert Douglas's *At Her Majesty's Pleasure* is a rare gem in the genre.[10] In the USA there appears to be more of a tradition of wardens and ex-officers being involved in writing history and memoir, as in the case of the very commercial subject of Alcatraz, for instance.[11] In other corners of the world their writings are very hard to find. The true crime genre appears to be the main outlet, as in the writings of professionals on the lives and executions of national hangmen.[12]

Taking all these factors into account, it is clear that prison written 'from the inside' will always have aspects of counter-philosophy, dissent and criticism. In the old debtors' prisons of the years before the late Victorian years, prisoners could sometimes live a reasonably normal life, some of them being allowed to spend some of the day outside the walls, working or relaxing. Prisoners in Siberia could escapein some contexts, but of course they escaped into a wilderness and most likely into starvation. On the whole, inmates have had to spend a lot of time in their cell, and creative expression has always been there. It is the case that the first topic a prisoner wants to write about is prison and their criminal experience. This obvious statement accounts for the massive number of memoirs being written inside the walls, not allowed to see print, for legal reasons, and that very fact brings to light the struggle between 'human rights' of self expression and the criminal legislations of various states in which such 'rights' are cancelled out by penal law.

This literature of resistance, part of a wider concept with that phrase as the key concept, has been gradually emerging into full discussion, even to the extent of academics working out prison poetics and attempting to find organising principles and elements of common material and structures in the literature. Prison writing is also more familiar now across the world, as usual with the internet as the educative medium. Thanks to essays and interviews regularly occurring online, it is not difficult to acquire a wider cross-cultural knowledge of this, as illustrated by the quite recent discourse on Chinese 'reform through labour' sentences which forms the focus for Zhang Chumlei's novel *Four Walls*, originally published in serialized form online under a pen-name of Gemenr. In an interview with *Southern Weekly*, Zhang points out that prison writing in China has a long pedigree, going back to Wenwang's *The Book of Changes* and the Juyou Cao lyrics, written while he was detained at Youli in the twelfth century BCE. The lyrics produced have been explained by the record compiled by Qin Lu: 'Wen Wang was detained in Youli. He was unhappy and dejected. He played his *qin* and sang... so it was called *Detained in Gloom*.'[13] Today, Youli is in the city of Anyang in Henan province.

The Euro-centred view of the history of prison writing perhaps centres on Boethius (AD 475-524) and his classic work *The Consolations of Philosophy*. He was appointed to a high position by the Goth Theodoric but was later accused of treason and imprisoned and tortured at Pavia before finally being executed. His book is in some ways a model for prison writing in that it deals with the sorrows of the loss of liberty, examines personal reflection and soul-searching, and introduces the discipline of philosophy as the route to survival. In other words, through prison thinking and 'time out' the prisoner searches for fresh knowledge, special insight and a strategy for comfort and consolation. His great book deals with the problem of evil, using the vision of a visit to him in his death row cell by Lady Philosophy, his Muse. This shows another aspect of prison writing through history: the use of the vision as a trope, a central metaphor as part of the structuring of thought.

In former times, prison writing went on largely unknown and for personal fulfilment and satisfaction only. Then the age of information engendered by the Victorians made documentation of facts prominent in reportage and official writing. Arguably, the second age of prison writing was of that time, something created by the urgent need for regulation ad social control in an age of Utilitarianism. The third age in terms of prison has surely been marked by the emergence of two organizations: Amnesty International and PEN.

Amnesty International, founded in 1961, began with an article in *The Observer* headed 'The Forgotten Prisoners' by Peter Benenson, in which he made an appeal for help in the case of political prisoners detained for their views and opinions. Amnesty was born, working to change laws where possible, and to raise awareness of injustice in imprisonment. Writings from prison played a key part in their development.

Even more directly involved in prison writing is PEN. Today there are 144 branches of PEN (Poets, Essayists and Novelists). It has existed for 90 years, being founded in 1921 by Amy Dawson Scott when she conceived the idea of the Tomorrow Club, a place where all kinds of writers could meet and share ideas. The Club's activities were extended after the Great War such as providing dinners for what Amy called 'my starving men.' The organization later became international, and the first meeting involving an international group of delegates was held in 1923.

PEN now has a Writers in Prison section which campaigns constantly on human rights issues for prisoners everywhere. As I write this in early 2011, Amnesty and PEN have applied their energy to highlighting the plight of Mao Hengfeng, for instance, a Chinese mother of three and former factory worker who, like Zhang Chunlei the writer, is held in a Re-education through labour prison. Under the present security system known as *laofiao*, the police may imprison anyone from dissidents to drug addicts for up to four years without court hearings. One report has explained what Mao has experienced: 'During her stay in prison she was beaten and choked, placed in solitary confinement and has been on hunger strike. She has spent part of her jail time refusing to wear clothes to protest at her treatment.'[14]

As these cases show very powerfully, writing in prison has always been there, from the time of the cell graffiti in Biblical times to the autobiographies of lifers in today's ever larger prisons. The alternative history of prison from these sources links with the vast literature of dissent and resistance across the centuries and offers another perspective at odds with the prison regimes. The situation regarding actual publication of prison writing today is complex and contradictory.

In prisons today not only are there classes in basic literacy, but there is also the Toe by Toe scheme started by Christopher Morgan and the Shannon Trust. The spur for this came from a long correspondence between Morgan and a lifer called Tom Shannon which became the book *The Invisible Crying Tree* (a new edition came out in 1996). The Toe by Toe idea is based on a 'buddy system' and a thick red handbook is used, so that in a twenty-minute session as often as possible (every day, in theory) two people work on the book, tutor and student. Prison officers may act as the buddy if they wish. Morgan has said that at its launch in H M P Wandsworth, there was a sense of challenge, but that more than 200 prisoners have completed the course. Christopher Morgan's initiative has had a profound effect on attitudes to prisoners' writing generally, and more particularly, to the benefits of literacy and the consequent opening up of language as a tool to express reflection, understanding and remorse.

There is also now the residences established by the Writers in Prison Network, in which writers spend two days inside working in all kinds of writing from drama groups to autobiographies, and from poetry to storytelling. Each year, six residencies are in place at prisons across the land, and products and results show that this work has a positive effect on the prison community.

All this has been in place for Noel Razor Smith, published writer and long-term prisoner. In a feature written by Erwin James in 2004, Noel explained how his writing began. James wrote: 'His writing activities began as part of a business enterprise while he was in Albany prison on the Isle of Wight in the 1990s. An associate made greetings cards to sell to fellow prisoners. Smith, who was writing poetry, "trying to win the prison's annual Christmas poetry competition," would write the verses. "I haven't got a clue where it came from," he says, "It was just something I could do.".'[15]

The rest is history. His books are now on every true crime shelf in the libraries and bookshops. That began with the help of Smith. Behind the book and the new life inside, there was personal tragedy.

Smith's son, Mark, took his own life after a spell in the young offender's jail at Feltham. Smith felt some responsibility for the death.

Smith is now notorious because of his transformation. His long criminal career began when he was a Teddy Boy and carried a razor. He later became an armed robber, working in a team to rob banks and enjoying a wealthy lifestyle on the proceeds. He and the gang used to take two banks a month. When he explains that life now he says: 'You've got to detach yourself. So you tell yourself you're a Robin Hood figure. If you sat down and told yourself the truth: I am a nasty, violent man, going out there and terrifying innocent members of the public.... you cut yourself off.'[16]

Smith's writing is, without doubt, something that aims to counteract the glamorous true crime volumes on the shelves, covers red like the blood described in their pages. The struggle to write has been tough. In his autobiography, he writes that he moved from small successes to large setbacks. Against the grain, he managed to be published in *Punch*, with help from John McVicar. But the first phase of the writing from prison was fraught with difficulties and even today, in 2010, the obstacles are still there. When Smith wrote his first book, he recorded there the massive resource his life supplies for a potential writer: 'Some people may wonder at my extraordinary memory of events, some of which occurred more than a quarter of a century ago. Part of it is that prison is so boring that we have little to do except remember...' He had the huge stock of writer's 'material' but prison regulations blocked the path.[17]

Basically, Smith was aiming to write for money and there is a prison service order against that. Writing is only a minor part of the never-ending action-response life of the prisoner and his keepers. For every strategy inside to overcome a problem, the authorities have to conceive of a measure to deal with it. The most irritating and potentially threatening example of this is the use of mobile phones inside prison walls. They are strictly forbidden, of course, but they are always there somewhere, secreted with great ingenuity and not always located in spins. Now, every prison has a device called a 'BOSS' – a Body Orifice Security Scanner. This scans for hidden weapons and other objects hidden in any dark place in the human physiology. It looks like a very uncomfortable armchair. Refusal to submit to such a scan means that there will be disciplinary action taken.

That is just one instance of something being done to prevent prisoners getting involved in undesirable activities. After all, there are cases in which a man inside has used a mobile phone to initiate a hit killing, so this is no laughing matter. But what about the use of a pen or a keyboard in order to express what is bubbling up in the prisoner's imagination? Writing is one of the most basic human needs in out society now: to be illiterate is the surest way to oblivion. We talk of 'rehab' and fail to see that creative writing, even for small profits which may be always given to charity, gives a person an immense injection of self-esteem – a kind of drug we like to think we all have, administered naturally.

Yet the obstacles remain, and Noel Smith is in the thick of the fight to write and be encouraged. Once again, he is in a scrap. One huge problem with this whole activity is nothing to do with the system and the regulations. It is that prison writing can become great literature, as in Dostoievsky's *House of the Dead* and Chekhov's *Sakhalin Island*, or more recently than these classics, Alexander Solzhenitsyn's book *The Gulag Archipeligo*. But that success is usually linked to political status and major events. Prison itself, as in the British establishment, is something we are forced to regard as uninteresting, static, despicable and rather embarrassing to contemplate. We have a communal sense of shame, unexpressed, because we feel that, as the statistics of people locked up tops the 580,000 mark (in March, 2011), there is a dark, nagging sense of failure and that we have all played a part. The politicians and papers tell us that it is down to poor parenting, the loss of family cohesion, the collapse of Christian ethics, and so on. What is forgotten or at least overlooked is the capacity for the people inside to effect a repositioning if at least the talented ones inside are given the chance to exercise their talents in creativity rather than in villainy.

Yet with an historical perspective, it is heartening to reflect that writing in prisons across the world is going on, in spite of rules, impositions and tough regimes. Not all such writing will sit in an honoured position along side the real classics, of course, but at least the activity is increasingly respected and given time and space. The very fact that a 'change through literature' concept is being applied in some American penitentiaries is an amazing step forward, and the Koestler Awards for prison creative activities carries on in Britain in spite of economic constraints. Some presses and publishers add to this, with the publication of writing anthologies by prisoners, often given media attention by the participation of celebrities with an interest in prison creativity.

The outlook is bright for the survival of the counter-history of being 'inside.' In past years prison experience was virtually a great silence, and only when such topics as biographies of conscientious objectors or spies, notorious gangsters or victims of miscarriages of justice made the headlines did prison life arouse any general interest.

Notes and references

1 *Parliamentary Papers:* Reports: Prison 1857 p. 212.

2 Rudolf Slatin, *Fire and Sword in the Sudan* (London, 1914 p. 251).

3 See www.bible-history.com/past/blinding_prisoners. html.

4 T P Cooper, *The History of the Castle of York* (London, 1911) p. 97.

5 Francois Villon, 'Ballade: Epistre' see www.poetsintranslation.com/PITBR/French/Villon.htm.

6 See 'A Prisoner of the Inquisition, Mexico City 1474-5' Miles Phillips, in Jon E Lewis (Ed.) *How it Happened in Britain* (London, 2001) p. 175.

7 Charles Bronson, *Bronson* (London, 2004) p. 3.

8 Vivien Stern *A Sin Against the Future* p. 25.

9 See *Female Life in Prison* (London, 1862).

10 Robert Douglas, *At Her Majesty's Pleasure* (London, 2007).

11 Alcatraz has spawned a number of staff memoirs, including writing by the warden, by prisoners and even by a doctor – no doubt prompted by the writers' acquaintance with such characters as Al Capone and the 'Birdman'.

12 Typical is T J Leech's book on executions, *A Date with the Hangman* (London, 1992) Leech was a former prison officer.

13 See 'Detained in Gloom' at www.silkqin.com/02qnpu/10gyy/tg05jyc.htm for a full account of the story on Wen Wang and Youli.

14 Clifford Coonan, 'Chinese Rights Defender Back in Jail' *Irish Times* 21 Feb. 2011.

15 For an account of help received in writing, see the acknowledgements for Noel's book, *A Few Kind Words and a Loaded Gun* (London, 2004).

16 Ibid. p. 7.

17 See profile of Smith by Erwin James, 'I'm on a Journey' at www.guardian.co.uk/uk/2004/may/26/ukcrime.biography.

Conclusions

Wh

When I began the research for this book my experience of working in prisons, along with the growing body of criminological research, confirmed my view that the history of prisons across the globe has been a woeful tale of trial and error, good intentions gone wrong, and theory dissolving in the face of actual penal reality. At the end of writing the narrative, this has largely been confirmed, and yet there is something inherent in penology that encourages optimism. That optimism is perhaps in the face of sheer economic necessity in most cases. For instance, it costs governments across the enlightened world today around £40,000 on average to maintain a prisoner for a year. Policies in practical everyday politics will always be ruled by figures, perhaps inevitably in opposition to the theories of penologists.

However, within the first years of the twenty-first century, with the exception of the repressive and backward-looking regimes still existing, the signs are that although alternatives to prison are being suggested and in some cases implemented, the ever-present problem of support after a prison stretch is still there and becoming increasingly insurmountable.

This is not a new problem. In past centuries, if there was a policy of after-care at all, it was left to charities and volunteers. Unfortunately, this may still largely be the case. Before probation became established in the first decades of the twentieth century, the church tended to act as carer; the so-called police court missionaries did what was essentially probation work. Currently, efforts are being made to work at the other end of the process – preventive measures. There is no doubt that reducing the number of sentences, or reforming sentencing generally, would have some impact, yet whatever changes are made, the issue of the nature of prison itself still remains.

History shows that there is a pulse running through penal thought and provision: a cyclical trajectory which reflects the ebbs and flows of humanitarian and repressive philosophies that applies only to prison within civil society, and the pattern still reflects Enlightenment attitudes to transgression. What is cause for real concern is the recurrent phenomenon of the prison camp, the penal estate neatly shoved out of focus and populated with those who 'disappear' in various locations. Prison history, perhaps more than any other aspect of criminal or social history, shines a torch on the darkest corners of the human capacity to show 'man's inhumanity to man.' The battle for human rights goes on, and almost every week there is a law report concerning the interplay between the rulings at Geneva and the criminal justice systems across the world.

Every counter-culture has a counter narrative, and that forms a shadow land often missing from the landscape of mainstream history. Prison experience and policy plays a major role in this, as is clearly seen in the shameful history of the Australian aboriginals or in the tribal history of Natal, Zululand and the Transvaal.

History is supposed to offer templates, patterns, models: all the aspects of human experience logging our mistakes, shortcomings and injustices. Prison history has ample material on this and the hope has to be that as time goes on, humanitarian thought and pragmatic exercise of power never drift too far apart. Punishment will always have to be in every criminal justice system, and attitudes to it will always be some kind of measure of that complex bundle of values which establishes legality at any one time. For that reason, built on shifting ground, the nature of a prison will inevitably be subject to radical change, but in the end, the deprivation of liberty is the focal concept. Every other punishment on top of that tends to provide endless fodder for human rights debate.

Clearly, I have had to be selective. In countless small domains over the centuries, tyrants have had no need of a prison 'system'. Yet, my selected case studies highlight the recurrent themes in the long chronicle of attempts to put in place a successful prison establishment – with the rider that 'successful' has always meant different things to different people who have the centre of power. These themes are:

• 1: The nature of punishments imposed in addition to the deprivation of liberty.
• 2: The use of power tempered by humanitarian concerns.

• 3: The reflection of perceived 'civilised' values within the prison system.
• 4: Methods of regulation.
• 5: The nature, duties and behaviour of staff.
• 6: The extent to which there is adequate provision for guidance: probation, after-care and support regarding prevention of recidivism.
• 7: In war conditions, the extent to which human rights are transparently considered by those imposing incarceration.
• 8: The relation of imprisonment at any given time *vis a vis* the current ideology of government.

There are more profound themes relating to global prison systems and specialists in that study have isolated various ongoing issues, including the link between economic factors and crime, expressed well by Weiss and Smith in their comparison of prison systems: '…we note that the mediating influences of changes in economic success and cuts in welfare services' in relation to a 'hardening of penal control.' In other words, a penal system will be repressive if seen as having that function, regardless of the broader social picture.

Glossary

Blockhouse
A term first used as a term for prison in 1624. But before that, a detached fort used to overlook a strategical point.

Categorization
The classification of inmates according to various defined offences of sentence planning trajectories.

Gulag
The network of early Soviet work camps, formed from the initials of the Russian *Glavnoe upravlenie lagerei* – Main Camp Administration.

Habeas Corpus
A writ, directed at anyone who has a person in custody, commanding the jailer to produce the body of the person, for a hearing. The full wording is *habeas corpus ad subjiciendum.*

House of Correction
Alternatively, referred to as a 'Bridewell' after the first such institution was established in London in 1555, this was the first type of local gaol meant to be part prison and part workhouse. It generally included debtors, those awaiting trial and convicted criminals.

Jail/Gaol
Historically a term used for a local or regional prison, as opposed to a national institution. The term could refer to anything from a Sheriff's cells in America to a local lock-up in any rural area of a country.

Local Jails
Temporary jails in locations away from central legal authority were referred to by various names, including: lock-up, toll booth, pledgehouse (for debtors), cage and round house.

Panopticon
The penal concept devised by Samuel and Jeremy Bentham in which

radial wings and a central observation point were intended to create an establishment in which cellular life and prisoners could be observed at all times.

Penal Labour

This has varied across cultures, but common tasks have been breaking stones, civil engineering, using the treadmill, picking oakum and turning the crank. The latter was an in-cell device involving a handle (called a screw) being turned a set number of times daily. Hence the term 'screw' for a prison officer.

Penal Laws

This is a general term of course, but specifically in British history, it refers to the series of statutes between Tudor times and the early eighteenth century by which measures were taken to imprison and impose limitations of civic and human rights on Catholics. Hence the term 'penal period' with reference to Irish history also.

Penitentiary

The name was originally used as a term to differentiate the institution from a prison *per se*. That is, the term implies that this was a house where a prisoner would be penitent. As a word devised to help with aspirational ideals in penology, it has assumed an ironical status in the modern age, of course, as they tend to be very large, with punishment higher on the agenda that reform.

Reconcentracion

The first form of 'concentration camp' for non-combatants, as created by Spanish forces under Marshal Weyser in the 1890s.

Supermax

Large-scale top security jails adopted across several countries after the first American versions post The Second World War.

Transportation

The transport of convicts abroad has been large-scale in imperial history, embracing the histories of Britain, France, Spain and Portugal, but the history of Australia has provided the most numerous examples, with convicts being despatched there from London between 1788 and 1868 in vast numbers, notably to Sydney and to Tasmania.

Bibliography

Note

Naturally, a bibliography for such a wide-ranging subject necessarily embraces several academic disciplines and also has to include a number of sources from ephemera, personal memoir and popular mass media. I have been selective in this, but items listed here are mostly referred to or discussed in the text. Hence full information on all texts listed in the endnotes is here. Arguably, of all the material in the literature of penology, the most informative and enlightening are the texts produced in official reports and enquiries and I have included the most voluminous of the parliamentary papers in this respect, excluding only the publications on transportation ad those on very detailed and specific topics such as the prison dietary.

Recent publishing developments have included a proliferation of monographs on individual prisons. I have written two of these recently – on Hull and on Northallerton – and I can say with confidence that this historiography has added new dimensions to our understanding of how and why recurrent problems in prison regimes happened. These texts also add considerably to the biographical element in our knowledge of the prison experience.

It has also been necessary to explore some by-ways of memoir-writing in American crime writing such as accounts by staff, governors and penologists in the USA. Notable in this is the literature concerning disorder and failure of course, but there is also a rich source of information on the logistics of high-security prisons in America from former governors, perhaps best represented by Warden Johnston, who explains the establishment of Alcatraz.

One outstanding feature of the sources here has been the vast body of material coming from dissident and minority writers and groups. Naturally, prison history has always created schisms, ideological alignments, political faction and philosophical perspectives in international political history which has constantly forced historians to take up opposing positions in order to see the writer's native metahistorical narrative from outside – classically, in the case of writing from post-imperial situations. I have included plenty of material from such sources here, and the reader is invited to search actively for the analyses from the cultural 'others' who have written in order to provide an axis for debate and dissent from the dominant narrative, which of course foregrounds accepted knowledge.

There is also controversy: one dimension of prison history is fraught with historiographical contention and debate, and that concerns the actual practice and administration of penal colonies within modern empires. From empires in the classical and ancient worlds, records are limited, but in the post Enlightenment world, there has been a plethora of documentation and this gives rise to the familiar aspect of revising history and revisiting old political controversy. I have included a representative sample of the texts at the heart of this source material.

For a fuller archival guide to penal history, the reader is referred to 'Your Archives' at The National Archives UK with a research guide: *Sources for the History of Prisons*.

Primary Sources
Books

Berkman, Alexander (Editor); *Letters from Russians Prisons* (Hyperion Press, 1999).

Bronson, Charles; *Bronson* (John Blake, 2004).

Burnley, James; *West Riding Sketches* (Hodder and Stoughton, 1890).

Czapski, Joseph; *Proust Contre La Decheance* (Noir Sur Blanc, 2011).

Charriere, Henri; *Papillon* (1969) (Harper, 2005).

Chekhov, Anton; *A Life in Letters* (Penguin, 2004).

Davitt, Michael; *Leaves From a Prison Diary or Lectures to a Solitary Audience* (Irish University Press, 1997).

De Windt, Harry; *From Paris to New York by Land* (Nelson, 1904).

Dostoievski, Fyodor; *Memoirs from the House of the Dead* (OUP, 2008).

Drabble, Margaret; *The Oxford Companion to English Literature* (Oxford, 1987).

Douglas, Robert; *At Her Majesty's Pleasure* (Hodder, 2007).

Ellis, John; *The Diary of a Hangman* (True Crime Library, 2000).

Gramsci, Antonio (Ed. David Forgacs); *The Antonio Gramsci Reader* (Lawrence andWishart, 1999).

Howard, John; *The State of the Prisons* (1777) (Everyman, 1929).

Johnston, Warden; *Alcatraz Island Prison* (Douglas/Ryan, 1999).

Levi, Primo; *The Periodic Table* (Penguin, 200?).

Lincolnshire County Council: *Convicts of Lincolnshire: 'Sentences'* 1988.

Lytton, Constance; *Prisons and Prisoners* (Virago, 1988).

Mayhew, Henry, and Binny, John; *The Criminal Prisons of London* (Griffin, Bohn and Co., 1862).

Melling, Elizabeth; *Crime and Punishment: Kentish Sources* (Kent County Council, 1969).

Morton, H.V.; *I Saw Two Englands* (Methuen, 1943).

Murton, Tom and Hyams, Joe; *Accomplices to the Crime: the Arkansas Prison Scandal* (Grove Press, 1969).

Orwell, George; *Decline of the English Murder and Other Essays* (Penguin, 1953).

Orwell, George; *Inside the Whale and Other Essays* (Penguin, 1957).

Phillips, Miles; 'A Prisoner of the Inquisition'. Quoted in Hakluyt's *Voyages* of 1589 reproduced in Jon E. Lewis (Ed.) *The Mammoth Book of How it Happened in Britain* (Robinson, 2001).

Rousseau, Jean-Jacques; *The Social Contract* (Penguin, 2006).

Slatin, Rudolph; *Fire and Sword in the Sudan* (Edward Arnold, 1914).

Smith, Noel Razor; *A Few Kind Words and a Loaded Gun* (Penguin, 2004).

Solzhenitsyn, Alexander; *The Gulag Archipelago* (Fontana, 1974).

Steevens, G.W.; *With Kitchener to Khartoum* (William Blackwood, 1898).

Stow, John; *A Survey of London Written in the Year 1598* (Sutton, 2005).

Thomas, Donald; *State Trials Vol.2* (Routledge and Kegan Paul, 1972).

Wilde, Oscar; *De Profundis* (Collins, 1948).

Periodicals and Official Publications

Anon.; *The New Newgate Calendar* (A. Ritchie, Fleet Street, 1880).

Morrison, A. C. L. and Hughes, Edward: *The Criminal Justice Act 1948* (Butterworth, 1948).

Secondary Sources
Books

Ackroyd, Peter; *Venice, Pure City* (Vintage, 2010).

Adams, Robert and Campling, Jo; *Prison Riots in Britain and the USA* (St Martin's Press, 2002).

Adorno, Theodor; *Prisms* (MIT Press, 1983).

Ahmed, Akbar S.; *Discovering Islam: Making Sense of Muslim History and Society* (Routledge, 2002).

Applebaum, Anne; *Gulag: A History* (Penguin, 2003).

Armstrong, Karen; *Islam: A Short History* (Phoenix, 2001).

Birkenhead, Earl of; *More Famous Trials* (Hutchinson, 1930).

Bresler, Fenton; *Reprieve: A Study of a System* (Harrap, 1978).

Burgtorf, Jochen et alia; *The Debate on the Trial of the Templars* (Ashgate, 2010).

Bury, J. B.; *A History of Greece* (Macmillan, 1966).

Butler, Anne; *Gendered Justice in the American West* (St Martin's Press, 1992).

Cadbury, Geraldine S.; *Young Offenders: Yesterday and Today* (Allen & Unwin, 1938).

Calder, Angus, Mojaddedi, Jawid and Rippin, Andrew; *Classical Islam: A Sourcebook for Religious Literature* (Routledge, 2003).

Carey, Tim; *Mountjoy: The Story of a Prison* (Collins Press, 2000).

Cheever, John; *Falconer* (Penguin, 1977).

Costin, W. C. and Watson, J. Steven; *The Law and the Working of the Constitution: Documents Vol. 1 1660-1783* (Adam and Charles Black, 1952).

Coulson, Noel J.; *A History of Islamic Law* (Edinburgh University Press, 2004).

Cyriax, Oliver; *The Penguin Encyclopaedia of Crime* (Penguin, 1996).

Denning, Lord; *Landmarks in the Law* (Butterworth, 1948).

French, Yvonne; *News from the Past 1805-1887* (Gollancz, 1940).

Fife, Graham; *The Terror* (Portrait, 2004).

Figes, Orlando; *Natasha's Dance: A Cultural History of Russia* (Penguin, 2002).

Fletcher, Anthony and MacCulloch, Diarmaid; *Tudor Rebellions* (Pearson, 1997).

Foucault, Michel; *Discipline and Punish: The Birth of the Prison* (Penguin, 1977).

Friedman, Lawrence M.; *Crime and Punishment in American History* (Basic Books, 1993).

Fromm, Erich; *The Fear of Freedom* (Routledge, 2002).

Fulford, Roger; *Votes for Women* (Faber and Faber, 1958).

Geltner, G.; *The Medieval Prison: A Social History* (Princeton University Press, 2008).

Grahame-Evans, Alex; *A Short History and Guide to Port Arthur* (Regal Publications, 2001).

Griffiths, Arthur; *Millbank Penitentiary: An Experiment in Reformation* (Grolier Society, 1890).

Grovier, Kelly; *The Gaol: The Story of Newgate* (John Murray, 2008).

Haralambos, Michael and Holborn, Martin; *Sociology: Themes and Perspectives* (Collins, 2008).

Haven, Cynthia L.; *Conversations with Joseph Brodsky* (University of Mississippi Press, 2002).

Heath, James; *18th Century Penal Theory* (OUP, 1963).

Henderson, Charles Richmond; *Modern Prison Systems* (Washington Government Printing Office, 1903).

Herrup, Cynthia; *The Common Peace: participation in the criminal law in Seventeenth Century England* (CUP 1987)

Hirst, Joseph H.; *The Blockhouses of Kingston-upon-Hull* (A. Brown, 1913)

Horn, Pamela; *Young Offenders: Juvenile Delinquency 1700-2000* (Amberley, 2011).

Hosking, Geoffrey; *Russia and the Russians* (Penguin, 2002).

Howard, D. L.; *John Howard, Prison Reformer* (Christopher Johnson, 1958).

Howse, Christopher ; *How We Saw It: 150 years of the Daily Telegraph 1855-2005* (Ebury Press, 2005).

Hughes, Robert; *The Fatal Shore* (Vintage, 2003).

Hurnad, Naomi; *The King's Pardon for Homicide before AD 1307* (OUP 1969).

Ingledew, C. J. Davison; *The History and Antiquities of Northallerton* (Bell and Daldy, 1858).

James, Trevor; *About Dartmoor Prison* (Hedgerow Print, Crediton, 2001)

Jewkes, Yvonne and Letherby, Gayle; *Criminology: A Reader* (Sage, 2008)

Justinian, (Edited by C. F. Kolbert); *The Digest of Roman Law* (Penguin, 1979).

Kadri, Sadakat; *The Trial: a history from Socrates to O J Simpson* (HarperCollins, 2005) .

Kelly, Ian; *Casanova* (Hodder and Stoughton, 2008).

Knightley, Phillip; *Australia: A Biography of a Nation* (Vintage, 2001).

Lilin, Nicolai; *Siberian Education* (Canongate, 2011).

Lytton, Constance; *Prisons and Prisoners* (Virago, 1988).

McLaughlin, Eugene et alia; *Criminological Perspectives: Essential Readings* (Sage, 2004).

McLaughlin, Eugene and Muncie, John; *The Sage Dictionary of Criminology* (Sage, 2006).

McNeill, J. R. and William H. ; *The Human Web: A Bird's Eye View of World History* W.W. Norton, 2003).

Marlow, Joyce; *The Tolpuddle Martyrs* (Panther, 1974).

Morris, Norval and Rothman, David J.; *The Oxford History of the Prison* (OUP, 1998).

Muhlhahn, Klaus; *Criminal Justice in China: A History* (Harvard University Press, 2009).

Neese, Robert; *Prison Exposures* (Chilton Company, 1959).

O'Shea, Kathleen; *Women and the Death Penalty in the United States 1900-1998* (Praeger, 1999).

Partridge, Col. S. G.; *Prisoners' Progress* (Hutchinson, 1900).

Porter, Roy; *Enlightenment* (Penguin, 2000).

Priestley, Philip; *Victorian Prison Lives* (Pimlico, 1999).

Rafter, Nicole; *Prisons in America: A Reference Book* (ABC Clio, 1999).

Robinson, Frederick W.; *Female Life in Prison* (Spencer Blackett, 1888).

Rogers, A. P. V.; *Law on the Battlefield* (Manchester University Press, 2004).

Rolph, C. H.; *The Queen's Pardon* (Cassell, 1978).

Rosie, George; *Curious Scotland* (Granta, 2004).

Roth, Mitchell P.; *Prisons and Prison Systems* (Greenwood, 2005).

Rutherford, Sarah; *The Victorian Asylum* (Shire, 2008).

Saunders, John B. ; *Mozley and Whiteley's Law Dictionary* (Butterworths, 1977).

Schama, Simon; *Citizens: A Chronicle of the French Revolution* (Penguin, 2004).

Sharpe, J. A. ; *Crime in Early Modern England 1550-1750* (Longman, 1999).

Smith, F. B.; *The People's Health 1830-1910* (Weidenfeld and Nicholson, 1990).

Solomon, Norman; *Judaism, A Very Short History* (OUP, 1996).

Spargo, Tamsin; *Wanted Man* (Bloomsbury, 2004).

Spierenburg, Pieter: *Disciplinary Institutions and their Inmates in Early Modern Europe* (Amsterdam Academic Archive, 2007).

Stern, Vivien; *Creating Criminals: Prisons and People in a Market Society* (Zed Books, 2006).

Stern, Vivien; *A Sin Against the Future* (Penguin, 1998).

Stokes, Anthony; *Pit of Shame: the Real Ballad of Reading Gaol* (Waterside, 2007).

Sullivan, Larry E.; *The Prison Reform Movement: Forlorn Hope* (Twayne, 1990).

Suvak, Daniel; *Memoirs of American Prisons* (Scarecrow press, 1979).

Templewood, Viscount; *The Shadow of the Gallows* (Gollancz, 1951).

Wade, Stephen,; *House of Care* (Bar None Books, 2009).

Walklate, Sandra; *Criminology: the Basics* (Routledge, 2005).

Waters, Malcolm; *Globalization* (Routledge, 1995).

Weiss, Robert P. and South, Nigel; *Comparing Prison Systems* (Gordon and Breach, 1998).

Wheatcroft, S. G. *Challenging Traditional Views of Russian History* (Palgrave, 2002).

Wilkinson, George Theodore; *The Newgate Calendar* (Cardinal, 1991).

Yarmolinsky, Avrahm; *Dostoevsky: His Life and Art* (Arco, 1957).

Younghusband, Sir George; *The Tower of London* (Herbert Jenkins, 1924).

Newspapers and Periodicals
Daily Telegraph
Freeman's Journal
Graphic
Illustrated London News
Inside Time
Social History
Southern Monthly
The Irish Times
The Times

Articles

Barker, Anna; 'Novel Sentences' *The Guardian* 21 July 2010.

Colley, Linda; 'Great Writs' *Times Literary Supplement* 17 Dec. 2010 pp. 3-4.

Daley, Larry; 'Documenting The Reconcentration: Cuba (1895-1898)' See http://www.amigospais-guaracabuya.org/oagld003.php.

Daly, Gavin; 'Napoleon's Lost legions: French Prisoners of War in Britain 1803-1814' *History* Vol. 89 no. 295 2004 pp. 361-380.

'Democracy, Human Rights and Prison Conditions in South America' at www.memoriayjusticia.cl/english/en_rights-tejas.htm.

Eisenman, Stephen F.; 'The Resistable Rise and Predictable Fall of the U.S. Supermax' *Monthly Review* Nov.2009 online pp. 1-15.

'First Indictments for Torture at tejas Verdes' op.cit above, memoriayjusticia

Forbes, Cameron; 'Palm Island case Study' at www.qsa.qld.eda.au.

Franklin, H. Bruce; 'From Plantation to the Prison-Industrial Complex' Paper delivered to the Modern Language Association Convention, Dec. 2000, on http://andromeda.rutgers.edu/~hbf/MLABLACK.htm.

Hardman, Philippa; 'The origins of Imprisonment' in *Prison Service Journal* no. 177 pp. 16-22.

Johnston, Helen; 'The Cell: Separation, isolation and space in the architecture of the birth of the prison' *Prison Service Journal* no. 187 pp. 9-14.

Kelly, Catriona ; 'No Coffins Provided' *Times Literary Supplement* 4 March 2011 p. 13.

Lake, Elliot; 'British Concentration Camps' http://elliotlakenews. wordpress.com/2007/03/17/ british-concentration-camps/.

Lally, Conor; 'Conditions in Republic's Jails Unsafe' *Irish Times* 9 Feb. 2011 p. 5.

Marks, Cathy; 'Aborigine Race Row Deepens as More Officers are Exonerated' *The Independent* 18 March 2011 p. 29.

Marx, Karl; Letter to L'Internationale 'The English Government and the

Fenian Prisoners' Feb. 21 1870 at www.marxists.org/archive/marx/works/1870.

Nicholls, Mark; 'Walter Raleigh, The Heroic Traitor' *BBC History Magazine* Vol.12 No.2 Feb. 2011 pp. 21-25.

Taylor, Alison; 'The Deviant Dead' *Current Archaeology* no. 244 Aug. 2010 pp. 20-25.

Techman, Milton; 'How Writers Fought Back' *Literature from the Nazi Ghettos and Camps* http://findarticles.com.

Varese, Federico; 'Tattoo Tales' *Times Literary Supplement* Jan. 21 2011 p. 23.

Web Sites

www.alcatrazhistory.com/mainpg.htm
www.americanheritage.com
www.amnesty.org.uk
www.blacksheepancestors.com
www.danwei.org/books/prison.html
www.englishpen.org/writersinprison
www.friendsofnormancross/a-detailed-history
www.history.ac.uk/reviews/reviews/805
www.hmprisonservice.gov.uk
www.howardleague.org./history-of-prison-system
www.museumstuff.com
www.silkqin.com/02qnpu/10tgyy/tg05jyc.htm
www.studymore.org.uk/crimtim.htm

Index

People

Ackroyd, Peter   37
Aikenhead, Thomas   23
Alcibiades   30
Arendt, Hannah   169
Avery, Denis   137
 -*The Man who Broke into Auschwitz*
   137

Bambridge, Thomas   75
Beccaria, Cesare   72, 83
Bentham, Jeremy   72
Berkman, Alexander   107
-*Letters from a Russian Prison*   107
Brannon, Peter   96
Brockway, Zebulon   115
Brodsky, Joseph   26
Bronson, Charles   179, 184
Bury, J B   14-15

Carey, Tim   175
Charlemagne   33
Charles I   42
Charriere, Henri   91, 92
 -*Papillon*   91
Cheever, John   182
 - *Falconer*   182
Chekhov, Anton   65, 190
Chesterton, G K   14
Churchill, Winston   153
Cicero   32
Cnut   45, 48
Cohen, Stanley   26
Coke, Sir Edward   50
Confucius   70
Coon, Darwin   120
Corso, Gregory   183
Cowper, William   73
Cubillo, Lorna   170
Czapski, Joseph   143

Dante,   9
Doomadgee,   171
Dostoievski, Fyodor   65, 190
Douglas, Robert   17-18, 185
Draco   29
Dreyfus, Alfred   91
Du Cane, Edmond   115
Dwight, Louis   114
Dylan, Bob   151

Edward II   36
Egerton, John   77
Esquirol, Jean-Etienne   82
Ethelbert   45
Evershed, Zofia   14

Fielding, Henry   73
Forbes, Cameron   170
Foucault, Michel   11, 26, 84, 87,125
   -*Discipline or Punishment*   11
Frenkel, Naphtali   103
Fromm, Erich   165
 - *The Fear of Freedom*   166
Fry, Margery   168

Gertner, G   38, 57
Gordon, General   180
Gratian   35
Grey, Samuel   179
Gui, Bernard   36
Gunner, Peter   170

Hadfield, John   80-82
Hall, Francis   52-53
Hammurabi   28
Henderson, Charles   116
Henry I   46
Henry VII   42, 49
Herrup, Cynthia   48
Hobhouse, Emily   134
Hosking, Geoffrey   67

Howard, John   66, 68,78, 82, 85
  -*The State of the Prisons* 85
Huggins, John   73-74
Hughes, Robert   96
  -*The Fatal Shore* 96
Hullock, Baron   16

James, Erwin   188
Johnston, Warden   116-117

Kafka, Franz   183
King, Martin Luther   155
Kitchener, Herbert   132-134
Knightley, Philip   169
Kolbert, C F   31
Kramer, Thomas   36

Lally, Conor   174
Leigh, Mrs   162
Levi. Primo   139
Lombroso, Cesare   86
  -*L'Uomo Delinquente* 86
Lytton, Lady Constance   161

McVicar, John   189
Mahdi'   180
Martin, William   21-22
Mayhew, Henry   97
Morton, H V   149
Maimonides, Moses   24
Muhlhahn, Thomas   70

Neild, Dr   77
Neville, A O   169
Nicholas I (Tsar)   65
Nihil, Daniel   110

O'Brien, William Smith   93, 151
Orwell, George   61

Penn, William   112
Perlin, Etienne   48
Peter I (Tsar)   66
Pinel, Philippe   82
Plato   29
Pope Clement V   36

Priestley, Philip   10
Proust, Marcel   143

Queen Mary   50

Raal, Sarah   135
Redfield, Senator   129-130
Redmond, John   162
Richard III   60
Robins, Nick   61
Rogers, A P W   137
Romilly, Samuel   84
Roosevelt, F. D   118
Rossa, O'Donovan   150
Roth, Philip   139
Rousseau, Jean-Jacques   115

Sadakat, Kadri   32
Shakespeare, William   66
  -*Coriolanus* 153-154
  -*Hamlet* 72
  -*The Merchant of Venice*   66
Sidorkina, Yelena   105
Sharpe, James   51
Skinner, Thomas   62
Slatin, Rudolph   180-181
Sleeman, William   62
Smith, Noel Razor   188-189
Socrates   14
Solon   29
Solzhenitsyn, Alexander   105
Spivak, Guyatri   61
Stalin, Joseph   107
Steevens, G W   132
  -*With Kitchener to Khartoum* 132-133
Stern, Vivien   183
Stow, John   58
  -*Survey of London* 58
Straffen, John   18-20
Suleiman   59
Sullivan, Larry   114-115, 121-122

Taylor, Laurie   26
Teichman, Milton   155
Tibi, Daniel   157
Tyrwhitt, Sir Thoma

Turpin, Robert 48s 146

Villon, Francois 182
Voltaire, (Francois-Marie Arouet) 114

Wilde, Oscar 9, 163
Wines, Enoch 115
Wolsey, Cardinal 42
Wyatt, Sir Thomas 49

Zhang, Chumlei 186

Places and General Reference

Aborigines 169
Alba fucens 32
Alcatraz 116-120
American War of Independence 109
Amnesty 187
Amur Cart Road 101
Ancien regime 53
Andaman Islands 65
Angevin Empire 42
Assize of Clarendon 47
Auburn 113-114
Auschwitz 106

Bay of Bengal 65
Birmingham HMP 178
Bit Kili 28
Black Hole of Calcutta 24
Blasphemy Act (1661) 23
Boer War 133-134
Brazil 156
Bridewells 10
Broadmoor 83
Byzantine Law 33

Canon Law 33
Canques 71
Chatelet prison 84
Cheka 102
Chile 156
China 151-152
Clinton State Prison 183

Colditz 13
Comitia Centuriata 31
Concordance of Discordant Canons 35
Criminal Cases Review Commission 21
Criminal Lunatics Asylum Act (1860) 83

Dartmoor, HMP 144-146, 147-148
Debtors 55-56
Desmoterion 29-30
Domostroi 67
Drury Lane theatre 80

Ecuador 157
Elmira reformatory 115
European Committee for the Prevention of Torture and Inhuman or Degrading Punishment (1989) 174
Enlightenment, The 84-85
Fleet prison 54-55, 73-75
Folsom prison 117
Frankland, HMP 19
French colonies 90-92

Gaol Act (1823) 178
Gentleman's Magazine 75
'Great Game' 62
Germany 56
Guiana 90

Habeas Corpus 43, 53
Halakha 24
Harmsworth's Magazine 104
Howard League for Penal Reform 167
Hull 52
Human Rights Act 27

International penal and Penitentiary Commission 167
Inside Time 176
International prison Congress (1872) 86
Irish Times 174
Islamic fortresses 54
Isle of the Dead 96

Keleska Ostrog 67

King's Bench prison   12
Koestler Awards   191

League of Nations   167
Les Isles du Salut   90
Local gaols   55
Louisiana State Penitentiary   121
Lucknow   64
Lunatics Act (1800)   81

Magna Carta   43
Mau Mau   168, 172-173
Millbank   110-111
Mishneh Torah   24
Mosaic Law   7
Mountjoy prison   175

Napoleonic War-prisoners   143-145
Netherlands   85
Newgate   110
NKVD   105
Norman Conquest   45
Norman Cross   144
Northallerton, HMP   22

Ottoman Empire   59
Oudh   63

Palm Island   169
Paris   82
PEN (Poets, Essayists, Novelists)   187
Pentonville, HMP   9
Petersburg   66
Pilgrimage of Grace   49
Plassey, battle of   61
'Pleading the belly'   51
Port Arthur   94
Presnya   105
Prison Discipline Society   114

Qing Code   70

Regulating Act (1774)   62
Roman Law   31
Royal Commission on Aboriginal
   Deaths (1987)   171

Royal Asiatic Society   10
Russian colonies   98-100
Rus   102

Salpetriere   82
Schuldturmen   56
Siberia   60, 185
Siena   38
Soviet Union   102
Star Chamber, court of   51
Suffragettes   158-160
Supermax prisons   122
Supreme Court (UK)   27

Tejas verdes   156
Templars   36-37
Theodosian Code   32
The Red Book   73
Thornton Hall   174
Thuggee   62
Tolpuddle Martyrs   94
Tower Hill   50
Tower of London   52, 153
Transport Board   144
Treadmill   22
Treason Act (1351)   152
Tullianum   32

Urga   10-11, 24

Van Dieman's Land   93-95

Walnut Street   112
Walton gaol   158
West Sussex Quarter Sessions   80
White Sea Canal   103
Writers in Prison Network   184

Xing   69

York assizes   15
York Castle   6

Zemstva   67
Zui   69